MW00957819

Holden Village - A Memoir

Holden Village - A Memoir

NEW LIFE - ENDLESS STORIES

Werner Janssen

Copyright © 2014 Werner Janssen
All rights reserved.
ISBN: 150334231X
ISBN 13: 9781503342316

Author's Notes

1. I'd like to recognize Mary Koch for her efforts in working with my rough drafts and painstakingly sifting through the pages, challenging accuracy and continuity. Mary is a gifted professional in terms of writing and editing, and she has also been a member of the Holden community sufficiently long to understand the unique character of this remote village struggling each day to live its mission. Mary urged me to write a memoir rather than a historical document. Thanks to Mary for encouraging me to share the stories that have remained in my memory over the past fifty years.

2. I request forgiveness. Holden Village has developed and grown through the efforts and lives of many thousands of people. Many of these people have never been acknowledged. In my memoirs I have added a few more names to the written documentation, but many more people, all making significant contributions to the Holden Village community, remain in museum documents or in the memories of others involved. Please forgive me for not being able to honor everyone. All guests, staff, and faculty have been critical to the overall development of the Holden Village community.

3. Holden guests, staff, and faculty have urged me to write my stories before I reached the age when memory seriously fades. What I have written has not been requested or authorized by Holden

Village or its board of directors. I have written this for our children, Kristy and Jeff, documenting the beginning of our family life for their enjoyment. I trust that others might be interested in the beginning years of Holden Village as experienced by one who lived in the community, managed its operational functions, and influenced some aspects of its life during the first twenty years of its existence. What I have shared is what I observed and experienced which I think approaches historical accuracy.

4. My wife, Claudia, has lovingly encouraged me in this project and provided technical assistance and emotional encouragement. Thanks to Don Wagner for graciously providing several pictures from his extensive library of Holden photos. Several others have shared photos, but the majority of the pictures included are from the Janssen family collection. The photos were scanned from photographs or slides taken in an era prior to digital technology.

Foreword

By Gene Sharratt

THIS ISN'T A HISTORY BOOK filled with facts and figures; instead it's a collection of stories reflecting one man's journey and his candid memories of how a community shaped a sense of place, one where building common purpose surmounted individual interests. Werner Janssen takes us back in time and opens a rare window into the human story of Holden Village.

This story is sometimes painfully spoken through the joys and struggles of real life. Holden Village developed naturally through the persistent efforts of determined people to survive and thrive in an often-harsh and remote environment. Residents of the Holden community united around a common sense of belonging to weave a fabric of interconnected social networks. These networks were especially strong within families and among friends and were most often based on the need to build community. These relationships enabled Holden citizens to navigate the difficulties and uncertainty of everyday living.

History is best told by those who lived it. Werner Janssen lived in and managed Holden Village for twenty years. He is certainly in a position to peel back the pages of time and share his frank observations about people, places, and events leading up to modern-day Holden Village life. His approach to storytelling is engaging, historically honest, and motivated by an authentic effort to present history as it was lived.

The fascination with the history of Holden Village is compelling as this demanding and isolated place has been the scene of historic events, sometime joyous, sometimes dire, but it's always been a place where history was made. Werner's journey isn't just sentimental or nostalgic: it does not assume the past was better. Above all, it's a journey to encourage deeper personal reflections while offering Holden as an inspiring example of place, community, and a commitment by residents to worthy accomplishments.

Dr. Gene Sharratt has been a personal friend for thirty years. We became acquainted when he served as superintendent of the North Central Educational Service District and I was a member of the Cascade District School Board in Leavenworth, Washington. Gene became well acquainted with Holden Village during his numerous trips there, enjoying his work with and observation of the Holden public school. He is currently executive director of the Washington State Student Achievement Council and a member of Washington State Governor Jay Inslee's cabinet.

—W. J.

Introduction

WHAT I HAVE WRITTEN IN the following pages is a memoir covering my twenty-three years of direct involvement with Holden Village plus the years that Holden Village directly influenced my work life following my retirement as Holden Village manager.

I am not claiming to write history. I have checked with a few people who were involved during those years to verify some facts, but I haven't attempted to fact-check everything written. A few dates may be slightly different but I think the stories I share and the people I credit are all accurate. Since retiring from Holden Village, I have recorded audio history stories on several trips back to the village. What I have written here is more accurate in terms of some details. If you listen to the recordings and then read the memoirs, believe what is written rather than assuming the oral recordings are accurate in every detail.

In the time since I retired as manager in 1983, many talented individuals have joined forces to continue developing Holden Village, its community, and its program into an increasingly exciting and complex operation. I had the privilege of being a part of the beginning of Holden Village, when everything was rather primitive and probably less complicated. It may be true that in the beginning God gifted Holden Village, but it's also true that God neglected to include electrical power, a bank account, heat and hot water in the buildings, transportation to get people from Lucerne to Holden, a method to deal with garbage, and the ability and insight to deal with the federal government, our landlord. We dealt with these challenges as best we could. I may not have the ability to be manager during these more complex times, but I'm thankful that I could assist Holden Village gain a foothold in the maturing process. I'm grateful that Holden Village has continued to expand its impact on society.

The stories of healing received and the hopes generated for many people have, for the most part, remained the private memories of those individuals. Too many people significant to the Holden Village history have been forgotten. It's impossible to document who was most important and who advanced Holden to where it's today. The real miracle is that Holden wasn't established to provide a spiritual or sociological experiment that needed to be closely documented. The Holden Village community developed very naturally and sometimes painfully through the joys and struggles of real life, not through the work of a church-established committee wishing to create a miracle.

Holden grew through community participation, and like any puzzle, each piece is critical in terms of the whole picture. I have tried to include a few people who have been left out of previous writings of Holden history and, at the very least, document a few more names. My memoirs include those individuals and those events that have, for some reason, remained in my thoughts. Unfortunately, many who were significant to the development of Holden Village may never be documented or remembered. I hope others will write their memoirs with different stories and a different emphasis, giving credit to more people who helped Holden Village develop and who helped Holden Village maintain its spirituality and its conscience.

Fortunately, so much of what makes Holden special was never recorded or documented. It's easier to write a memoir. A couple of books about Holden unfortunately include what I consider some fantasies that the author or sources think occurred. Some people who have been elevated to Holden "sainthood" in reality displayed serious flaws. Saints most frequently are genuine sinners with their flaws forgotten. I have been concerned that the few books/documents and even recordings that have been preserved about Holden have been based on the particular bias of a few people and too-often based on second or third person accounts. What I have written are my memories of events and people. My memoirs are, of course, also biased, based on my observations and mental imprint. I have tried my best to be honest, even if it hurts.

Holden continued to impact my life for another twenty years after my official retirement in 1983. My time as Holden Village manager ended in September of 1983, but I remained as a paid consultant for the next twelve months. The last chapter of my memoir shares the Holden influence and connection that continued during the years 1984 through 2008. I served as Holden Village manger from age twenty-four until age forty-five. I'm writing this at age seventy-five. I consider my memory for details to be reasonably sharp.

I don't know exactly what originally drew me to Holden Village. Since the jobs I really enjoyed through my life were those that approached me rather than jobs I obtained through application processes, I credit my mother, who fervently prayed for me. My mother didn't have any knowledge of Holden initially, but I think she kept praying that I would somehow be involved with a church-related activity since I chose not to attend seminary and become a pastor like multiple generations of our family previously. I never asked my mother if she didn't trust me to reach my potential as an engineer, but my conclusion is that Mother lived each day in the hands of God, and prayer was an important part of that relationship. My brother became a medical doctor and psychiatrist, and I elected aeronautical engineering. However, I did end up at Holden Village, so perhaps my mother won. Time spent in the Rocky Mountains at Estes Park, Colorado, where my father was in charge of many Central District Luther League conferences, very likely impacted my emotions regarding the excitement and beauty of life in the mountains.

In 2012, I was very appreciative that Stephanie and Chuck Carpenter, Holden executive directors, invited me to go to Holden to share stories covering my years of involvement. The Carpenters are the first directors since I retired who helped me to again feel more a part of Holden

Village. Over these fifty years, I had never been invited to be on faculty or teaching staff, so I greatly appreciated this new opportunity. At the conclusion of the first vespers, when Claudia, my partner, and I were in the village for the fiftieth anniversary of Holden, the community honored me for my Holden involvement. Stephanie read a letter from my dear friend, Pastor Jim Fish. Since Jim's letter spoke of the larger Holden history, I'm including most of it as a part of this introduction. The letter helps set the stage for my memoirs, and besides that, his thoughts and comments touched me deeply.

The following was written by Pastor Jim Fish, Holden volunteer, family sabbatical participant, and village pastor. Jim and his wife Kay, are to me, heroes in the church. They highly respected the church organization, but they were also willing to share their thoughts and convictions even if it raised the eyebrows of those in power. Jim sent the following letter to Holden in connection with the fiftieth anniversary observance:

> The two key figures in Holden history these past fifty years are Carroll Hinderlie and Werner Janssen. About that there should be little disagreement.
>
> It is impossible to miss the impact of the first person. It's very possible to miss the story of the second.
>
> All that Holden is—a worship/education/celebration center at odds with the world and passionate about the Gospel—all that comes directly from the odd and wacko vision of Carroll Hinderlie. Carroll didn't fit into the traditional slots assigned pious Norwegian clergy in the 1960s. He was all over the map, delighting many and puzzling even more. He didn't fit into the mold of a traditional pastor nor that of a theological professor. All that is well documented. Subsequent directors, including my beloved friends John and Mary Schramm, with whom I worked for three years, didn't shape the fundamental character of the Village more than Carroll. If the Hinderlie story isn't told, the passion and oddity that is Holden will not be understood.

However—and here is where my primary emphasis is placed—it is the life and work of Werner Janssen that must also be held up, along with that of Carroll and Mary Hinderlie, as primary creators of the Holden brand. Knowing the Werner Janssen story is essential to fully appreciating what it is. But, since he was only the business manager, well…

Here is where some of Werner's impact is seen today:

* Garbage/recycling—care of the earth. On this Werner was way, way ahead of his time.
* Ministry of the laity. He knew Holden would grow, not because of clergy, but in spite of them.
* Using the gifts of all God's people. Werner was amazing in seeing sacred gifts in everyone. He let me run the backhoe!
* Working for the joy of it, not the salary.
* Gathering around him a team of very smart, science-oriented, dedicated laypeople to solve huge problems, e.g., how to keep the hydro running all winter.
* Hilarity. If the Village knows how to laugh, it's in large part thanks to Werner. How could hilarity be central to an institution's life and mission? Not by accident, but by the spirit of a person's life. Werner was, and is, funny! He made Holden funny. He named Wes Prieb "Ph.D.," Pool Hall Director. He came up with the Fourth of July parade. Without Werner, Holden would be just another self-righteous Bible camp.
* Worship centered on scripture, scholarship and grace.
* That's the beginning of the list. All the things Holden stands for, all the traditions quaint and wickedly funny, at the root of nearly every one of them is Werner.

So in these years of celebration, the one person not to be missed, if the story is told with love and care, is the funny, little, wise, stubborn, Purdue-educated engineer from DeWitt, Nebraska, who gave decades of service to Holden. He was there from Day One. His vision and passion for doing the impossible, with no money, with a group of amateurs, while loving every minute of it, is the Holden story.

Ultimately Holden isn't about clergy. Thank God! It doesn't belong to the church; it's a gift to the church from a million hands volunteering over decades, led forward primarily by one individual, Werner Janssen. He did more than put wheels under the vision of others. (no small job given how odd the vision was) He directly shaped the vision and mission every step of the way. Get his story straight, and you understand how Holden came to be...

Jim was very gracious with his comments, and his thoughts are humbly and gratefully accepted. I admit that I have felt somewhat left out of the Holden community since retiring in 1983. I did appreciate a great e-mail exchange with Paul Hinderlie, son of the former director Carroll Hinderlie, during the years he co directed Holden Village as we exchanged memories and lessons learned from our shared Holden history that applied to ongoing community challenges. Paul invited and even urged me to come back several times, but for some reason a return trip during his tenure never materialized.

Over the twenty-plus years of direct involvement, I experienced too much human history within the Holden Village community—and not all of it good. The few times I did return to Holden, I felt that I was still the keeper of secrets that had been imposed on me, and it was more comfortable not to return. When I met Stephanie and Chuck, I felt an immediate and honest welcome, and I gained a new appreciation for the Holden ministry. It's because of Stephanie and Chuck and the encouragement of other Holden Village friends that I began writing my stories. Mary Koch, Holden's communications coordinator and my associate in this project, encouraged me to write the stories in the form of a memoir rather than attempting to document history.

Much of what Holden Village has become has been a gift from others. Even the prayer that has been designated the "Holden Prayer" was written by the Reverend Eric Milner-White, a priest of the Church of England and first published in 1941: *O God, you have called your servants to ventures of which we cannot see the ending, by paths as yet untrodden, through perils unknown. Give us faith to go out with good courage, not knowing where we go, but only that your hand is leading us and your love supporting us; through Jesus Christ our Lord. Amen.*

It is ironic, but appropriate, that the Holden Prayer was written by an Anglican priest in England twenty years before Holden Village, the spiritual community, was conceived. The miracle of the Holden Village community has been totally dependent on accepting the generous gifts of countless others.

Holden has been a celebration of mystery from the very beginning, the mystery in terms of the original gift, as well as the mystery of how Holden impacted the spiritual, mental, and physical lives of so many people. We should never claim to understand or be able to explain the mysteries associated with Holden Village.

The following are my stories. The vast majority of the memoir, I feel, is factual history. Some things that I'm sharing are probably meaningless trivia, but all that I have written is a part of Holden Village as I experienced it. Enjoy the stories and continue to celebrate the mysteries.

Werner Janssen, 2014

CHAPTER 1

Wes Prieb—Divine
Intervention

WES PRIEB WAS AN ENIGMA who believed with all sincerity that God directed his life. Wes would never question the significance of the burning
bush. I'm sure if Wes saw a burning bush, he would immediately pause
and patiently stand and wait until the bush stopped burning or until
God finally spoke. While waiting, Wes would perhaps recite the words
of a hymn or verbalize several favorite Biblical passages, but he would
never doubt that God was trying to speak to him.

While Wes was working in Alaska in 1957, he read an article in the
Anchorage paper concerning the termination of the Holden Mine, located in the Cascade Mountains in Washington state and belonging to
the Howe Sound Company, with headquarters in Canada. He wrote his
first letter to the Howe Sound Company inquiring as to their asking
price. He was informed that it was available for $100,000. Wes leisurely
pursued the Holden Mine idea, apparently writing only one letter each
year for three years.

He finally received a telegram from someone representing the Howe
Sound Company indicating the company would donate the Holden
buildings and Holden mine claims. The only requirement was that Wes
needed to find an organization that could officially accept the gift with
the capacity to meet the financial requirements for a US Forest Service
permit. Howe Sound owned approximately 240 acres of patented mine

claims, including mineral rights. Howe Sound also owned the buildings
in the company town that we now call Holden Village, but those buildings were located on forest service land, and a special use permit would
be required for any operation. Over the years I consistently heard that
there was a financial transaction of one dollar to make the sale official.
However, I saw a letter in the files documenting that it was a pure gift
from the Howe Sound Company. Not even one dollar was exchanged.
Wes and God negotiated the best deal.

When he received the gift offer, Wes was a student at the Lutheran
Bible Institute (LBI) in Seattle. He approached the LBI president, Dr.
E. V. Stime, and informed him that he had just been given a mining
town in the North Cascade Mountains, 150 highway miles East of Seattle
and accessible only by a forty-mile boat trip followed by a ten-mile ve-
hicle trip up the Railroad Creek Valley to an elevation of 3,200 feet.
Wes asked if LBI would be interested in accepting the gift. Fortunately,
Dr. Stime was tuned into the miracles that occur through prayer and

persistence and not as concerned as to the gift being practical from an operational consideration. He approached the LBI board. Gil Berg was chairman of the board and sufficiently interested to approach some of his acquaintances and investigate the options. Many of Gil's acquaintances were successful business owners and were willing to share their knowledge and time and perhaps a little financial assistance to launch this unique project. Receiving a gift involving a town in the mountains with a capacity for four hundred people was too good to ignore.

The Lutheran Bible Institute wasn't flush with cash, and the agreement called for LBI to accept and hold the gift until a new nonprofit organization could be established. Holden Village, Inc., was established February 2, 1961, and took over the ownership of the new project. The only request from LBI was that it retain 50-percent ownership of the mineral rights of the mine. I have wondered if the forest service ever investigated the financial stability of the Lutheran Bible Institute as an organization that was supposedly financially responsible to accept the gift from Howe Sound. It's possible that the forest service was more interested in finding an organization to take responsibility for the closed mine facilities off the back of the government. The forest service faced some costly obligations if Howe Sound abandoned the entire site.

Wes wasn't an entrepreneur. Wes wasn't a theologian. Wes wasn't a businessman. Wes wasn't a project developer. Wes was fortunately naïve and believed without doubt what he heard in church and read in the Bible. Ask and you will receive. The Bible didn't say how many times you should ask, so Wes assumed you just keep asking. Wes was a person who could see an article in a newspaper about the closing of a mine and immediately think that it might make a great church camp. Wes wouldn't think of potential hurdles, but it's likely Wes would think of drinking coffee and enjoying conversations and singing church songs and sharing religious phrases around a campfire. The improbability of a church camp accessible only via a forty-mile boat trip located in an area without any communications didn't discourage Wes from writing letters to the mine company. Logic and in-depth analysis didn't interfere with Wes's determination to ask for the gift of a town. It's my impression that Wes would have continued writing letters if he hadn't received a positive response from the Howe Sound Company.

When Wes read the story concerning the closing of Holden Mine, he was a civilian employee of the government. He shared with me that at one point the government hired him as a courier. I guess a courier doesn't need to sell anything or express deep thoughts or have the ability to direct people. Wes merely needed to faithfully transport materials from point A to point B. Wes could follow directions, which would make him a good courier. Wes could ride the train or bus for hours or days and enjoy whatever life generated. It is my understanding that Wes also served as a purchasing agent with the government. I don't remember Wes ever mentioning that he had driven a car or even had a license. I never noticed Wes being bored. He must have found it easy to observe life and nature and sit alone and listen to internal spiritual songs and spiritual phrases. He found it easy to talk with a variety of people. Wes seldom initiated a conversation, but he was always willing to listen and respond when appropriate.

After Wes approached Dr. Stime concerning the possibility of the Lutheran Bible Institute accepting the Holden gift, Wes was more or less ignored in terms of any further discussions or decisions concerning the future of Holden. He wasn't an aggressive person, and he would basically wait until being approached before he reacted. I don't recall Wes ever being invited to participate in any planning meetings or even asked to share his thoughts and dreams concerning the development of Holden. He basically became an outsider in the process. I never asked him if he felt left out, but he was human and I'm sure he was somewhat hurt that he was never included. On the other hand, Wes was unique. Rather than being hurt over being ignored, he may have been thrilled that people were seriously pursuing his dream for Holden and that a nonprofit organization was established, a true sign that people were seriously working on this gift.

We talk about Holden being a miracle, but the gift might have been more of a long shot than many realize. Before Wes received the telegram from Howe Sound, several other groups were actively raising funds to buy Holden at the stated price of $100,000. One group was formed to raise funds to purchase Holden and develop a Father Flanagan–type facility for boys. There was also a public announcement that a group was putting a down payment on the facility to develop it into a high-end, year-round recreational area. The Boy Scouts were also interested in the facility for the ultimate Boy Scout camp.

Since Wes wasn't involved with the beginning of this new project he headed to the Southwest after his time at Lutheran Bible Institute and worked at a Navajo Indian Mission. Wes was a good storyteller and had many stories of his working in a distribution center, sorting items donated to the mission by churches. He said he was amazed at how many pairs of high-heeled shoes were sent to the Native Americans, who lived in the desert. He returned to Seattle after his time working in the mission.

To my knowledge, Wes never engaged in political or theological discussions. If the subject of religion was initiated, he was a great listener and could offer religious comments and an affirmation of his faith. Perhaps his genius was that he waited for others to define him in any particular situation, and then he determined whom they wanted him to be. He could easily change from being the proprietor of the popcorn concession to the collector of meaningless memorabilia for the Prieb museum or assuming the character of Santa Claus or a monk. He loved to impersonate W. C. Fields. With Wes being totally responsible for the gift of Holden but not involved in any of its operation or management, there was a lot of speculation about him and his relationship to Holden Village, Inc.

Wes was a sensitive person and he appeared to me to be lonely. This was perhaps why it meant so much for him to be an icon in the Holden community with friends all over the country. He probably appeared in as many photographs as the mine itself or Bonanza Mountain. He wasn't an entrepreneur, but he did firmly believe that God was active in his life. He merely had to wait until God led him in a specific direction. I'll speculate that he had a positive experience at a Bible camp when he was young and therefore had a passion to expand church-related camping opportunities. On the other hand, Wes might have been a shy child and prone to being bullied and was never given the opportunity to attend church camp, so this was his chance to live his dream.

Much of Wes's life became speculation by others. No matter what Wes thought of, it had to be related to God's work. He was always looking for something that might be free or very low-cost. He told me that while in Alaska, he and a friend noticed huge piles of wood shavings from the sawmills—free for the taking. They decided to initiate a business making sweeping compound. (In those days, the main ingredient in sweeping compound was wood shavings.) The name of the new business was Alaska Clean Sweep. They rented a warehouse and began production. The business was short-lived. It's likely they didn't put together a business or marketing plan before beginning production.

Holden wasn't the only item that Wes pursued as a possible gift. Wes was on the mailing list for government surplus property. He shared with me that he bid on a navy ship, moored on Lake Union. I asked him what bid he submitted, and he said one dollar, thinking that if no one else bid he might win. He had no plans for utilizing a ship. He also shared with me about working on the possibility of a small estate or castle on the coast of California. Wes also was in contact with the Lone Star Brewery in Texas concerning the liquidation of its executive retreat. The Lone Star Brewery actually contacted Wes and began to negotiate with him. We acknowledge God was instrumental in the Holden gift, but I also think God was involved in preventing the possibility of Wes owning of a navy ship, a castle, and a Lone Star brewery retreat. Wes was rather naïve, but he was a dreamer and had a strong faith in the mystery of how God works. We are glad that the dream of Holden materialized for Wes and society.

Wes lived a life full of stories. I don't know if he attracted other characters because of his own uniqueness, but he always had great stories. He shared with me that one time he joined a tour going to Europe. He didn't know the nature of the tour until he boarded the ship. It was a tour set up by a national association of undertakers. They apparently had a few rooms left, and that is why Wes got a good price. He indicated that the conversations seemed to concentrate on day-to-day experiences in mortuaries. Wes also frequently rode the bus; invariably he would have a seat partner who also had a unique life and lots of stories.

The first Holden office I occupied was located in the second floor of the Berg Fuel office building in Ballard, Seattle. The office address was 2036½ NW 56th Street, Seattle. Since the Holden office and the house where Wes lived were in relatively close proximity, Wes and I would occasionally meet for lunch. To my knowledge, he never had a job, but he always seemed to manage financially. I always assumed that he must have been living off a trust from his parents. I'm not aware that he worked with the government sufficiently long to receive a pension or retirement. I can't imagine Wes living off of his own investments. I know his father had died some years earlier and his mother remarried. Occasionally he would return to Webster, South Dakota, to visit his mother.

I knew Wes was interested in keeping track of activities involving Holden, but he wasn't really involved in any official way. I got the impression that Gil and the others didn't make an effort to involve Wes. On the other hand, what skill could Wes contribute? I don't think anyone was trying to eliminate him, but he just didn't have any of the skills needed during those early years of activating the facilities. If I was making a trip to Holden, I would invite Wes to join me. We had many enjoyable conversations on the trips to and from Chelan.

During the summer of 1965, we invited Wes to come to the village, but I don't recall if he was immediately asked to run the pool hall. He stayed in the village for a portion of the winter of 1965. Early that winter, Holden experienced a damaging avalanche that took out the electrical power lines between the footbridge across Railroad Creek and the village about a quarter mile away. Holden Village itself was comprised of twenty four buildings. We never found the power lines after the snow melted. We strung temporary power lines in the trees until we could make permanent repairs in the spring. The avalanche also destroyed a two-car garage on the north side of the main road and to the west of Lodge 2. Also destroyed was the "Fire House" on the south side of the main road. It still housed a truck bed originally used on a Holden Mine fire truck and a used jeep given to Holden the previous summer. The jeep survived. The avalanche also filled the north bedroom of Chalet 11 with approximately three feet of snow. The back screened porch on Chalet 10 was also damaged.

During the mine operation, families living in Winston Camp, the housing areas where families lived, had feared this same avalanche path. Parents had volunteered for safety patrols, walking their children through that area in the mornings and afternoons as they walked to and from school.

Oscar Getty, the only resident of Lucerne, the port on Lake Chelan providing access to Holden, sent a message to the forest service, reporting an avalanche had hit the village. I received a call in Seattle from the forest service but, of course, had no details. Oscar actually called from Lucerne to the Chelan Forest Service station via a crank phone over a wire that ran from Stehekin, the remote community at the Northern end of Lake Chelan to the city of Chelan. This phone line was attached to rocks and to trees and needed constant repair, especially after each winter. I drove to Chelan, and the next morning chartered a helicopter and flew into the village, landing east of the schoolhouse. The avalanche had emotionally impacted Wes, and I instructed him to ride the helicopter back to Chelan. It was evident that it wouldn't be physically or mentally healthy for him to remain in the village. Wes spent the rest of that winter in Chelan. When it was clear that the three other staff members who were living at Holden Village at the time were OK and that the village had basically survived,

I snowshoed to Lucerne on the next boat day and caught the boat to Chelan.

We all marvel at Wes and the miracle of his procuring Holden Village. I know Wes prayed a lot and had an unshakable faith in God. When Wes conducted matins, he sounded like a mild-mannered fundamentalist preacher. I don't recall that he ever attended a lecture or presentation. Listening to lectures and discussing subjects such as history, art, and science wasn't of specific interest to him. I'm not sure if he even attended many, if any, Bible studies, not because he didn't have an interest in the Bible, but I assume Wes was comfortable with his knowledge of the Bible and didn't want to be challenged with new information. He never missed a worship service, but he wasn't an early riser. He was seldom seen until coffee break unless he was conducting matins.

When we first invited Wes to live at the village in the summer months, it was a matter of finding something that he could do that would give him a feeling of making a contribution to the operation and community. The pool hall and bowling alley turned out to be the perfect match. I arranged to have Wes receive a small stipend, which was increased over the years. I still don't know what other sources of income he had. The amount he received from Holden would have made it difficult for him to survive. On the other hand, Wes lived a simple life. While in Holden he had very few expenses since coffee, pop corn, lodging, and food were free. His life in the village became centered in the pool hall / bowling alley, more specifically, running the popcorn concession. He was initially the sole proprietor of this concession but later was assigned a volunteer staff member to assist with sales, especially prior to and following vespers.

In 1977, Fritz Norstad was selected as the interim director following Carroll Hinderlie's departure as the first paid Holden Village director. Although Fritz had spent much time in the village over the years as a member of the faculty/teaching staff, he had never had any responsibility for the staff or the village in general. During the summer of 1977, Fritz had a conversation with me about a concern relating to Wes's relationship with the younger boys that spent time in the pool hall. Over the years, I had never received any comments of concern from parents, but apparently at least one couple approached Fritz and raised a concern about the relationship between their son and Wes. Fritz decided that Holden should have Wes evaluated. If any parents raised this concern with Carroll, I was never made aware of it and it was never pursued. The conclusion was that there was no valid concern, and it was OK for Wes to continue operating the pool hall.

Holden Village developed a community over the years that seemed to generate icons or heroes. Wes Prieb and Carroll Hinderlie easily fit this scenario. Wes was recognized as the person who gave birth to Holden Village, and he was elevated to a hero status. Carroll had an extremely strong personality that dominated any conversation or discussion. Carroll became an icon partially through the admiration many had for him and his ability to proclaim the gospel with the clarity of understanding and forgiveness. Wes was perhaps the single-most person identified with Holden Village over the longest period of time. Although he didn't always live in the village on a year-round basis, he was always in residence from mid-May until early winter. This is the period when the village had the highest population and also the greatest turnover of guests. Before Wes retired and moved permanently to Chelan, he had met and become acquainted with parents, grandparents, children, and then grandchildren of families coming to Holden.

Wes in some ways became the Holden mascot. This shouldn't be taken in a negative sense. Wes helped to create this image as he assumed several characters, with appropriate costumes. His early performances in the village talent shows were always eagerly anticipated, not because of the quality of the performances but because everyone wanted to honor Wes for the part he played in Holden history. He wasn't a demanding person and didn't require much attention when in the village. I don't recall Wes ever asking for anything for himself. He appeared to be grateful for having the village as his community and as his home for a portion of each year. The danger for Holden was that heroes or icons can be created but not always comfortably integrated in all aspects of the Holden community.

The pool hall was the hangout for many of the younger guests. Wes was around 45 years of age when he became director of the pool hall but he was someone the younger people could joke with and easily talk to. Since Wes was a Holden hero, their acquaintanceship with him made it easier for them to feel at home in the village, especially when they first arrived. If Wes was your friend, it elevated your status in the community. This phenomenon was also true for some of the staff who became acquainted with Wes. Wes had a personality that didn't vary too much in terms of one being a long-time acquaintance or a new arrival. The main difference was that if one was previously acquainted with Wes, one could immediately greet him with a phrase or a joke that confirmed one to be a member of the unofficial pool hall fraternity. Wes for many years appeared at the bus departure in his monk's robe costume, which maintained his Holden image even as the buses left for the dock on Lake Chelan. There were many questions about Wes over the years. In reality, he remained somewhat of a mystery and, at the same time, one of the central Holden images that shaped Holden in a unique way.

Holden Village always lived and celebrated with a certain degree of make-believe. The worship life was of course genuine, and the lectures covered significant areas of life and faith, offered by very competent people. Perhaps due to the remote site and lack of external news and entertainment being piped into the Railroad Creek Valley, a sense of make-believe either emerged naturally or became a necessity for the mental health of the people and a healthy community spirit. This is especially true during the winter months.

In 1990, the series *Northern Exposure* began running on network TV. It was about the small, remotely located, make-believe Alaska town of Cicely. I loved this series because it reminded me of the life that I knew at Holden Village in the 1960s and 1970s. In *Northern Exposure*, celebrations were instituted to fit the people and location. Strong personalities ran the town but not the community. The town included the very conservative and the very liberal. Organized religion wasn't central to Cicely, but spirituality was an important part of life in the community. Cicely, as well as Holden, had strong characters that created real life. Cicely was a community that celebrated make-believe as reality. I sometimes wondered if the writers of *Northern Exposure* had at some point visited Holden Village.

Wes was one of the characters in the real-life story of Holden. He created characters that he also acted out within the community, bringing smiles to many young people and adults alike. His make-believe gave permission for others to be themselves or take on new identities while at Holden and celebrate life within a community. Wes was very important to the overall success of Holden Village, not only in terms of his writing those letters but also for his view of life. Life could be filled with jokes and meaningless memorabilia. Life could be filled with prayers and religious phrases, but it could also be filled with make-believe. Wes made sure that Holden didn't become too serious even though the program centered on themes and subjects filled with spiritual depth. Because Wes could graciously act out various characters in the village, it allowed Holden to be full of frivolity, encouraging all the youth and adults to celebrate life without the community losing control.

Wes once gave me his recipe for Rye Wine. I don't recall if this was a family recipe or if he knew we were making elderberry wine and thought we needed another option.

Wes's Rye Wine
1 pound of raisins
4 cups of rye
4 quarts of boiling water
8 cups of sugar

Mix—let cool.
Add 3 pkg. yeast.
Let stand two weeks.

Stir once a day.
Strain and put into bottles—do not cap tight.
Siphon off the settlings.
Cap in two weeks when wine has cleared.

Wes was unique to the success of Holden and its psychological well-being. Since he was the only person involved in the acquisition of Holden, it would be evident that human ingenuity and business expertise couldn't be credited with Holden's gift. Until Wes approached Dr. Stime concerning the gift, it's likely that no other person knew that he was writing letters to Howe Sound Mining Company. There were no committees meeting to strategize an acquisition plan, no business consultants outlining the financial pathway to a successful future, and no pastors or bishops gathering to give a spiritual direction and blessing to the program outline. Besides the low-key effort by Wes, Holden began through the efforts of many young adults and retired or semiretired individuals who were given the opportunity to celebrate their talents and abilities.

Holden Village was born through the naïve efforts of a humble servant of God and put into daily operation through the involvement of a maverick theologian who was considered by many to be an outcast in the Lutheran Church and a recently graduated aeronautical engineer who had no experience managing volunteers or facilities. Miracles happen when freedom within nature and the human life are allowed to develop through relatively free interaction but without too much organizational interference.

CHAPTER 2

Discovering A New Future

I CAN'T DOCUMENT THAT ATTENDING church has changed my life, but I can document that a bulletin insert that I never read powerfully impacted my life from age twenty-two until the present.

Ron Lenz, my roommate at Purdue University, accepted a job at the Boeing Company in Seattle in 1960, six months before I graduated. Upon graduation, I also received a job offer from Boeing, as well as from companies in Los Angeles; San Diego; and Hampton, Virginia. I studied the offers carefully, and although the compensation offered by the Boeing Company was slightly lower, I decided to move to Seattle. To be honest, my reasoning wasn't based on a detailed analysis of how Boeing might launch my exciting engineering career, but more along the lines that Ron had a two-bedroom apartment with one bedroom available for my use. If I hadn't moved to Seattle and not worked for the Boeing Company, I would have missed the opportunity to experience the excitement of Holden Village for twenty years and the impact Holden continued to offer throughout my life. Ron belonged to the Lutheran Church–Missouri Synod, and I belonged to the American Lutheran Church. Ron and I never discussed theology or church doctrines. He was rather conservative, and I was an emerging liberal. It's my understanding that he continued working with Boeing through his entire career. I lost track of Ron over the years, but I'm forever grateful for his involvement in my life.

One Sunday in early September 1961, Ron read a bulletin insert from his church inviting people to Holden Village to participate in the dedication of the newly installed diesel-electric generators. I attended Cross and Crown Lutheran Church in Renton, but either they didn't have the bulletin insert, I missed church that Sunday, or I was too caught up in the power of the sermon to read the bulletin. Ron was intrigued by the possibility of visiting Holden and urged me to join him for the weekend of September 30. I was interested, but I was also scheduled to work two consecutive eight-hour shifts involving airfoil testing. I would get home at two o'clock Saturday morning, and we would leave for Lake Chelan at six. I'm forever grateful that Ron encouraged, or perhaps insisted, that I join him for this trip. Without Ron being my Purdue roommate, and without his working for Boeing, and without his having a two-bedroom apartment, and without his faithful attendance of a Missouri Synod Lutheran Church and reading a bulletin insert, my life would have be very different.

Holden Village and the Railroad Creek Valley are examples of God creating and then God encouraging creation to venture into the unknown. I think the Railroad Creek Valley, the Howe Sound Holden Mine, and the eventual development of what we now call Holden Village provided God with many laughs and a few tears over what we know as the period of recorded history.

God may be the Creator, but God also has the courage and the humor to give the creation total freedom to erupt into volcanoes, get covered with snow and ice, and then celebrate the power of gravity moving the ice, carving out the valley with powerful rivers and marvelous lakes, and then even leaving exposed minerals to be visually discovered. Freedom, not control, was the modus operandi allowing curious animals and humans to roam the wilderness seeking needed sustenance and chasing dreams. And God looked at the work that had been accomplished and probably said, "With the resources available and with the limitation of human wisdom, I think this is as good as can be expected."

Probably no humans came up Lake Chelan until our Native American brothers and sisters responded to their curiosity to determine if anything of interest could be at the end of a very long and often-wild body of water. Originally there weren't many fish in the lake, so the lake had little value except for transportation into the unknown and wonderfully clear, cold water. I don't know the stories of the first people to understand if their curiosity got them into trouble or perhaps even into physical peril. We do know that it always takes a few individuals with unending curiosity to step out into "ventures of which they cannot see the ending, by paths as yet untrodden, through perils unknown" before others follow. The Native American community was probably the first in the Railroad Creek Valley. Archeological surveys confirmed that Native American activities were in the Refrigerator Harbor area, a natural camping area in Lucerne, as well as a short distance up the valley.

It probably took only one successful canoe traveling up Lake Chelan to determine there were no monsters in the lake, thus encouraging many others to follow. It didn't take long before those responding to the urge to locate the ideal living site, especially with freedom to live and celebrate the sustainability of nature, traveled uplake. Pioneers began settling in Stehekin around 1883. I'm guessing those seeking the beauty and isolation of the Stehekin valley might have been people who were trying to find a place where nature was untouched and where government interference was minimal. They wanted to live in an area where they could partner with nature and celebrate the daily newness of life. Certain people have a desire to develop a one-to-one relationship with nature; interrelationship with larger numbers of humans doesn't have high priority. It's amazing that people build home sites or small cabins along Lake Chelan without any communications and with total dependence on the commercial boat service. There are always people who enjoy isolation and others who are looking for riches from hidden minerals or the opportunity to homestead and for the first time occupy their own land.

Adventurous people from Seattle who could afford to travel soon discovered it doesn't rain as much in Eastern Washington. If a summer outing was on the docket, a camping trip up Lake Chelan would offer the ideal experience with the added benefit of providing bragging rights at winter dinner parties. Some people enjoy traveling in style even when seeking a wilderness experience. Status requires help to do the menial tasks such as rowing the boat, securing the camping location, cooking the meals, and organizing happy hours. Those with financial means can afford to hire people to do the work. All people have sensitivities and generally agree that their household associates deserve a little free time for physical and mental rejuvenation.

In the late 1890's, along comes J. H. Holden, employee of the wealthy Denny family from Seattle. J. H. was a curious person. Wilderness is an ideal location for those with curious minds. J. H. was an amateur prospector and a professional dreamer. On his days off during the Denny family's Lake Chelan camping trips, J. H. wandered up the Railroad Creek Valley and, after several summer camping trips, made it to what we call Copper Mountain, across Railroad Creek from the current location of Holden Village. If J. H. knew anything about geology, it was through curiosity, independent reading, and perhaps talking with Denny household visitors who might have had an interest in geology or actual mining experience.

Observation of the discolored rock on the slopes of Copper Mountain piqued curiosity of J. H. and elevated his testosterone level to the point where he knew being a household associate was in his past and owning a mine was his future. J. H. marked out his claim on one of the trips and officially recorded the mine claim with the appropriate government department.

In the "good old days," our government didn't have many rules and regulations that were adequately patrolled. Extraction of minerals has always been encouraged by the government, including financial incentives. Prospectors in some remote areas, including the Railroad Creek Valley, were more concerned with convenience in getting to prospecting sites in the upper valley than they were in preserving timber and the environment. The accepted prospecting practice was for the last prospector out of the valley before winter to set fire to the undergrowth to burn off all the brush that made walking or riding a horse up the valley in early summer difficult. No concern for preservation of other resources! Dreams of riches were their only interest. Mine claims still exist in the valley, including claims up toward Bonanza Mountain a few miles to the West of the Holden mine. The Crown Point Mine just below Lyman Lake at the base of Bonanza Mountain actually operated. The rumor is that a German company operated the Crown Point Mine during World War I, for molybdenum ore extraction.

When J. H. Holden got serious about mining, the Denny family thought they should share in the potential riches, since it was their trips and their money that allowed J. H. to discover the outcropping of what he thought was valuable ore. The courts in Chelan County didn't agree with the Denny family, and J. H. was left as the sole owner of the mining claims in Railroad Creek Valley. J. H. did what all prospectors do when they don't have any cash reserves to pursue an actual operation: he sold stock. He was probably a better stock salesperson than developer of a new mine. Eventually, the Howe Sound Mining Company became owners of the mine in the Railroad Creek Valley.

Howe Sound spent several years gathering information to help determine the profitability of an actual mining operation. The ore needed to end up at a smelter in Tacoma, Washington. The mine had no road or rail access. Even an uneducated developer could tell that the financial challenges to realize a profit from an operation this remote were severe. Howe Sound executives knew that unless the ore would assay out to a specific level, with indications that sufficient ore would be available for twenty years, it would never be a viable operation. By a narrow margin, exploration indicated that the mineral content and the estimates of total ore available confirmed the information needed to proceed. The early mining community was located on the hillside on the south side of the valley above Railroad Creek and was called Honeymoon Heights. Some relics and foundations still exist at the Honeymoon site.

Before the mining operation could be turned over to the operations division of Howe Sound, there was a major fire in Copper Basin and the lower slopes of the Railroad Creek Valley. Howe Sound had been doing test borings in Copper Basin, and with prospectors not having a good reputation concerning the care of nature, the forest service naturally assumed that the Howe Sound exploration crews were responsible for the fire. The story, as told to me by William S. Barquist, the exploration mine engineer for Howe Sound between 1928 and 1932, was that the forest supervisor from the Wenatchee National Forest office was on his way to deliver documents holding Howe Sound Mining Company responsible for the fire in Copper Basin.

Gordon Stuart, forest service ranger at Lucerne, escorted the supervisor and his entourage to the Howe Sound mine manager to present him with a bill for $50,000 for the cost of the fire. As they entered the area of the burn, Stuart discovered a tree that had been struck by lightening, which meant that Howe Sound was no longer deemed responsible. When they rode down to the office of the exploration crew, it was reported that the supervisor tore up the bill covering the fire costs in front of Mr. Barquist and indicated how close they had come to being charged $50,000. Mr. Barquist related that if the cost of the fire had been the responsibility of the mine, Howe Sound would have pulled out, since it appeared to be a marginal ore deposit to begin with. Now we see that, without the sharp eyes of Gordon Stuart, the future involvement of Howe Sound and Holden Mine in Railroad Creek Valley would never have materialized. Without the love of the valley and the keen observation by Stuart, there would be no Holden Village retreat center. Many years later, Stuart was always skeptical of the religious activities at Holden Village, but he never realized that he was partially responsible for the retreat center now in existence. God works in mysterious ways.

Before a full scale mining operation could begin a complete town was built to house, feed and provide recreation activity for the miners. Twenty four building were constructed. The buildings included a dining hall and kitchen, a hospital, a recreation building with full size basketball court and 35 mm movie projector plus a bowling alley pool hall and an area for gambling tables and slot machines. They also constructed fourteen chalets for the management staff and six lodges to house single miners. A school house was added after wives and families were allowed to join the men working in the mine. When families moved into the valley, a second village was built, called Winston Camp. Winston Construction was a contractor for the mine. Winston Camp was located approximately one half miles west of the management town of Holden. Winston Camp and Holden were constructed on the North side of Railroad Creek which flowed approximately twenty miles from Lyman Lake at the west end of Railroad Creek valley to Lake Chelan at Lucerne.

Access to Holden was by a passenger ferry on Lake Chelan. The Lake Chelan Boat Company operated the Lady of the Lake and the Speedway, the two passenger boats used on Lake Chelan until 1976 when a new vessel was added. All freight was shipped by motor barge also operated by the Lake Chelan Boat Company.

When the Holden division of the Howe Sound Mine Company shut down in 1957, the mine workers had a difficult time accepting that the mine was closing. Finally the mine management announced a date when water and electricity would be shut off. The mine management offered to transport homes owned by miners downlake if the homes were dismantled. A few homeowners actually made use of this offer.

Oscar Getty, resident and landowner in Lucerne, was hired by the Howe Sound Company to keep an eye on the Holden facility after the mine closed. Lucerne is the port allowing access up to Railroad Creek Valley as well as the Domke Lake area. Oscar wasn't what you would identify as the ideal caretaker or bouncer, but he was a resident of Lucerne and could easily keep an eye on traffic in and out of Holden. Oscar at the time was probably in his sixties and stood at least five foot four, had a winning smile, and knew that anyone tying to take things from Holden would require a trip on Lake Chelan, giving him plenty of time to alert authorities.

Holden Village now had the opportunity to be a part of the uplake Chelan and Railroad Creek Valley history with a very unique social fabric. Holden Village, the retreat center, moved into this geographical community that many had occupied before Holden Mine became operational. Holden as a retreat center was in many ways an intrusion into their community, just as the mine had been. Between Gordon Stuart and Oscar Getty, who were the real residents of the Railroad Creek Valley, only Gordon would at times make comments about the activities at Holden and the religious nature of the program. I hope Holden in some way gave back something positive to these special people over the years. Oscar and Gordon weren't religious men, but I'm sure that God found delight in their unique lives and probably gained some new insights from what had been created in these two special individuals. Since God gave complete freedom to creation, God also delighted in some unusual results.

The Howe Sound Mine Holden Division closed in June of 1957. A new nonprofit corporation, Holden Village, Inc., legally came into existence in Washington State on February 2, 1961. At the closing of the mine, the Chelan County Public Utility District (PUD), which owned the electrical system providing power to the mine and concentrating mill, removed the electrical distribution yard. Washington Water Power originally owned and operated the hydroelectric installation at Chelan Falls, which had also involved the building of a dam at the south end of Lake Chelan, raising the level of Lake Chelan by twenty-two feet. This dam had been built in 1928. Power lines from Chelan to Holden had been built along the north shore of Lake Chelan, crossing the lake in the area of Domke Falls and proceeding up Railroad Creek Valley to Holden Mine. The removal of the transformers and switches at the mine in 1957 meant no electricity was available within the Railroad Creek valley.

Holden intrigued me for several reasons. It's located in, reportedly, one of the most spectacular areas of the North Cascade Mountains. As soon as I moved to Seattle, I joined many other wannabe mountain climbers. I joined the Seattle Mountaineers and enrolled in the basic climbing class. When I joined REI (Recreation Equipment, Inc.), my membership number was below fifteen thousand, and REI was still located in a small upstairs room in the heart of downtown Seattle.

Involvement in church activities was certainly a factor that influenced my early life and probably my interest in Holden Village. I was motivated to read and study, to help answer questions clarifying the mystery of faith and determine the validity of my spiritual life as it related to my quest for meaning. My father was a pastor, and my mother was the daughter of a pastor and the sister of three other pastors. My father's father was also a pastor. Dad was very involved in the youth program and was one of the leaders of youth activities in the Central District of the former American Lutheran Church. It was serendipitous that Dr. Marcus Rieke was the youth director in the national office of the American Lutheran Church, and Dad worked with him coordinating the youth work in the Central District.

Marcus Rieke was the father of Mary Schramm and John Rieke and the brother of Vern Rieke. Mary Schramm and her husband, John, were directors of Holden the last five years of my employment as Holden manager. John Rieke and his wife, Karen, were volunteers for a year at Holden and then moved to Leavenworth, where they continued to positively impact my life. Dr. Vern Rieke was a professor at the University of Washington Law School and was the first chairman of the Holden board, serving for at least fifteen years in that capacity. I met Marcus Rieke on a family trip to Columbus, Ohio, in perhaps 1949, but until my time at Holden I had never met Mary Schramm, John Rieke, or Vern Rieke.

Our family moved from Denver, Colorado, to DeWitt, Nebraska, in 1944, and I spent the twelve years of my initial schooling in DeWitt. A rural town with a population of 530, DeWitt was unique for a small town as it was the home of the world famous Petersen Vise-Grip wrench factory. I think DeWitt had a 100-percent employment rate. My early life was shaped by friendship with the Petersens, enjoying flights in their Piper Tri Pacer and traveling to dirt track races to watch the race car they had built.

My first official job, when I was in eighth grade, was as janitor of the DeWitt State Bank. Bob Berkley, the bank manager, gave me the key to the bank, which definitely built my self-confidence, knowing that I was trusted with access to the bank at age twelve. When I reached age sixteen, I worked summers in the Vise-Grip wrench factory and earned forty-nine dollars per week alongside the other full-time workers with the same pay. This money helped pay for my early college education.

Growing up in a small community allowed me to participate in many school activities. The school was so small that I lettered four years in football, basketball, and track. I also played trombone in the band. I chose the trombone because I was attracted to the girl playing first trombone. I had the lead in the musical *Hansel and Gretel* and considered the girl playing Gretel very interesting. I graduated in a class of seventeen. My first two years of college were at Wartburg College in Waverly, Iowa. My greatest accomplishment at Wartburg was winning second place in the homecoming beard growing and shaving contest. I then transferred to Purdue University to complete my degree in aeronautical engineering. My greatest accomplishment at Purdue was graduating.

Worship and church activities were literally the core of our life in a parsonage in the 1940s and early 1950s. Many of our summer vacations meant attending the Bible camp organized by my father at the YMCA Camp in Estes Park, Colorado. I loved the main lodge at the YMCA Camp with its huge fireplaces at each end of the room and fires always lit. Perhaps my enjoyment of the mountains began on those trips, and my first mountain hikes occurred around Estes Park YMCA Camp. The books I really enjoyed while growing up included the Sugar Creek Gang series. I didn't realize until I recently Googled them that these were Christian books with moral and religious messages. I had thought they were pure adventure stories. I really expected my parents, at some point, to put pressure on me to attend seminary. Thankfully they believed in the guidance of the Holy Spirit, and the Holy Spirit never communicated with me—at least in terms of becoming a pastor.

Perhaps the most profound spiritual experience I encountered in my life occurred while working at Boeing. Our group was moved from the main engineering building at Plant 2 to the Second Avenue building in downtown Seattle. I began commuting via the city bus. One of the books I read on the commute was *Mere Christianity* by C. S. Lewis. I still have my original copy. I assume that my interest in engineering and technology resulted from a somewhat curious and questioning mind. Although I never had problems with a belief in God or the virgin birth or the mystery of faith, I still continuously was mildly preoccupied with seeking clarification of religious concepts based on a certain element of logic combined with faith that is accepted, not proved. C. S. Lewis, through his writing of *Mere Christianity,* made that connection for me. Shortly after completing *Mere Christianity,* I decided to volunteer for a summer at Holden.

I began working for The Boeing Company in February 1961 in the aerospace division. I graduated with a degree in aeronautical engineering, and yet when I arrived at Boeing it was clear that my education was merely an indication that I had the capacity to learn but would need to start basically from scratch as an engineer. In 1961 we were still using the slide rule. High-speed electronic calculators were available if checked out and their use justified. Computers were just in the process of being discussed but weren't available. On my first day at Boeing, I was informed that our group hadn't yet assembled and I was the first one to arrive. I was given multiple sets of manuals and told to read the manuals until other members of the group arrived. I don't recall that the manuals had anything to do with our group or the work we would be doing.

The work involved applied research dealing with aerothermodynamic issues as related to shock-wave impingement on airfoils. Boeing was working on a US Air Force study contract to investigate the feasibility of designing an aerospace plane. The plane would fly into orbit from an existing Strategic Air Command base, deliver supplies into close earth orbit, and then return to the base. The aerospace plane was never built.

I really enjoyed my brief career at Boeing. The group I worked with never grew beyond five people; it was easy to develop a meaningful working relationship among them. In a very short time, I accomplished what I had imagined was the work of a lifetime in engineering, so it wasn't hard to start thinking that I may not stay in engineering until retirement. I was able to be involved with testing projects at Boeing involving their new-concept wind tunnel, simulating conditions above Mach 15. I also had the opportunity to be involved with airfoil testing at the US Air Force research facility at Tullahoma, Tennessee. As a result of the work of our team, I was listed as a coauthor of a technical paper titled "A Study of Shock Impingements on Boundary Layers at Mach 16." It was printed and distributed by the Stanford University Press for the Heat Transfer and Fluid Mechanics Institute at its 1962 meeting, held at the University of Washington.

Shortly before resigning from my engineering position and accepting the offer to become the first full-time general manger of Holden Village, I received an offer from Boeing for a lead position for the testing portion of a new project. I never regretted my move from engineering to managing Holden at age twenty-four. The engineering and technical background served me well in terms of studying and implementing various projects at Holden over the next twenty years. Science and technology have been a continuous interest in my life.

For Holden Village to begin operating a source of electricity was critical. Diesel-electric units were the only option for quickly providing electric power needed. Two reconditioned diesel-electric units, from a fishing village in Alaska, each generating fifty kilowatts, were installed during the summer of 1961.

The diesel generator dedication was set for Saturday afternoon, September 30, 1961. Ron and I arrived at Lucerne after an enjoyable ride uplake on the old *Lady of the Lake*. The dock at Lucerne was the dock used by the mine for twenty years. It was oil soaked, the deck functional but well worn. The old crane that loaded the barges with the seven-ton vats of copper, gold, silver and zinc concentrate from the mill was still sitting on the track. The aroma of aged grease and old mechanical equipment hung heavy in the air.

My first trip from Lucerne to Holden was on the back of a new 1961 International flatbed truck. Luggage was loaded first and then the thirty of us occupied the rest of the available space. Gil Berg, volunteer Holden manager/director, was the driver. I learned later that Gil didn't have the best reputation as a driver, but outside of being dusty and bumpy with a few unannounced quick stops to share points of interest, the trip was enjoyable. The flatbed truck was the first Holden Village–owned vehicle and was purchased through a loan from Gil. That loan of $1,500 was the only loan Holden incurred, at least through the twenty years I was involved. I'm not even certain that Gil was paid back. Holden had no money at the beginning. Over the years, the operation lived from day to day, paying bills and activating the facility through a few donations and an increasing number of paying guests.

I was new to the Seattle area and had little knowledge of the Lutheran tradition in the Pacific Northwest nor the Norwegian section of Seattle called Ballard, nor the KING-TV station, nor the Lutheran Bible Institute. I really don't remember too much during that first weekend at Holden Village, but I do remember that the dedication ceremony was held in the gymnasium, which was dark and cold. In September 1961, the village facilities were without heat or hot water. Sufficient light came through the upper windows of the gym to allow adequate illumination for the afternoon dedication service. Pastor Brown of Phinney Ridge Lutheran Church in Seattle was invited to officially bless the units. The dedication was rather traditional, with a brief service and prayer.

Stan Boreson, entertainer with a greatly loved program on KING-TV, was the warm-up act prior to the religious portion of the dedication. I found out later that Stan was a rather well-known personality in the Seattle area. He was also a member of one of the Lutheran Churches. He had a rich Norwegian heritage and found his niche as a performer, singing Norwegian songs and telling Scandinavian jokes. The Stan Boreson TV show not only featured Stan but also his famous basset hound named Slo Mo.

Slo Mo hadn't made the trip to Holden. Stan was volunteering his time for the weekend, and to my knowledge it was the only time Stan Boreson visited Holden Village. I later worked for Harriet Bullitt, owner along with her sister Patsy, of KING Broadcasting after their mother died. Harriet's mother originally hired Stan Boreson and launched his rather long career at KING-TV.

Pastor Brown offered traditional and appropriate words during the official dedication. Prayers were offered and, I'm sure, received, but when Pastor Brown gave the signal for the electricity to flow, nothing happened. I think God was letting us know that in the years ahead we shouldn't expect smooth sailing and that extra patience would be required in all we did. We nervously waited. Finally Reuben Thompson, village caretaker, appeared and informed us that a wire had burned off and there would be a slight delay. No major problem since Stan Boreson took charge of the silence during the delay and offered more Norwegian songs and jokes. Soon the lights illuminated the gym, and the Holden Village operation began its journey forward.

Before we left Holden that Sunday, Vic Nelson, a friend of Gil Berg and a faithful Holden volunteer, made a presentation after lunch encouraging any and all to volunteer in the work of launching the future of Holden Village. I responded to the "altar call"—actually it was more like a volunteer request. I was appointed to join the Development Council and also the Promotion and Finance Committee. Vic was typical of many volunteers who launched Holden Village. He owned Victor Nelson Furs at 611 Pine in Seattle. His shop was located just across the street from the famous Frederick & Nelson store in downtown Seattle. Vic was well connected with important people in the Seattle area, which was most convenient when needing specialized help or contacts. Two or three Holden planning meetings I attended were held in his fur store. Having grown up the son of a pastor in rural Nebraska, I was amazed there were stores devoted to selling, storing, and repairing expensive furs.

I visited the village again in 1962 and, in fact, introduced my brother and his family as well as my parents to the excitement and beauty of Holden. My brother, Erwin, was moving his wife, Maurine, and daughter, Julie, to Seattle to begin his medical internship at King County Hospital. Following his internship he began a research residency at the University of Washington Hospital before being inducted into the navy at the beginning of the Vietnam War. My parents, my brother, and his family visited the village frequently during the ensuing years.

Rueben Thompson was the first resident of the new Holden Village and was the village caretaker for several years. Rueben shouldn't be forgotten, as he was one of the Holden pioneers who helped shape its future. For at least two winters, Rueben stayed at the village as the lone resident. He was the brother of Stan Thompson, who managed a print shop in Seattle and was an acquaintance of Gil. Stan assisted in the graphics and printing of many of the initial brochures and basic promotional material for Holden. Rueben had a challenge with alcoholism and was the first person that came to Holden with the hope of healing. He was a great person and was loved by all staff and guests. Rueben's small dog, named Bugger, was a faithful companion for Rueben and a mascot for the village, appearing in many early photographs. During the winter, Rueben would snowshoe down to Lake Chelan at least once a month to pick up mail and visit Oscar Getty.

During the winter, Rueben lived in Chalet 1 with heat from the inefficient wood fireplace in the living room and the wood cookstove in the kitchen. Running water was provided from a spring behind the chalet. A hose from the spring ran into the kitchen. The village water system had been drained to avoid freezing, since the main water pipe was unprotected under the footbridge. Electricity for Ruben, the only oc-cupant of the village the first couple of winters, was available via a small Briggs and Stratton gas generator. Before daylight disappeared each eve-ning, Rueben would fill the small gas tank and then time his evening activities so he was in bed before the gas was consumed and lighting was lost until daybreak.

The celebration of Christmas in July began as a loving gesture to Rueben. He was in the village by himself for at least two Christmases. The staff decided that the village should celebrate Christmas on July 25 so Rueben could enjoy a Christmas celebration with his extended family and surrounded by a community. Christmas in July became a tradition, and in the early years was the one time of the summer when all of the rooms would be occupied. Rueben was a great caretaker and public rela-tions person, welcoming people who came to visit when Holden had no reputation in terms of a significant program. People recognized Holden as a people place partly because of Rueben, who shared his infectious smile and a willingness to serve and help everyone. It was obvious to me that Rueben lived in constant gratitude for the opportunity to live and work at Holden. For many people, Rueben was the image of Holden dur-ing those initial years.

Virtually all of the early work and volunteer activity took place in the Northwest. It was easy to become a member of a Holden committee with the only requirement a willingness to participate. A donation wasn't required for committee membership but was encouraged. I recently found a thank-you letter, signed by Gil, for a twenty-five-dollar donation I made in 1961.

During my first weekend at Holden, I heard the name Wes Prieb, but he wasn't in the village and not much information was offered in terms of his relationship with Holden. I wondered why, if Wes was so important to Holden Village, he wasn't around. Only later did I learn that Wes had played the pivotal role in obtaining Holden Village as a gift from Howe Sound.

The opportunity to volunteer and work on several of the Holden committees was a marvelous way for me to get acquainted with some of the movers and shakers within the Lutheran Church in the Seattle area. Wes's success in obtaining Holden predated the merger of several of the Lutheran Church bodies nationally, but in the Seattle area there didn't appear to be much competition or separation of the Lutheran groups. I was elected to the council of the Pacific Northwest District, which gave me an opportunity to meet and get acquainted with many pastors and laypeople in the district. I soon learned that the Northwest was one of the least churched areas within the United States. The speculation I heard indicated that the Northwest was the area where many young individuals and young families moved in order to get away from some of their over religious parents and families in the Midwest. That theory was never confirmed, but it's entirely possible that there was some basis for it.

The success of Holden might have derived from this theory and would help authenticate its validity. People living in the Northwest but not active in congregational life seemed to be willing to volunteer and participate in the Holden activities. Holden was perhaps one way for displaced Midwest Lutherans to deal with buried guilt without the necessity of becoming too involved in organizational activities, which too often became the main emphasis in many of the churches.

Gil Berg was definitely the "main man" initiating the Holden dream. Wes didn't have any money and wasn't really considered an entrepreneur with contacts or leadership skills to motivate people in joining a challenging cause. If a businessman with a business plan had seen the newspaper article concerning the closing of Holden Mine, it's likely that he would have attempted to purchase Holden for $100,000, and Wes's effort would have failed. I think Wes assumed that if God wanted Holden to be involved in the work of the church and society, God would make sure that Howe Sound Mining Company gave the property to the right organization. Wes was the perfect candidate to pursue an unreasonable idea. Gil was the person to bring the people together to implement an idea that was beyond comprehension, located in an area that was almost impossible to access. Simple faith may not be a business plan, but with Wes involved, it gave birth to a powerful community and ministry.

Gil owned and operated a very successful home oil-distributing business in Ballard. He was sufficiently wealthy and generous to his church and to the Lutheran Bible Institute (LBI). Gil had the respect of many people in the Seattle area even outside of the Lutheran Church. In general, Gil was a person who knew people. Some of them had money, and all of them appeared to have talent and skills, allowing Holden to be born again. Gil was sufficiently close enough to retirement that he had trained his son-in-law, Clyde Lohman, to run the fuel business, giving Gil the freedom to spend time with Holden activities on a volunteer basis. He made numerous trips to Holden beginning in 1960 and was more or less in residence at Holden during the summers of 1961 through 1963.

He wasn't a program person but had the ability of knowing people and meeting new people who would be instrumental in activating the village, thus allowing a program to begin. Gil was a good salesperson. If he thought someone had the means to benefit Holden Village, he was an excellent "closer" and convinced him or her to join the team. He had respect and admiration from people who came to do the dirty work of making Holden Village useable.

Gil began gathering a group of men that he called the Development Council, primarily people who had the skills to deal with facilities, vehicles, and the overall infrastructure needed for a village to function. The Development Council was a unique and eclectic group of volunteers. Some wives were involved to a minor extent, especially when there were questions with interior furnishing, etc. Only one woman was officially a member of the Development Council. No excuses offered. That was just how life was in the early 1960s.

The need for electricity was one of the first challenges the new Development Council addressed. Gil traveled around the state visiting pastors and being introduced to people who might help financially or technically to solve problems. Lou and Jerry Sheffels, father and son from Wilbur, Washington, became very involved. They owned extensive wheat land in eastern Washington and Montana. They gave a financial gift, allowing Holden to purchase a ten-passenger Ford Econoline van that could transport people between Lucerne and Holden more comfortably than the flatbed truck.

Lou and Jerry also located some used hydroelectric equipment stored in a warehouse in Idaho; it had originally been used in an irrigation project. The Sheffels purchased the hydro equipment, consisting of two Pelton wheels, two generators, mechanical governors, and electric switchboards, for $1,200 and gave this valuable find to Holden. The Sheffels also gave the village a four-wheel-drive military-surplus vehicle we called the "bomb truck." It had several winches and lifts. They also made arrangements for the village to obtain a bus that the Hanford nuclear operation in Kennewick, Washington sold as surplus.

Lou and Jerry also involved others, including Terry Sverdsten from Cataldo, Idaho. Jerry and Terry had been classmates at Pacific Lutheran University. The Sverdsten family owned and operated a large logging operation, owning and maintaining heavy equipment. Terry would bring several of his mechanics to Holden in the spring to go over our equipment to assure its integrity for the coming year. I heard some years later that Terry was elected to the Idaho State Legislature and served for a number of terms.

In mid-May each year, when the roads were snow-free, a group of volunteers would spend a weekend opening the village and checking equipment. When opening the village for the season in mid-May 1964, Rueben mentioned that his Briggs and Stratton generator had quit working. Lou went to work and took apart the one-cylinder engine. He determined that the valves needed to be ground but had none of the specific equipment needed. That didn't stop Lou. He made a little grinding compound with fine sand grit and oil and used a makeshift device for rotating the valve. When the operation was complete, he reassembled the engine. With the first pull of the rope, the engine sprang to life. It was evident to me that with people like Lou and the other volunteers, Holden had the possibility of a future life.

The Sheffels, the Sverdstens, and some of the other miracle workers on the Development Council gradually dropped away from participating and supporting Holden Village after what they perceived as a lack of appreciation for the work and leadership of Gil and the fact that Gil was put out to pasture when Carroll Hinderlie arrived.

The Development Council also included Bernard Anderson, insurance executive with Frank B. Hall Insurance Co. in Seattle; Burton Appelo, commercial real estate specialist; Fred Carlson, generation equipment sales- and service; Walt Jesernig, heavy construction project manager; Ralph Peterson, infrastructure specialist and consultant with Pacific Pipe and Supply Company; Henry Schwecke, hydro generation engineer; Stan Thompson, printing and publications adviser; and Erik West, telephone and communication engineer. The others on the committee that need to be documented included Easter Anderson, Dick Brynestad, Melvin Brynestad, Robert Chervensk, Warren Dewing, Clair Grahn, John Hill, Herman Johnson, Clyde Lohman, Harold Miller, Lloyd Nelson, Ed Ottum, Gail Peck, Erik Pihl, Bill Guenturn, Max Ritter, Henry Streitz, Orin Thykeson, Charles Tuvey, Art Torvie, Lyle Undlin, and Al Walker. There were others who contributed to the early resurrection of Holden Village, and I think it's important that these people at least be mentioned so they are never forgotten. To my knowledge, only one or two of these people are still alive at this writing.

In June 1963, Carroll Hinderlie arrived as the new executive director of Holden Village. For the first time in the brief Holden Village history, full-time paid management was involved. The Development Council was more or less disbanded within six months after Carroll arrived as director. When I became manager, I continued to consult with many of these people even though the council was no longer officially functioning. Many on the Development Council were extremely talented individuals, and many became my close friends. To me, the people who volunteered on the council were miracle workers. They didn't lecture about miracles; they performed miracles. It was most unfortunate that those with expertise in facility, equipment, and activity requiring manual labor were not-so-quietly eliminated from those who were vital in bringing Holden back to life. It was almost a case of class warfare between the intellectual emphasis and the technical and manual labor aspect of Holden Village. Carroll was comfortable dealing with and debating theological issues, but he appeared to be very uncomfortable dealing with those with technical expertise and construction backgrounds.

CHAPTER 3

Summer of 1963

DURING THE WINTER OF 1962–1963, Gil sent out a letter to the Holden mailing list requesting volunteers for the 1963 summer operation. I was employed at the Boeing Company but was intrigued with the thought of volunteering at Holden Village. I discovered Boeing offered the option of a leave of absence, although I was told that employees seldom used this option. I applied for a three-month volunteer position at Holden and was accepted. I applied for a three-month employment leave from Boeing and was approved. The leave of absence began Memorial Day weekend and ended the day after the Labor Day holiday.

I was familiar with the physical surroundings of Holden but had no experience in terms of the operational activities or the uniqueness of living in a community that was struggling for its identity and working through the challenges of establishing its management style. I was initially assigned to live in a second-floor bedroom of Chalet 2 and then later moved to the hotel for the summer. In 1963, the village was without heat in the buildings and hot water was only available in the dining hall and a couple of chalets. In the hotel, I lived above the kitchen; heat from the oil cookstove and ovens provided some heat to the upstairs rooms. I was living in luxury in the wilderness and even enjoyed hot water.

While staying in Chalet 2, I had an interesting experience that would help me appreciate one of the special aspects of Holden Village. The early summer was cold and wet. I was in my room, and in walked a small, elderly man wearing a red jumpsuit, dripping wet. At perhaps five foot three, he was essentially hidden by a full-size cruiser pack on his back and a smaller pack on his chest. Burr Singleton introduced himself and indicated that Gil invited him to use one of the spare bedrooms. Burr was from Manson, Washington. After he retired as the manager of a large orchard he decided to take up hiking and climbing. His wife of many years had died, so he was alone. We proceeded to have a lengthy conversation, became well acquainted, and quickly developed a genuine friendship.

Burr had just returned from an extensive hike into Lyman Lake, Cloudy Pass, Hart Lake, Holden Lake, and then into Holden Village. Much of the trip was in wet and cold conditions. He said he hiked alone because he didn't want to slow down fellow hikers who were generally more interested in quickly getting from one location to the other. Burr was interested in the trip rather than the destination. Burr hiked to celebrate and document the beauty of what he observed.

His camping gear filled the cruiser pack, which was about equal to his height. The front pack contained all of his photographic equipment, which included a Hasselblad 500C camera, multiple exchangeable camera backs, and exchangeable lenses. I later discovered that Burr was becoming well known as one of the great mountain photographers as well as a formidable Cascade Mountain Range hiker and climber. When Burr was on a hike or climb, his food consisted of cured sausage, cheese, and crackers. He indicated he didn't want to waste time cooking. In 1958, Burr climbed Mount Rainier at age seventy-five and for a number of years held the record as the oldest person to have made the climb. Burr was eighty years of age when we had our chance meeting in Chalet 2.

We invited Burr to visit the winter community the first couple of years of winter operation and enjoyed his sharing of photography and life stories. He was a great teller of stories and teacher of life. He was someone with no "title" but was powerful through his friendship and all that he shared with others. Burr was among many who benefited from the openness and inclusion offered by the Holden community.

A year after our first meeting, I was downlake and decided to visit Burr. He lived on fifteen acres of meadowland just outside of Manson, a small community a few miles north of Chelan. Right in the middle of his acreage, there was a small building that looked like a garage. In fact it was a garage but also his house. The only walls inside the house were to provide privacy for the bathroom. The rest was all open. Garage doors at the end of the living area could be opened to give the feeling of being outside. His bed was right in the middle of the open space with windows lacking shades. I was going to stay at a motel, but Burr insisted I stay with him. He had one bed, and he gave me no choice but to take his bed. That night he slept on a lounge chair outside. Burr was a wonderfully unique individual. When he died in 1973, he left his fifteen acres to the Manson Little League baseball team. I hope the field has remained a baseball field for youth and not developed for vacation rentals. It was appropriately named Singleton Field.

That summer, my volunteer position was an assignment as food department coordinator. I can't remember all of my responsibilities, but I ordered food and supplies and set up schedules for short-term volunteers who assisted the main cook, Bertha Pearson. Bertha was one of the early heroes of Holden. She was originally associated with the Lutheran Bible Institute, and Gil recruited her to head up the Holden kitchen staff. In fact, for some events she was the entire kitchen staff. In September of 1962, the pastors from the Pacific Northwest District of the Lutheran Church held their fall conference at Holden. Holden was working to get more churches acquainted with its new ministry. Not much was functioning in the kitchen, but Bertha cooked a memorable fried-chicken dinner on a wood stove in what is now known as the village sauna. Bertha's woodstove became an item in the original Holden museum. I hope it was saved for inclusion in the new museum.

The pastors had a reasonably good time at Holden, but later, when they were approached to take over operation of Holden—including the financing—they decided against it, calling it a potential white elephant. It turned out that, at least in the early years of Holden's development, some Lutheran pastors questioned the value of Holden as it related to the work of the church and at times resented Holden as an intrusion on church activities. Their hesitation to embrace Holden might have been out of fear of the financial drain it might have been within the life of many congregations if members were supporting the village. It turned out that the impact of the Holden program brought new life to the laity, but this impact was wrongly interpreted as a threat and inconvenience to parish ministry.

In my second week as a volunteer, Carroll Hinderlie arrived in the village. At its winter meeting in January 1963, the board had selected him as the executive director. They had held this meeting at the Masonic Temple in downtown Seattle and included a fundraising dinner. I participated in this event. Upon Carroll's arrival in the village, tensions began developing within the community almost immediately. The staff and community knew Carroll was coming, but at the time, the staff loyalty was with Gil. After all, Gil had chosen the staff members and was the only person they knew and related to in terms of the Holden operation.

Upon Carroll's arrival at Holden Village, the volunteer registrar initially refused to allow him into the dining room, telling him he had to wait until the meal had concluded. This didn't create a smooth entrance for Carroll. In retrospect, a representative from the Holden board should have arrived with him and officially introduced him to the community. The remote location and lack of communications added a definite element of inconvenience for the Holden board, but hurt feelings and tensions in the village could have been eliminated if Carroll had received a more official introduction and welcoming.

The importance of the physical labor and technical expertise for the rehabilitation of the facility and infrastructure aspects of Holden were obvious. The approach to program development wasn't as clear. In the late 1950s, national church leaders were becoming increasingly concerned that young adults were drifting away from the church, which created a concern for future membership but probably even more so in terms of a concern for the financial future of the organization. As more

young adults were attending college, the family and home congregations were losing their normal control over the young adult membership. Because of the location and lack of easy access to Holden Village,
the board quickly realized that the precollege youth wouldn't be the
program emphasis.

The first program the youth departments developed was called The
Young Adult Stehekin. Stehekin is the name of the community at the
head of Lake Chelan and was also the Native American name meaning
"the way through." It was a good name for a young-adult program. My
observation was that the Young Adult Stehekin wasn't successful because
it duplicated a Bible camp format but with a young adult emphasis. This
program was the responsibility of the youth departments and occurred
at the same time Carroll was conducting the overall program for the
summer. The hope was that the unique location of Holden Village would
improve the outcome of the work of the youth departments. It didn't.
However, the Young Adult Stehekin brought Karen Strom to Holden, for
which everyone is forever grateful.

The volunteer staffing plan for that initial summer involved a core
group of seventeen young adults who would provide leadership in the
various work areas. Thirty additional volunteers would arrive for a
one-month involvement. The national youth departments chose them
through their own promotional activities. I trust that the museum will
document all of the volunteer workers over the years. I can't do that
here, but I do want to list the seventeen core volunteer staff participants
I served with during the summer of 1963. The following was taken directly from the listing furnished by Gil:

Rueben Thompson	Year-round custodian—Holden Village
Jim Felton	Mechanic—Udell, Iowa
Curt and Mary Nelson	Carpenter and snack bar—Barnesville, Minn.
Bertha Pearson	Chief cook—Lutheran Bible Institute, Seattle

Esther Besonen	Second cook—Farmington, Conn.
Werner Janssen	Food department coordinator—Renton, Wash.
Carol Ann Oversvee	Dietician—Seattle, Wash.
Jeannine Lundahl	Kitchen staff—Pipestone, Minn.
Elizabeth Lindholm	Laundry and linen chief—Pecatonica, Ill.
Carol Lind	Summer secretary—Waukegan, Ill.
Pat Stuart	Registrar and household chief—Rockford, Ill.
Carol Nolte	Utility—Sun Valley, Calif.
Jim Donald	Chief, trails and mine area—Minneapolis, Minn.
Bill Jiran	Chief, painting and utility—Minneapolis, Minn.
Allan Tweite	Grounds chief—Minneapolis, Minn.
Otto Bloedow	Utility in several areas—Minneapolis, Minn.
Fern VanCura	Head nurse—Jackson, Minn.

By 1964, the mergers within the various Lutheran churches had evolved into the Lutheran Church in America, the Evangelical Lutheran Church in America, and the Lutheran Church–Missouri Synod. The original staffing approach was an attempt to recognize the involvement of the three national youth departments. The staffing of the village for its summer operation as originally proposed didn't work since the youth offices, especially the LCA and Missouri Synod, didn't carry through on their agreements to supply a certain number of staff members. After the summer of 1964, we informed the youth offices that we would take charge of the volunteer staff program and promote and select the staff out of the Holden office.

Gil remained as volunteer Holden manager during the summer of 1963, but following Carroll's arrival in the village it was made clear, in no uncertain terms, that Carroll was the director and that Carroll would be calling the shots. It was my impression that Gil understood and accepted this change in leadership, but Carroll remained overly sensitive as to who had the respect and leadership in the Holden community. Tensions immediately developed between Carroll and Gil. In hindsight, the conflict was totally unnecessary and destructive to the community. The clarification of Holden being centered in worship and program was made crystal clear in terms of the purpose of the community. This was important and was never again questioned during the first twenty years. Too often the church and its organizations have become enamored by concentrating on organizations and fundraising rather than a total emphasis on mission to build the worth of people rather than facilities.

I really admired Carroll for his insistence on a people- and program-oriented mission. I was totally in agreement with Carroll's approach. That didn't mean that the facilities and infrastructure should be ignored. Without an effective physical operation, no one could enjoy the program.

During the first twenty years, we basically made do with facilities that existed. When we needed a laundry expansion, we excavated the dirt space under the hospital building, mostly through manual labor. No offices were added or constructed. We did add the museum to expand the program possibilities and put an addition on Koinonia, a building developed from one of the mine housing lodges, to increase sleeping rooms and craft rooms and especially to provide dining space for the winter community.

The program aspect of Holden would be the dominant force and would prioritize all decisions concerning community life. The tension that surfaced when Carroll arrived set the atmosphere for that entire summer of 1963. There was major tension between the manual-labor activity, which Gil directed, and the program emphasis, which was the specific concern of Carroll. Carroll, as executive director, was of course in charge of all aspects of the operation. Carroll never trusted Gil in terms of his understanding of the village priorities and also his loyalty.

Prior to Carroll being chosen as executive director, the board had offered the position to Dr. Wilton Bergstrand, retiring youth director following the merger that formed the Lutheran Church in America. Dr. Bergstrand considered the job offer for over a year before the board withdrew it and selected Carroll. It was my impression that Dr. Bergstrand didn't have a significant impact on the future planning for Holden and its program. I'm sure there were many discussions that I wasn't aware of, but once Carroll was selected as executive director and I was working with him as manager, I never saw and didn't hear anything that related back to the period involving Dr. Bergstrand.

Carroll's availability was also a result of another national church merger. Carroll wasn't chosen as the new youth director for the recently merged church. It was obvious from his comments that this hurt him and again reinforced his fear of not being wanted. Carroll was first offered a temporary teaching position at Luther Seminary in St. Paul. Dr. Al Rogness, president of Luther Seminary, was a close friend of Carroll and Mary Hinderlie. Some years later, Dr. Rogness shared with me that Carroll wasn't first and foremost a seminary teacher, but he offered Carroll the faculty position on a temporary basis since the church didn't know what to do with Carroll.

Carroll's wife, Mary, was the daughter of Dr. Johan Aasgaard, who had been the bishop of the Norwegian Lutheran Church of America. Carroll was therefore known within the inner circle of the church, and he was admired by many because of his powerful proclamation and his ability to motivate people. Some involved in the church resented Carroll because he was a maverick in a conservative organization and often got away with doing as he pleased. He wasn't concerned with permanency in any one job, while others felt restricted by their allegiance to the organization. Carroll was always Carroll and didn't care if he said things or acted in a way that didn't meet organizational approval. As a serious maverick, Carroll had difficulty remaining a parish pastor and therefore bounced around with various positions in the church until Holden became his employment home for thirteen-plus years.

Carroll originally planned to be a missionary and had a specific interest in going to China. He once told me that while at seminary he had requested that the bed and mattress be removed from his room so he could sleep on the hard floor in preparation for going to the mission field. Following Carroll's graduation from Luther Seminary, he and Mary were accepted for the mission field in China. This was during World War II, and they made it to the Philippines before being captured by the Japanese and sent to a prison camp. He and Mary—and their daughter Marin, born in the prison camp—were rescued by the American armed forces. This experience obviously had a profound impact on the future life of Carroll and Mary, as well as their entire family.

Carroll had a great mind and was one of the few pastor/theologians in the church who never held back his thoughts or convictions. He had done graduate work at the University of Chicago but to my knowledge never received an advanced degree. Dr. Rogness told me that Carroll was generally considered to be a reasonable theologian, but it was really his wife Mary who was recognized by the leaders in the church to be a much more brilliant theologian. In those days the wife was still more or less subservient to the husband. Mary, especially in the earlier days of Holden, stayed in the background and allowed Carroll to be the leader and theological image for Holden. Toward the end of their time at Holden, however, Mary appeared to be much more motivated to freely offer her thoughts, comments, and direction concerning the program.

Carroll was both positively and negatively impacted by his previous life experiences. His exciting life provided powerful examples for his proclamation. It wasn't only his prisoner-of-war experience but also his seeming inability to find his place in the church that shaped his life and his fears. Until Holden came along, Carroll was too much of a maverick and loose cannon to fit into any other position within the organized church. It appeared to me that Carroll suffered from what I would call an exile syndrome throughout much of his life. He loved the church as an organization and a community but resented it when the organization put demands on him to remain a controlled, card-carrying member.

Holden turned out to be a reasonable match for Carroll. He had freedom to work in the manner he desired without too many demands from the

Holden board. He had a pulpit and a podium that reached many people but also independence from the national church organization. He was sufficiently tied to Lutheran theology so that the national church leadership hoped he wouldn't develop a destructive cult at Holden Village but rather would provide an arena for other mavericks in the church to lecture and worship and explore new thoughts without dividing the church.

The one unfortunate result of Carroll's freedom and his notoriety within Holden was his inability to establish limits on some of his actions with other people in the community. I loved Carroll, but I also at times lived in fear of him. There is definitely a potential danger when a person is considered an untouchable personality. Holden, stuck in the middle of the mountains without any form of easy communications in or out of the valley, was for the most part a safe haven for a maverick theologian.

The initial problem experienced in the summer of 1963 was Carroll's fear of those who had the abilities to deal with the village's infrastructure challenges. Carroll knew he was the director, but he was uncomfortable with so much effort being spent on activities outside the realm of program and worship. We worked well together because the division of responsibilities was clear, and Carroll had no interest in the physical aspects or infrastructure unless it related to the program. When Carroll first arrived in the village, he failed to understand that the work of rehabilitating the facility, making it usable and comfortable, had a two-year head start and therefore was what staff and guests had experienced to that point. Carroll saw the manual labor of improving the facility only as the source of power for Gil.

When I started working with Carroll, I think he trusted me to understand the priority of the program and worship. The facility maintenance and development would never take on the prime importance in the life of Holden Village or become a source of tension. Even though Carroll had experienced work camps in Europe, he apparently didn't see that the blending of work, study, and worship were the real program and impact that volunteers and staff would experience. Since it took the Holden board almost two years to hire a director, the facility activation and cleanup moved ahead with only minimal program, primarily worship. Gil didn't wait until a director was hired. He moved ahead with the work that obviously needed to be done. No one made a conscious effort to place daily work at a higher priority than worship and program but there were more people involved with the physical work than with program activities.

The summer faculty in 1963 consisted of Carroll Hinderlie, Howard Hong, Rudy and Doris Edmund, Beany and Gertrude Lundholm, Fritz Norstad, Armin Grams, and Jean Swihart. Rudy, Doris, Beany, Gertrude, and Jean, together with Carroll, were in the village the entire summer. Howard, Fritz, and Armin were involved for shorter periods of time. Shortly after my arrival, Jean Swihart introduced herself to me and suggested we take a walk around the village. We walked to the top of Chalet Hill, sat on a stump next to Chalet 9, and talked for several hours. It was primarily Jean who did the talking. She shared her life's story, which was most interesting. I didn't know how much to believe but later learned that most, if not all of it, was true. Jean shared that she had been raised within a wealthy family. Her father was a famous attorney in Oklahoma, involved with the oil industry. She attended private schools, became a climbing guide in the Rocky Mountains, trained horses, and I can't remember all of the other accomplishments. She lost her inheritance when her mother died and father remarried.

Jean's husband, Al, was back in Oklahoma City, where they owned a small restaurant in a large medical clinic. Jean didn't think Al would ever come out to Holden because, as she said, he wasn't really an outdoors person. Ironically, it later turned out that Al was the one who made such a significant impact on the village. Jean and Al were close friends with Doris and Rudy Edmund, who introduced the Swiharts to Holden.

In the 1987 book *Surprising Gift*, written by Charles Lutz, Jean was quoted as saying she was the one who encouraged or convinced Carroll to submit my name to the board as the first general manager of Holden. I wasn't aware of this until I read it in the book, and I never checked the authenticity of Jean's statement.

I never did understand why I was invited to join what I called the core faculty gatherings in the evenings, but I felt honored and delighted to be involved with this group. It wasn't only the delightful conversations that I enjoyed but also sharing a little wine to stimulate the conversation. I was the only one from the volunteers to be invited to join these gatherings. Since I was listed as the food service coordinator, perhaps they thought I would have access to food. Worship and the evening program concluded by nine o'clock in the evening, and the electricity was turned off each night at ten.

With the cost of diesel fuel at seventeen cents a gallon, Gil Berg made the decision to operate the diesel generators providing electricity for the village from five in the morning to ten o'clock each night. This power schedule continued for several years until the hydroelectric plant became operational in August of 1964. When all electricity was off, the evenings became magical. Stars in the dark sky appeared to be within easy reach. Everyone coming to the village was asked to bring a flashlight. Many of the great conversations began after ten p.m. That is also when any wine or beer that might be available was enjoyed. During my time at Holden, I never observed any problems through the consumption of alcohol. Even though Holden was open to those who were trying to deal with an alcoholic sensitivity, alcohol was never outlawed for those of legal age.

The unofficial gatherings of the core faculty generally involved the Edmunds, the Lundholms, Jean Swihart, and most of the time also myself. In 2013, I'm the only one of this group still alive. Many of the conversations at these social gatherings dealt with Carroll and the tension in the community. There was a noticeable division between those who supported Carroll and those who had loyalty to Gil. I found myself in the middle and seemed to get along well with both sides. I think I understood both sides. To me, the division of power and responsibilities was clear. Carroll was the director of Holden with specific interest and responsibilities for the program. Gil was the manager and had responsibilities for the operation of the physical plant and the continuing work to bring the facilities up to an operational level. Gil remained a volunteer; therefore, Carroll had less organizational power over him. Perhaps this was part of Carroll's problem. Carroll was officially Gil's boss, but because Gil had operated all aspects of Holden until this time, Gil had the knowledge and identity as Mr. Holden.

Carroll remained in the village until around Labor Day that year and then headed back to Minneapolis. I gained a real admiration for Carroll that summer primarily through his sermons and lectures and also because of the unique characters he brought to the village as faculty, specifically Howard Hong and Fritz Norstad.

In 1963, Holden had little reputation in the church and only minor name recognition in the country—primarily the Northwest and portions of the Midwest. However, Holden came to life at just the right time in history. The Village had no money or even a mailing list with which to launch its entrance into the world. Fortunately, the 1962 World's Fair in Seattle brought many people from the heavily populated Lutheran Midwest to Seattle. One article about Holden appeared in the *Lutheran Standard* and perhaps other Lutheran periodicals late in 1961 or early 1962. The article encouraged those traveling to the World's Fair to take a side trip to Holden. According to the records, sixteen hundred people visited Holden that summer. In 1961, five hundred people had visited Holden. By1963, Holden had a mailing list and excellent word-of-mouth promotion. The word began to spread, which increased attendance and the needed numbers of volunteer staff.

Carroll had the impossible task of bringing faculty members who would begin to develop its reputation as the place to visit if you wanted to experience community while sitting at the feet of teachers beyond what any one college could offer. With Carroll in charge of developing the program there was no doubt that it would involve the most interesting teachers with exciting lectures and discussion on all subjects taught in a liberal arts college. Potential faculty participants were initially hesitant to participate since Holden was an unknown entity and no recognized faculty had ever lectured there. Carroll made use of his friendships to more or less strongly encourage some of his close friends to join him on the faculty. Fortunately, most of these friends were highly respected people, known in the church and academia. Their participation opened the possibility for others to consider volunteering their time on the faculty. Without Carroll's unique circle of friends, Holden Village may not have developed the quality program that it did and may have had difficulty attracting the numbers of people needed to become financially viable.

In the early 1960s, there was a new yearning within the church and society to share in the conversation that up to then had involved only the professionals, leaving out those in the pews. Holden Village was part of a movement that was changing this old model.

Rudy and Doris Edmund and Beany and Gertrude Lundholm were invited to participate in the faculty prior to Carroll's involvement. Rudy and Doris were introduced to Holden through friends in California. They had been going to visit the World's Fair and were encouraged to take a side trip to Holden. During that short Holden visit, Rudy discovered the valuable mine records left unprotected. He strongly suggested to Gil and Dr. Bergstrand that these records be saved before they disappeared or before the weather destroyed them. Gil urged Rudy to return the next summer and make sure the records were properly preserved. That began a thirty-plus year involvement with Holden for Rudy.

It is my understanding that the Edmunds encouraged the Lundholms to join them at Holden in 1963. Both the Edmonds and Lundholms were extremely gifted and generously continued to share their lives and abilities during a significant portion of the first half of Holden's current existence.

Rudy had his doctorate in geology and was at one point the chief exploration geologist for Standard Oil of Ohio. Rudy shared in conversation that, as chief exploration geologist, he was assigned a corporate airplane and private pilot to literally fly around the world looking for future deposits of oil. It's my understanding that Rudy reached a point where corporate success was at its pinnacle, but his life wasn't providing the passion of fulfillment that his soul desired. He made the switch to teaching and encouraging students who would become future leaders. He resigned his corporate position and became the head of the geology department at Augustana College in Rock Island, Illinois. It's ironic that several of the leaders in the mine and tailings remediation project are former students of Rudy Edmund. He was a highly qualified and greatly loved Holden faculty member. Each year he led mine tours, which were the most popular program offering. He lectured and led discussions and was a founding member of the Holden Science and Technology Committee. He was such a humble person but was also knowledgeable, not only about geology but also organization management. He became a valued consultant to the board, which relied on his advice on many issues.

Rudy was also a talented artist with a fly rod. He had fly-fished in some of the best lakes around the world but still claimed that Domke Lake was his favorite. He also gave birth to the Holden Museum. One of his requirements was that if he was in charge of preserving the mine records, he would need one or more volunteers assigned to help in the work. Holden didn't have any ideal storage for all of this valuable material, but one of the lockers in the basement of the hotel provided a relatively dry and safe storage location. If volunteer staff members weren't available on a particular day, Rudy recruited his young daughters as well as the Lundholm boys. Over seven thousand pounds of maps, assay notes and miscellaneous mine records were saved. Most of this material was transferred to the archives at the University of Washington with the provision that items could be loaned back to Holden for its museum.

Since Holden was officially considered to be on the east side of the state, the mine materials would normally have gone to the archives at Washington State University in Pullman. However, Nigel Adams, son or a former Holden mine employee, was working on his doctorate at the University of Washington, dealing with the early history of Holden and the success of the mine. He requested that the Holden materials be assigned to the UW archives for convenience in his research work. I received a letter from the archivist at the UW, and I turned the matter over to the Holden board. The board really didn't care where the Holden material was housed as long as it would be safe and also accessible.

Two people from the UW archives first visited Holden to determine the value of the material. Later they came back to haul the material to Seattle. Nigel had grown up in the village until he was in high school. He loved what had become of the Holden facility but for years couldn't get his mother to return to the village. She wanted to remember it as it had been when they were there as a family. One Christmas, he finally convinced his mother to join their family at Holden. After that his mother had no hesitation about going back. Nigel finished his first book on the history of Holden Mine prior to the production years. Unfortunately, he died before having a chance to complete the next volume, which would have covered the production years. Nigel was a faculty member at Green River Community College in Auburn, Washington.

Beany Lundholm was the most beloved of the Holden musicians. Beany was a church musician from Rock Island, Illinois, and also taught at Augustana College. Beany was famous in Rock Island for, among many other accomplishments, his conducting Handel's *Messiah* each Christmas. At Holden, Beany was the music director for all worship services and assembled a new choir each week even as the population changed. Beany was small in stature but displayed a powerful command of the piano and organ.

He was best known at Holden for his *Beany Sings*. For at least the first twenty years, we ate all meals family style with multiple settings when necessary. Beany began each meal with one of the sung table prayers. Following the evening meal, everyone remained in the dining hall for *Beany Sings*. With the help of Doris Edmund, appropriate words were set to known music, and the *Beany Sing* was born. Others, such as Phil Brunelle, later worked with Doris on writing more song words that were specific to Holden and the mountain valley.

You will recognize the name Phil Brunelle not only from his numerous times on the Holden faculty but also his association with Garrison Keillor and *A Prairie Home Companion*. Other guests and faculty joined in writing additional songs, resulting in a rather extensive booklet available on each table. Even after the increasing population necessitated a second setting at the evening meal, *Beany Sings* continued and was an important part of creating the community spirit.

A financial gift allowed Holden to purchase an electronic organ, and several years later the electronic chimes were added to the organ through a memorial gift. Beany played the chimes each morning approximately five minutes before the bell rang for breakfast. *Beany Sings* and the morning chimes became one of several delightful traditions remembered by generations of visitors to Holden.

At one point, there was an offer by Pacific Lutheran University involving the gift of a pipe organ. A new pipe organ was being installed at PLU, and they offered to give the old pipe organ to Holden. The artist/technician and also a faculty member at PLU offered to install the organ at Holden at no cost. Pipe organs are temperamental and very dependent on temperature and humidity control. Holden could assure neither of these requirements, so a real pipe organ for Holden didn't become a reality.

Doris Edmund was one of the people who, early on, set the tone of celebration in all that Holden offered. Doris was overflowing with ideas and creativity. At Augustana College she established and operated a pre-school education program called Red Shoes. It was a model for early-childhood education. Doris was the leader in establishing the young people's program at Holden that later became known as Narnia, after the C. S. Lewis children's stories.

Gertrude Lundholm was the ultimate hostess for Holden. I first got acquainted with her during evening conversations in the summer of 1963. Gertrude hosted many of these conversations. The first interesting thing I noticed was that the napkins she initially used were folded sheets of toilet paper that had dainty decorations on them, to add an element of class.

Gertrude was a genius at making snacks from the very little that was available, being fifty miles from a grocery store. My favorite was Gertrude's Coconut Crackers:

1 stick of margarine—melt.

Thicken with about 1 cup of sugar.

Sprinkle with coconut until it gets thick like paste.

Add cardamom.

Spread on saltine crackers.

Brown under broiler.

Gertrude became the official hostess to the many guests by having an open house in Chalet 7 each Sunday morning after the matins service. She initiated the open house to make sure Holden guests had an opportunity to personally meet more of the faculty but also an opportunity for guests to see the inside of the chalets since the chalets were generally occupied by faculty and management staff.

Gertrude also had the ability to make use of the appropriate flowers, grasses, and even weeds to put together center pieces for the dining room tables. She would take her frequent walks to the former miners' village (Winston Camp) to see what nature could offer to beautify the daily life at Holden. The miners' village, even after the homes were removed, still had flowers in the flower gardens that were initially planted by those living in the homes during the mine operation. Gertrude was sensitive to the special lives of wild flowers. She reminded guests that wild flowers were meant to be enjoyed in the wild. They didn't last when picked. Since other women often asked Gertrude if they could walk to the miners' village with her, she started calling the group the Women's Wild Flower Club. Before long, the name somehow changed to the Wild Women's Flower Club, which was perhaps more appropriate.

The summer of 1963 was in many ways the beginning of Holden Village as we know it. Many of the traditions that remained for many years started with Doris or Gertrude or Beany—implementing an idea without any discussion or approval. There were no committees to discuss and vote on what would happen next. Carroll Hinderlie may have had a program concept for Holden in his mind, but to my knowledge he never prepared or shared a written outline. It was my observation that at least initially, Carroll concentrated on people rather than subject content. One of the challenges was that Holden had no money and decided to create a first-class program with quality faculty based on their willingness to volunteer their time and pay their own transportation costs to and from Holden. This concept worked by inviting faculty families to stay in the village at no cost but with no stipend or pay. The minimum faculty stay was usually three weeks, with a few staying for two to three months. Carroll involved faculty members who were first of all friends but secondly had name recognition within the church or society, so Holden could begin gaining a reputation for attracting a quality faculty, which would in turn make it easier to encourage new faculty. Once the process started, faculty members would recommend faculty they knew and who might consider coming based on their words of encouragement and personal testimony. It took a few years, but soon potential faculty members were writing Carroll asking how they could join the volunteer Holden faculty.

Carroll outwardly appeared to have tremendous self-confidence. He presented a formidable presence in terms of size and vocal power. Although Carroll had a volatile personality, I personally found him supportive and accepting. The inconsistency of his moods and the difficulty of understanding his sensitivities made it difficult for some within the community to deal with his style. I observed Carroll verbally lash out several times at an individual in almost a violent outburst over what might have been a very innocent comment, and immediately Carroll was over his emotions. For the person on the receiving end, the hurt and emotional impact lingered for days and sometimes for a lifetime.

Holden Village in many ways was the ideal ministry for Carroll since it allowed a maverick voice in the church to have a platform, sometimes not so gently stirring the church organizational and theological thinking. I also think Holden turned out to be the downfall

of Carroll. It provided a location where Carroll was elevated to something approaching sainthood and hero status. It allowed him to
think he could do no wrong, always protected by a strong family presence and guest support and admiration. Even his friends, brought in
on the faculty, were grateful that Carroll finally had a community.
Actually his friends failed him by failing to act as his conscience and
keep him aware that he was very human and had fragile emotional
tendencies.

The worship and program of Holden Village was the reason for
Holden's existence, but it was also a fact that without a safe and comfortable facility the worship and program would be less effective. Holden
Village was a remote town that needed to operate its own infrastructure. Commercial transportation was available to the port of Lucerne,
but from that point on it was up to Holden Village, Inc., to provide for
the ten-mile road trip up two thousand feet. In the winter this involved
dealing with snow and snowslides. Holden also had to operate its own
water and sewage system as well as waste disposal. Because of its remote
location, even fire and medical concerns were the responsibility of the
community. No communication was available initially outside of the US
Postal Service. For six months of the year, mail service was six days each
week. The other six months it was three times each week. In the winter,
orders for critical parts might take a week or more to arrive. The commercial boat service on Lake Chelan dictated our access to the outside
world.

The summer of 1963 was really a delightful experience, even with
some of the obvious tensions. Howard Hong, professor at St. Olaf College
in North Field, Minnesota, had agreed to join the Holden faculty initially
out of respect for Carroll and at Carroll's urging. The next year, Howard's
wife Edna would also be a valuable addition to the faculty. Carroll had
promised Howard that if he agreed to be on the faculty, Holden would
make sure a sauna was in operation. I suggested we use the enclosure
behind the hotel that had been the garbage shed during the mine days.

The garbage shed was a concrete structure built into the hillside and with a metal sliding door that made it bear proof. The building also had a smokestack, since wood heat had been needed in the winter to keep the garbage from freezing. It made an adequate and quickly prepared sauna. Howard was a sauna fanatic, and it was an important part of his life. He was convinced his health was dependent on frequent saunas. Howard had a tradition of making "sauna nuts" by deep frying wheat kernels and then salting them. The sauna nuts were eaten in the sauna while also encouraging drinking plenty of water. It became a Holden tradition for several years. Howard Hong became known as "Sauna Claus" and was one of the people who brought levity to the community that summer.

I had never heard of Howard Hong until he arrived at Holden. He was a world-recognized scholar of Soren Kierkegaard, Danish philosopher. A student of Howard's showed up on the volunteer staff and was amazed by how different Howard was at Holden than at the St. Olaf campus. Howard was a beloved teacher but also one whom students feared because of the demands for excellence he put on each and every student. Howard was an example of the quality of teacher and person Carroll attracted to Holden.

Fritz Norstad was another notable character who became closely associated with Holden initially through his friendship with Carroll. Fritz, an ordained pastor, had a PhD in physiological counseling. He taught at Luther Seminary and worked at Lutheran General Hospital in Park Ridge, Illinois, designing and implementing a new approach to hospital care involving a coordinated team approach. It was my understanding that Fritz was responsible for developing the Department of Human Ecology at Lutheran General. He and his wife, Gertrude, were frequent members of the faculty and were also asked to be the interim directors of Holden during a particularly sensitive time of administrative transition.

One of the first years Fritz was on the Holden faculty, he brought a 16-mm film that had been made at Lutheran General Hospital, showing

a live human birth. Fritz had raised money to have this film produced with the idea that it be shown on television to help people understand the miracle of human birth. At least up until 1963, no TV station could get permission from its legal department to show the film. I recall that we showed the film several times in Chalet 2. Even at Holden there was some hesitation to share what now can be seen on the Internet.

Fritz had a very recognizable name in the church and in many parts of society. Lauris Norstad, brother of Fritz, rose to be the commander of United States forces in Europe and also commander of NATO. With a brother like Lauris, Fritz had contacts in many areas of society, which was a help to bring credibility to Holden and its program. Fritz also served as a military chaplain. Lauris visited Holden the summer Fritz served as interim director.

Having the opportunity to meet the people who were on the faculty in the summer of 1963 was an amazing experience for me. The faculty members were all excellent teachers. They were people who valued each person and communicated with the young and old. It was an amazing experience for the guests of Holden as well as the staff to have an opportunity to have face-to-face conversations with these people and not be intimidated by their titles or stature. When Holden anointed a Kierkegaard scholar as Sauna Claus, it was easier to have a conversation or even play a game of pool with Howard Hong.

During the summer of 1963, I also had the opportunity to do a lot of hiking and climbing. None of the climbing was very technical, but it allowed great views and a feeling of accomplishment. Early in the summer I climbed Buckskin Mountain, overlooking Holden. It was really more of a difficult hike than a climb. After my first climb, I had requests to take others on the climb. Before the summer was over, I'd been to the top of Buckskin at least twelve times.

I got well acquainted with Carroll and Mary Hinderlie during that summer, and on a couple of occasions Carroll briefly talked with me about the possibility of my working with him as manager. A conversation with Carroll was frequently one-sided. If he had in mind that I should be the manager, then it was more a statement of what would happen rather than a discussion of what might be possible or even desirable. Gil remained volunteer Holden manager through the summer, but as the summer progressed, he spent less time in the village.

The summer came to an end. On Labor Day I returned to Seattle to resume my employment at Boeing. After my return, a fellow engineer heard that I had spent the summer at Holden and told me about an earlier plan involving Boeing investigating the use of the Holden as an aboveground Minuteman Missile site. I assume the plan was no longer classified since the idea had been abandoned. Although all of the sites had been below ground, the air force was interested in the Holden site because it was remote but potentially accessible. The investigation indicated that the main shaft of the Trinity mine, north of Leavenworth, and the Holden mine main shaft were only a couple of miles apart. The consideration was to extend the Trinity tunnel to the Holden tunnel, thus giving vehicle access to the Holden site. The missile control room would be underground in the abandoned Holden Mine. The missiles would need to be above ground and camouflaged because of the impossibility of developing the silos below the surface. Obliviously the plan was only a slight possibility and not very practical.

Because of the brief conversations with Carroll during the summer, I left Holden assuming there was at least a slight possibility I might be offered the manager's job. Until I received the call from Vern Rieke, Holden board chairman, it was only a remote thought that kept surfacing in my mind. The call from Vern came at the same time I had been offered the new job responsibilities at Boeing, and it made the decision a little more difficult. My heart was with Holden, but it seemed obvious that the more stable and lucrative future was with Boeing.

One of the first things I did after receiving the offer involving employment with Holden from Vern was to call Rudy Edmund. I highly respected his opinion and, with his experience at Holden, he was the one person I felt would be honest with me concerning my being a fit for the Holden position. I knew I wanted to take the Holden job, but I was concerned about my qualifications and lack of experience. I was twenty-four years old and had no training in business or management. My rationale for finally accepting the job was that if Vern, who was such a highly respected figure in the church and in the state of Washington, felt I could do the job, I would give it a try.

CHAPTER 4

An Opportunity to Bring About Change

I was twenty-four years of age. I'd just resigned from my first job after two years and eight months as an associate research engineer with the Boeing Company. It's very possible that I could have remained with Boeing my entire working life and comfortably retired. I had no guarantees of a career with Holden Village, especially with the uncertainty of working with Carroll and/or the Holden board. With the experience at Holden as a volunteer during the summer, it was clear that life at Holden held many uncertainties, and personalities were volatile. I was single and had no debt. It's likely that my excitement over living in the mountains and basically managing a small town with unlimited possibilities overshadowed the logic of taking a job for which I had absolutely no experience or training and which offered no job security.

My first day as a Holden Village employee was November 22, 1963. My office was located on the second floor of the Berg Fuel office building in Ballard. Until we moved our office permanently to Holden Village in May of 1966 the winter office was in Seattle. I didn't have any manuals to read and didn't know what I was to do. Carroll, my boss, was in Minneapolis, and I don't recall receiving any instructions from him as to how I should begin the work as business manager. This initial relationship with Carroll was an indication of how our relationship would continue and perhaps why I was able to work with him for thirteen years.

Carroll's former assistant in the National Youth Office, Ray Johnson, visited Holden some years later and told me that I held the record as the person who had been able to work with Carroll the longest. He had had the record to that point. I think Carroll trusted me and had little interest in or knowledge of the physical operational aspects of Holden. The responsibilities were easily divided. He was interested in the program and worship life of Holden. As long as the facility and infrastructure work allowed his program and worship activities to function without interference or distraction, he was a happy camper. The main factor in our working relationship was that Carroll realized that I understood that worship and program had the highest priority in the Holden Village operation.

At the beginning, the board had set up no major fund drives. There were no major donors who pledged money to underwrite the initial costs. There were no board members who made large financial donations, but the board was enthusiastic about Holden's potential. Carroll had a few contacts who were helpful in the initial fundraising, and Holden Village had a mailing list of perhaps twenty-five hundred names and addresses of people who had visited the village in 1962 and 1963. Holden had no credit established at any financial institutions, but everyone who visited left with enthusiasm and a willingness to see that the village survived. Repeat registrations and word-of-mouth promotion were perhaps the most important factors that allowed Holden Village to move forward.

In December 1963, we received information from the forest service that the agency had burned Winston Camp, or as we had called it, the miners' village. The miners' homes were built on forest service land. Once the miners who owned the homes abandoned them, the liability and responsibility for the buildings had returned to the forest service. Before the burning, Holden was given the opportunity to salvage any materials from Winston Camp but with the limited staff during the summer of 1963, we were able to complete very little salvage work. We were able to procure some lumber and some sinks and toilets, but it was only a small portion of what was available.

The forest service made the decision to burn Winston Camp as soon as sufficient snow had fallen to reduce the possibility of a forest fire. For several years the charred ruins remained on the hillside. The forest service later received a special grant to clean up the site and attempt to return the area to its natural condition. Prior to the agency bulldozing the site, volunteer staff and guests made multiple trips to salvage daffodils, irises, and other perennials that the miners had planted around their homes in Winston Camp approximately one half miles from the village. The flowers that bloomed around the homes of miners could now enhance the beauty of the buildings in the Village. The grant that the forest service received also included money to do some cleanup around the mine. A large hole was opened in the tailings above the hydro plant and "junk" was dozed into the hole then covered with tailings.

Initially, Carroll and I were Holden's only full-time salaried employees. We were both paid on the basis of a twelve-month salary. Since Carroll was on the roster of the ELCA, he also received benefits in terms of health insurance and pension payments made directly to the ELCA. Carroll being an ordained pastor also had the advantage of having his salary divided into a nontaxable portion to cover housing and a taxable portion covering employment. He didn't have any housing costs at Holden, although he did maintain a home in Minneapolis. I have heard stories that initially Holden couldn't afford to pay Carroll year-round for full-time work, which isn't true. I do remember that for tax purposes, the board was willing to adjust the payments for housing and salary, but Carroll was always paid for full-time employment. The board approved what I considered some questionable arrangements between salaried and housing payments which Carroll requested to reduce tax liabilities initially, so perhaps this resulted in confusion as to what was considered payment for employment. I wrote and signed all of the salary checks for both of us. I received a salary, but for a number of years, neither health insurance nor any type of pension were included as part of my compensation. Some years later, the Holden board did add health insurance and allowed me to establish a tax sheltered annuity but didn't increase my salary to cover it. Perhaps after ten years, an additional amount was added to my compensation that was considered pension.

It was initially uncomfortable to be working in the Berg Fuel office building. After all, Gil had been the hero who elevated Holden from Wes's unrealistic dream to a level approaching reality. Gil had volunteered his time and generously contributed personal finances to cover the tasks as the Holden Village director/manager. He had all of the contacts and respect of many local people who helped launch the project. And he was deservedly the Holden Village hero. Now I was in Gil's office building as the new Holden manager, serving in the position that had elevated Gil to a miracle worker for many in the church. On that November 22, 1963, Gil was in his office at the bottom of the stairs. Around midmorning, he yelled up the stairs that President Kennedy had been shot. That was the end of my first day of work as a Holden employee. I went home to try and understand what had just happened.

I don't recall officially meeting with Gil to arrange an exchange of Holden operational information. Even though I had always had a good relationship with Gil, I was hesitant to assume that he was enthusiastic about assisting me in getting started because of the way he was treated during the summer when Carroll arrived. Gil and I probably shared similar personalities in that neither of us was very aggressive in developing friendships. I probably missed a great opportunity to work more closely with Gil, but again, he was very helpful to me when I approached him. He was an interesting person: climbed Mount Rainier at age eighteen, developed a successful fuel distribution business in Ballard, and was passionate about his hobby of needlepoint. In his retirement he was asked to do a needlepoint that helped refurbish a chair in the home of Governor Dan Evans.

There was no transition team to help guide me into the new position. Gil was very gracious, and I always knew if I needed help or had questions he was more than willing to help. I can't imagine Gil wasn't emotionally hurt by the way he had been treated by Carroll during the summer of 1963, but if he was hurt he never showed it outwardly. He wasn't an emotional man, at least not in public, and I don't recall that he ever made a negative comment about Carroll. Gil loved Holden, and I was convinced his greatest interest was to help Holden Village succeed. To my knowledge, he encouraged all of his friends and associates to continue supporting the work at Holden and me as the new manager. I was aware of only a very few people who disassociated themselves from Holden over the way Carroll treated Gil. At the fall Holden board meeting in 1963, Gil was named Holden Village mayor. He was the only person to officially hold this post. Even though he died in 1996 at age ninety-six, he will remain the only designated mayor of Holden unless the Holden board names a replacement.

The Holden office later moved to a small office space that was owned by Gethsemane Lutheran Church in downtown Seattle. It was an interesting location, and it was especially handy to the Swedish Café, which held many official and unofficial meetings. It has since moved because of major real estate developments.

Gethsemane Lutheran had a Wednesday lunch that was open to all, and I frequently joined them. At one of these lunches, I met Mike Griffin, a Missouri Lutheran layman who was in charge of sales at one of Seattle's largest furniture stores. He and his family became involved with Holden and later purchased the Lucerne Resort, which they ultimately donated to Holden.

Perhaps the miracle of Holden Village was that the program, combined with the unique location, developed strong relationships and adequate financial support for Holden to advance. Strong and controversial personalities such as Carroll were important, but the love and support people felt for Holden fortunately went beyond any personalities. Even though Carroll was a strong personality, he didn't dominate the daily activities, and the community developed in spite of him, not because of him.

Since I had served as a volunteer with at least two of the planning committees, I was acquainted with some of the important contacts and the basic knowledge of what planning was under way. I had attended several of the Holden board meetings, including the January, 1963 meeting with a concluding banquet at the Masonic Temple in downtown Seattle. It turned out to be the occasion when the board introduced Carroll as the new director. As I recall, there were perhaps two hundred people in attendance. Holden Village was beginning to attract an increasing number of interested people and supporters in the Seattle area.

After Christmas in 1963, I joined village caretaker Rueben Thompson's nephew, Mark Thompson on a visit to Rueben at Holden. The only transportation from Lucerne to Holden at that time was via snowshoe. I had never used snowshoes and a trip up two thousand feet covering ten miles with two feet of fresh snow at the village elevation was perhaps not the wisest decision for an initial snowshoe trip. We arrived at Lucerne at noon and finally took off our snowshoes at Chalet 1 at midnight after a twelve-hour trip.

This is one of several times while manager of Holden that I was lucky or protected by a guardian angel, allowing for my survival. At one point I got so tired I desperately wanted to lie down and sleep, which may have resulted in death. It was probably a mistake to attempt this trip, but we survived and it was a good introduction to winter at Holden. We encouraged one another along the way and finally made it to the Ten Mile Bridge. During the final four miles of road into Holden Village there was a creek crossing about each mile. We reached Ten Mile creek at about eleven that night. We heard a gunshot—our only form of communication—from the direction of the village. We knew Rueben was expecting us, and he was apparently getting worried. Rueben's nephew had a pistol and fired a shot in return to let Rueben know we were on the road and still alive.

Rueben insisted I take the "master bedroom" in Chalet 1. I initially wondered if he gave me the privilege of the master bedroom because I was the new manager. It turned out that the master bedroom designation didn't have much meaning. It did have a private bathroom with tub and shower, but of course there was no running water in the house. The only heat came from the fireplace in the front room and the wood cook-stove in the kitchen. There was a thermometer in my bedroom; the first morning I noticed it was eighteen degrees. This was the first time I saw Holden in the winter, and it started the thought process about the possibility of Holden being open for winter activities. The one factor that had not occurred to me was the realization that the sun did not shine on the valley floor for a portion of the winter because of the elevation of the mountain peaks to the south. We enjoyed a delightful two days with Rueben and then returned by snowshoe to Lucerne.

The hydro was the primary work project in 1963. Construction had begun during the prior summer. The board made a commitment to complete the first phase of the project, and if all went well, the first electricity would flow into the village in late summer of 1964. A new oil boiler had been installed in the dinning hall/hotel, and plans were being made to activate or replace the boilers in some of the lodges. The boilers would provide heat as well as hot water. Those paying to visit Holden and participate in the program would begin to have some of the basic comforts as well as a healthy living environment. If the Health Department had initiated inspections before 1965, it's possible that Holden wouldn't have received authorization to serve the public.

Thinking back on that tenuous beginning, I'm amazed that it all worked. Trying to write these thoughts actually scares me and makes me wonder why I took this job, leaving a job with stability and a future for a job that was completely foreign to me without any guarantee of stability. It may go back to my receiving the key to the DeWitt State Bank, an act of trust expressed by the bank manager. At this point, Vern Rieke was offering me the "keys" to Holden.

The easiest task to initiate was lining up promotional presentations in churches around Seattle and the state. Holden had a set of slides that had been assembled for promotional use. The other promotional item available was a commercially produced 16-mm film called *Alps of the Stehekin*. This film was produced by the Sierra Club, a national environmental and conservation organization to help with its efforts to have the North Cascades designated as a national park. The film made negative remarks about the damage caused by Holden Mine, but most of the film did an excellent job of showing the amazing beauty of the North Cascades. (While writing this, I Googled "Alps of the Stehekin" and was able to watch this film online. It brought back many memories. I showed it so many times, I memorized much of the narration, which quickly came back as I was watching this film fifty years later.)

The effort of the Sierra Club was successful, and North Cascades National Park was established in 1968. A spectacular and frequently photographed view is that of Glacier Peak with its reflection in Image Lake—a must for hikers to experience. So many Sierra Club horse pack trips came to Image Lake to build public support for the national park that the area around Image Lake was severely damaged. The area directly around the lake was placed off-limits for camping for many years, giving the fragile grasses and flowers time to reestablish their natural growth. It's easy to love nature to death.

The many committee volunteers were helpful in providing access to congregations. The need to inform as many people as possible was critical to increase the summer attendance as well as make contacts with individuals who had the skills needed to activate the facilities. With no money in the till, it was necessary to make maximum use of volunteers. Perhaps, due to the uniqueness of the location and the excitement for a new program, young adults responded to the concept of volunteering their labor in exchange for the opportunity to participate at Holden Village.

I sent letters to many of the Lutheran colleges, requesting they post information concerning our need for volunteer staff. Rudy Edmund and Beany Lundholm were well known on the Augustana College campus. It was convenient for them to handpick a few students whom they considered excellent prospects for the staff. Carroll was also giving frequent promotional talks to raise money and promote the village. He had good contacts with Augsburg College in Minneapolis. St. Olaf College in Northfield, Minnesota, was another fertile area for volunteers, especially with Howard Hong already having been on the Holden faculty. Luther Seminary and later Wartburg Seminary were also good sources for volunteer staff recruits. Once students from a college or seminary served on the staff and returned to the campus, it was much easier to get students interested in the Holden staff opportunities.

Following the summer of 1964, we notified the national church youth offices that Holden would take over the promotion and selection of the volunteer staff. Since I was supervising the staff once they arrived in the village, it was great to be able to correspond with potential staff members and get somewhat acquainted with them prior to their arrival. We established a three-week minimum for the staff participation. The maximum more or less controlled itself since the initial operation was seasonal.

For approximately ten years, Carroll and I were the only salaried employees. The summer cook was given a small stipend. After a couple of years, we added a registrar, mechanic, and carpenter. None of these were salaried but rather considered stipend positions. Carroll and I always shared a secretary and made this one of the few positions initially receiving a stipend. Holden may not have been able to survive financially if all positions had required salaries and benefits. The Holden staff had a very small line item in the budget. No salaries. No benefits. Period. Perhaps we were taking advantage of the willingness of volunteers to become involved. More volunteers initially applied, and because Holden didn't have sufficient money to consider paying even stipends, the positions were strictly volunteer. This is one reason that Carroll encouraged staff to attend lectures. He let them know numerous times during their stay that the excellence of the faculty and program were their paychecks. If they elected not to attend lectures, they were missing out on their payment for work.

I went through files to get acquainted with the vendors. On trips to Wenatchee and Chelan, I would introduce myself in hopes of developing a more personal relationship. Lake Chelan Lutheran Church in Chelan was most helpful in assisting us to become acquainted in the community. Renie Riddle, a member of the congregation, had a couple of extra bedrooms in her home, a comfortable couch, and a very generous heart. As soon as volunteers began passing through Chelan on their way uplake to Holden, Renie offered her home to provide lodging and generally breakfast to those in transit. I'm sure that some of the Forerunners, the first volunteer workers, stayed with Renie. I don't know if Renie kept a guest book or list of those who stayed with her, but the beginning of Holden owes much to Renie Riddle. I was privileged to stay with her several times, and her generosity should never be forgotten. While writing these memoirs I read that Renie Riddle died. God bless her memory.

Prior to 1965, Chelan and Lake Chelan Lutheran Church became Holden Central as the community at Holden was being established. Many arrived by bus. Once they arrived in Chelan, it was generally Lake Chelan Lutheran or one of its members who provided transportation, making sure that volunteers got overnight lodging as well as food. The *Lady of the Lake* originally left from the dock in front of Campbell's Lodge, which made it easier for those arriving by bus and staying in a Chelan home to catch the boat. The parsonage in those years had an unfinished attic. I slept several nights in the attic because the other rooms were full of other volunteers. The basement of the church was small, but it included a kitchen, restrooms, and floor space for many volunteers to sleep. Without the generosity of Lake Chelan Lutheran and its members, the beginnings of Holden Village would have been an even greater challenge.

It became apparent that Holden Mine had been very important to the life and the economy of Chelan. The Howe Sound Mining Company, Holden Division had an office in Chelan providing communications and coordination for shipments of ore to the smelters. Vendors in Chelan and Wenatchee enjoyed large volumes of sales involving the mine operation.

Keith Krebs was the pastor of Lake Chelan Lutheran. It was great that he was on the liberal side of life and theology. In the first several years, it wasn't clear how the Holden Village program might develop, but with Keith as the contact pastor in Chelan, it was easier to celebrate a new and unusual project. When I found out that Keith made beer in his bathtub, I knew he was sufficiently open-minded to help add levity and not get too serious with our efforts. Keith made it easier for Carroll, the maverick, to feel comfortable being the first director of Holden Village. Initially Carroll, Mary, and I joined Lake Chelan Lutheran since we had no congregation at Holden Village. We had very poor church attendance, but we did worship twice each day at Holden so our guilt factor was minimal.

Clyde Green was one of the first vendors I met. Clyde owned and operated Green Petroleum and was also a member of Lake Chelan Lutheran. As Holden Village increased its activities, we needed more and more fuel. We needed diesel fuel for the electric generator and gasoline for the vehicles. Initially no gas pump was available at Holden. Gas and diesel were shipped in five-hundred-gallon tanks and pumped directly out of the tanks. The mine had used diesel fuel to heat buildings as well as domestic water. The mine had an underground pumping system so diesel fuel could be pumped to each chalet and lodge from a central fifteen-thousand-gallon underground tank located just to the south of Lodge 4. Some fuel was left in this underground tank from the mine operation. When this system was activated, we could fill the underground tank by gravity as the five-hundred-gallon tanks remained on the flatbed truck. In the early 1970s, when the first fuel crisis occurred and prices were escalating with warnings of limited supplies, Clyde offered to allow us to use one of his fifteen thousand gallon storage tanks and have it filled with diesel so it could be purchased at the best price with a guaranteed and uninterrupted supply for Holden. Clyde allowed Holden to pay as needed and he didn't charge for the storage. Any question we had concerning fuel or pumps or storage, Clyde was right there to help us in any way needed.

I discovered that business people in the Wenatchee and Chelan areas were most interested in helping us succeed, not only to enhance their businesses, but because the mine operation had meant so much to many people in the area. Many people in the local area had worked at or with Holden, and they all seemed to have very fond memories of the experience. When I visited with business people, it was frequently time-consuming. They all had stories to share about their experiences with the mine and were anxious to engage in conversation.

Money was always a major consideration for any aspect of Holden in those days. At the beginning of the summer of 1964, I went into Wenatchee and negotiated with Pacific Fruit and Produce Company (supplier of our produce and much of our food) and also Wells and Wade Hardware (suppliers of just about everything else) to see if we could get delivery of food and maintenance supplies but delay the payments until the end of the summer. I convinced them that we had good registrations for the summer and money would be available before fall. Fortunately they agreed with the plan. Neither of these businesses exists at this time; I hope our delayed payments didn't contribute to their demise.

One of my favorite people was Bill Bumps. Bill owned Craftsman Office Supplies and Printing. He had actually worked underground in the mine when he was quite young. He shared with me the story of his underground accident. He fell down one of the shafts and injured his back but survived. I think Bill said he started to work in the mine shortly after graduating from high school. Craftsman Printing helped with some of the printing of brochures and other promotional materials. Bill was a great friend of Holden and someone I greatly appreciated. He had numerous contacts with other business people in the area. Whenever I stopped at Craftsman for office supplies, Bill would appear and share another Holden story, extending my shopping time by at least thirty minutes. Some twenty years after I retired as the Holden business manager, I ran for a seat on the Chelan Public Utility Board of Commissioners. Bill was one of my best supporters, financially as well as gaining votes. He was an adventurous person, having worked underground in Holden Mine, but also riding motorcycles until a stroke created some problems with his mobility. Even after his stroke, he had dreams of buying a three-wheeler so he could continue to ride.

Art and Dan Campbell, owners of Campbell's Lodge in Chelan, were also good friends and most helpful. Art and Dan were the sons of Campbell's original owners. They knew everyone in the area and were influential in introducing us to others who could be of help as we began the process of building support for Holden. I frequently stayed at Campbell's on the many trips to Chelan, prior to boarding the boat for Lucerne. In the early 1960s, they were still renting rooms in the original lodge. I was always looking for the least expensive lodging. I recall that one night they gave me the "suite" in the original lodge. The cost was $4.50.

Holden perhaps helped the Campbells as well as Chelan to integrate the area. We frequently recommended Campbell's since, in the early days, the commercial boat dock was immediately in front of the lodge. In the late 1960s, the first African-American faculty member arrived at Campbell's to seek lodging before heading to Holden the next day. He was refused lodging. Carroll made a special trip downlake to have a "come to Jesus" talk with the Campbells, and as far as I know, Chelan was totally open to African-Americans following Carroll's visit.

Howard Kingman, owner of the Chelan Lumber Company, was also a great friend. As Holden Village began remodeling and improving facilities, we had increasing requirements for building material. Howard wasn't only knowledgeable concerning his trade, but he was more than willing to give free advice as to what was the most efficient or the best product and how best to utilize materials. We were frequently asking for the unusual. As we remodeled and repaired, we made an attempt to stay with what had historically been used by the mining operation. The Holden buildings were originally constructed between 1934 and 1936. Twenty-eight years later, we were trying to find materials that would match the originals. Howard worked magic in many cases.

He was also known to kid and challenge me concerning my knowledge of the building trade. I gradually gained knowledge and occasionally could outsmart Howard in terms of his mentally jousting with me. Howard was the brother of Kathy Woods, the wife of Wilfred Woods, owner/editor of the *Wenatchee World*. When Howard died, I was honored to have Kathy ask me to say a few words at his funeral. It wasn't difficult to remember interesting and humorous stories concerning Howard, his relationship with me, and his cooperation with Holden.

It didn't take long to get acquainted with Wells and Wade Hardware in Wenatchee. Wells and Wade was one of the "real" hardware stores that had items in bins without plastic containers and literally had everything, including the kitchen sink. They had items by the piece or by the carton. It was my experience that they never disposed of any items they ever had maintained in their inventory. On more than one occasion I went to Wells and Wade and describe a piece of equipment in the buildings at Holden. Invariably, I would be directed to a person who knew exactly what I needed and where it was still located, sometimes in the first or second basement with single light bulbs hanging by cords from the ceiling. During the mine days, Wells and Wade had a salesman who made regular trips to Holden. He would stay in a room in the Holden hotel and meet with various departments to take orders, which he then had shipped. Wells and Wade didn't have a frequent turnover of employees. In fact, it wasn't unusual to meet a son working as an apprentice in one department, with his father still working—often as department head—in another department. At one time in its history, Wells and Wade Hardware was literally a family-oriented business.

When we began activating the GE Downdraft oil boilers that heated and provided hot water for the lodges, I paid a visit to Wells and Wade. It turned out that Wells and Wade had originally supplied the boilers and still had a small inventory of some replacement parts. Wells and Wade was truly one-stop shopping. The store had a sheet-metal fabrication shop, a heating and cooling department, and a complete plumbing and electrical department. One of the most important services Wells and Wade provided was a telephone that I could use for making long-distance calls. I made so many trips to Wells and Wade that whenever an office was available, they invited me to use it while in Wenatchee. Wells and Wade even contributed some financial support to Holden.

In the mid 1960s, the telephone calling card was just starting to become available. Since we had no phone service at Holden, I always had a long list of phone calls to make, either for general business or sometimes calls that the registration office requested to more quickly solve communication challenges. Burton Appelo was a successful commercial real estate specialist in downtown Seattle, working with Yates Wood and McDonald. Burton was one of the early Holden volunteers, a man full of energy, life and—more importantly for Holden—contacts. His family owned the Western Wahkiakum Telephone Company in Naselle, Washington.

Burton's family had an army surplus jeep that was a fixer-upper. I traveled with Burton to Naselle, and we towed the Jeep to Seattle and then to Chelan, where we loaded it on the barge. While in Naselle, Burton indicated that the family telephone company was just starting to distribute telephone calling cards. He thought I should have one for making long-distance calls. The Western Wahkiakum Telephone calling card was invaluable when making calls at Wells and Wade Hardware or when standing in telephone booths. Burton was a great friend and a faithful Holden volunteer. He was a good example of a rather conservative Lutheran, who at least initially worked with Holden even as it began to emerge as a more theologically open program, leaning toward the liberal side. The contacts Burton made for Holden were extremely valuable, and his energy helped Holden develop and grow.

The summer of 1964 was the first summer I would be in the position as Holden manager. Fortunately, the Holden Village operation had some internal momentum to propel it along without too much effort. The main effort was assuring adequate staffing for all aspects of the operation. Even though the Lutheran Church of America and Missouri Lutheran Church youth offices didn't fulfill their obligations with staffing, we were able to operate through the summer partially because we discovered that even the people paying as registered guests were willing to assist in the community as needed. A new volunteer work opportunity was beginning to emerge. We discovered that the young adults weren't the only group in society excited about an opportunity to be a part of a community on a volunteer basis. An increasing number in the retired population were becoming available and interested in using their talents and be a part of a community.

There was limited money to plan for the future, but we did what we could and celebrated each day. Community celebrations and spontaneous levity go a long way in hiding fear and uncertainty. I guess our business plan was that a new song for *Beany Sings* or a talent show or planning for Christmas in July or initiating a July Fourth celebration lifted the spirits for all involved. That even solidified financial support as people began experiencing Holden Village as a unique place of community with intellectual challenge and celebration through daily worship. When Holden provided a unique opportunity in a unique setting, it was relatively easy to build support and involvement.

The completion of the first phase of the hydro project was the emphasis for the summer of 1964. We were still using the diesel generator and getting by on forty-five-to-fifty kilowatts of electricity. The hydro installation was completed mid-August. When electricity was available from the hydroelectric plant, electricity was available twenty-four hours, seven days a week. The first phase of the hydro project was utilizing the diversion dam originally used by the mine for both domestic water and water to run the mine operation. It flowed into a seventy-five-thousand-gallon tank and then out of the tank, either to the mine or to the company town and Winston Camp. Ralph Peterson was a salesman/consultant with Pacific Pipe and Supply Company in Seattle, dealing with large municipal water and sewer projects. Ralph was our go-to person whenever water, sewage, and anything dealing with commercial-size pipes were involved.

He designed a diversion valve system so we could divert water from the original waterline before it entered the storage tank and guide it to a fourteen-inch line that was added to bring water to the hydro. This system would provide only a two-hundred-thirty-foot dynamic head of vertical drop from the diversion dam to the hydro. The hydro turbines were designed for a six-hundred-forty-foot head. Therefore this first phase would provide only approximately a hundred kilowatts of electrical power, which was still twice the electrical power we used from the diesel generating system.

When electricity was available over the entire twenty-four hours, people complained and asked that we turn off the electricity at ten o'clock each night, which had been the procedure when using the diesel generators. They wrote letters to the board, requesting that management be instructed to restore "dark skies" at ten o'clock. The decision came down to our insurance policy and the liability issue.

Bernard Anderson, executive with Frank B. Hall Insurance Company, was our insurance agent and consultant. Bernard was a member of the Lutheran Church and volunteered to work with Holden, even though an upstart, remote retreat center wasn't his normal client. It's fortunate that we could work with Bernard. He was well respected in the insurance field and was able to get liability insurance for Holden. I suspected that Bernard also delayed having any inspections by the insurance company until we were a bit better organized. Bringing guests up a mountain road on the back of a flatbed truck may not have passed inspection. Dormitories without any fire alarms and only the very basic of fire fighting equipment probably wouldn't have been accepted. It's possible that the insurance companies didn't realize that Holden didn't have electricity from ten at night to five each morning. Bernard was definitely working on behalf of Holden Village and its need for liability insurance. A good broker can work with an insurance company in a way that benefits both the company and the client. Bernard made it clear that once the hydro was operational, it would be required that electricity and lights would be available twenty-four hours a day. We really didn't have a choice.

Holden was exciting in the initial years. Everything was new, and whatever we initiated frequently became traditional in future years.

Community is more than just being in one location together. Community is the sharing of common experiences, experiences that are repeated so new arrivals can easily feel a part of common activities that bond everyone together without any required initiation. Christmas in July, the tradition that started out of a love for Rueben Thompson, became an important one. For a while it drew the largest crowds to Holden. Christmas in July also generated national attention.

One summer, a retired but well-known writer for *The Wenatchee (Washington) World*, Hu Blonk, was going uplake with friends in a private boat. Hu wrote many of the stories that promoted the government financing of Grand Coulee Dam. In his retirement, he continued to write stories that were almost always published. The private boat with Hu aboard arrived at the Lucerne Dock just as the *Lady of the Lake* was arriving. It happened to be July 25, and Wes was at the dock in his Santa Claus suit to welcome the arriving Holden guests. Hu had a nose for a good story. He decided to leave his friends and take the bus to Holden to investigate the background of a Santa Claus meeting the boat on July 25. He arrived in the village and interviewed me.

The story appeared in *The Wenatchee World* the next day. United Press International (UPI) picked up the story, and it started appearing in newspapers all over the country. Many former Holden guests, who read this unique story in their local papers, sent copies of the article to us. A couple months later, I received a letter from one of our faculty members living in Pennsylvania. He said he was driving down the turnpike in September listening to National Public Radio. NPR began playing Christmas music and told the story about Christmas being celebrated in July in a remote mountain village called Holden Village.

It was primarily the volunteer staff who initiated ideas for more Holden celebrations. Part of the celebrations or festivals was to join the nation but also sometimes to make fun of traditions in the outside world. The Fourth of July celebration was a natural. We suggested staff in each work area put together floats based on their work. Materials had to be scrounged, and not too many were mobile. Wagons, wheelbarrows, and other wheeled devices were common. I thought we needed a band and started the tradition of the Holden marching band. Most years few instruments were available; we concentrated on intricate marching maneuvers while we hummed band music. The July Fourth celebration concluded with a barbecue and village talent show, which also became a tradition.

The July Fourth talent show is how Wes became famous for his portrayal of Florence Nightingale. His act is too difficult to explain, although many will remember it and, I'm sure, smile. I also began making appearances at the talent show. Donn and Dottie Rosenauer joined the volunteer staff and established a more organized registration office. Donn was a delight in terms of his humor and positive personality. He approached me and suggested that the two of us be masters of ceremonies for the show and take on the characters of Rowan and Martin of television's *Laugh-In*. I didn't know who Rowan and Martin were since we didn't get TV. Donn explained the program format and the nature of the banter. Since it was Donn's idea, he chose to play Dan Rowan, which left me to play Dick Martin. We pulled it off in a most enjoyable way.

The celebration of Christmas in July or a tongue-in-cheek Fourth of July parade tied the community to the outside world and yet allowed the Holden community to create its own version of popular celebrations. There was a desire to imitate normal society, and at times poke fun at a society that was operating in another world, providing us an opportunity to make social statements within the safe confines of the isolated Railroad Creek Valley.

One of the early responsibilities that I assumed was working with the forest service. Holden Village was operating under a special-use permit from the forest service because the company town, now called Holden Village, was on forest service land. This required an annual inspection. There was never a written outline of our working relationship, but it became clear that anything we did dealing with facilities, forest service land, or transportation would require involvement with the district ranger.

Bill Rines was the district ranger in Chelan when I became manager. We were on uncharted ground in terms of operating a retreat center at the location of a mine operation. Bill and I developed a good relationship and a genuine friendship. It became apparent that Carroll was someone who shouldn't work with the forest service. Carroll's personality definitely didn't mix with federal authority that took precedence over the authority of God, at least in terms of government real estate and forests.

There was no manual to guide my relationship with our landlord, so it was learn while doing. Without communications other than the US Postal Service, requiring transport by boat, it was very inconvenient to get any quick response to questions. I took it upon myself to decide what we could do without permission and what would require formal forest service input and permission. Basically I decided that if a project or change wouldn't noticeably show as a change or addition, and if it wouldn't in any way negatively impact the forest or nature, we could proceed and take a chance. That system seemed to work. I did send letters to request input and permission for many projects until finally Bill told me on the QT during a visit to the village that I shouldn't send anything in writing unless it was major. He said that anything he received in writing would have to go through the official process and have a written response. Unofficially, he said, he trusted me and I should ask for permission only in major projects. That made it easier.

After seven years of my working with the forest service, the agency sent a letter to the board asking for a more formal indication of who would be the official "agent" for Holden. At this point I was officially declared the Holden Agent. During the first several years of operation, the personnel in the Chelan District Ranger office didn't think Holden Village would last. They had an office wager concerning our life expectancy. The longest bet was three and a half years. Since they didn't expect the Holden operation to last, they paid minimum attention to us. It made it easier, and we could more or less operate as if we didn't have a landlord. The hydro project was of course on their radar, but it's amazing that even that major project had very little involvement by any of the government agencies.

The summer of 1964 was cold and rainy. The only heat was from the oil stoves in the dining room and fireplaces in some of the chalets. We designated Chalet 1 as a location for guests to sit and talk in front of the living room fireplace. In August, the national youth board met at Holden. Willis Shellberg, an architect from Forest City, Iowa, was caring for his child while his wife attended the meetings. Carroll and I talked with Willis to get ideas on how we could remodel Lodge 5 to make it into a hotel lobby, where guests could warm themselves with a fireplace and also a building that could be used for lectures and gatherings. Willis volunteered his time to put together a couple of options.

In January 1965, I traveled to Forest City to meet with Willis. Originally, Carroll outlined the basics of what he thought the area should be. In order to encourage community and conversation, an area should be developed to minimize rows of chairs but rather seating should be encouraged so people were looking at each other. Willis presented two main options, primarily with two different fireplace locations: a standard rock fireplace at the end of the room which would allow chairs to be set up in rows, and a large circular fireplace in the middle of the room to force people to face each other. He informed me that he would do the construction drawings if we picked the circular fireplace. If we wanted the other fireplace location, we could find another architect to finish the project. The design Wills completed included the circular fireplace, with a museum and library on the West end of the building on the ground floor. Sleeping rooms would be included in the west half of the upstairs.

Construction on Koinonia (Lodge 5) began during the winter/ spring of 1965. I submitted the plans to the Chelan County Building Department and paid fifty dollars for the building permit. I inquired as to the frequency of their inspections during construction. They said they hadn't sent an inspector up Lake Chelan for fifteen years, and they would have the PUD check over the electrical when the PUD did the electrical connection. I informed them that we produced our own power and the Chelan County PUD wasn't involved. The county planner informed me that we should proceed with the project and not expect any inspections.

During the summer of 1965, the fir poles were cut that would form the structural integrity in the open meeting room, with the second floor becoming the balcony. The four logs were hauled next to Lodge 5. Elenore Orlow and her three daughters spent the better part of six weeks peeling bark off the logs. They were left to dry.

In September, the Nazerene district pastors had their conference at Holden. We suggested that a great community project would be their helping us carry these rather substantial logs into the building. We removed one of the first floor windows and, with the Nazerene pastors chest to back, literally picked up each log and walked it into the room. Without the Nazerene pastors, the construction of Koinonia may have been delayed a year. The meeting room was completed early summer of 1966. The cedar lumber used in the interior of Koinonia was cut in the Railroad Creek Valley by the Swiss loggers, milled at the Chelan Box Company mill in Manson, and then shipped back to Holden.

The circular fireplace necessitated a rather large, circular hood, seven feet in diameter. Teeter Sheet Metal in Seattle had been recommended to us. They had built a smaller version of what we needed for a University of Washington fraternity. The hood cost $1,500.

Walt Olson was a volunteer whose family had arranged for him to come to Holden because he had a challenge with alcohol. He was also a licensed electrician. Walt expressed a concern to me on the morning of July 4: he didn't think we had sufficient funds to pay for the hood. He gave me a hundred-dollar bill and told me to ask for fourteen other donors at the noon meal. I told him we had a policy against fundraising at Holden when people were more or less captive. He insisted, and Carroll gave me permission to ask for fourteen donors following the meal. Within several minutes we had our fourteen donors. I thought it was going so well that I announced that we also needed money to pay for the carpet. In another couple of minutes we had an additional twelve donors. The guests found this so amazing and exciting that we had requests that each Fourth of July we repeat this opportunity for guests to help the village with specific needs.

The subsequent "auctions" were held in connection with the Fourth of July talent show. In subsequent years, we raised $2,800 for a greenhouse and $6,500 for a portable saw mill. The largest amount contributed in this way was $12,500 for the purchase of a grand piano and final payment on a Snow Trac vehicle. All of this started with Walt Olson, who was seeking healing in the community and exhibited his generosity and concern for Holden.

In 1967 we began work in the Koinonia museum and library. Rudy Edmund had been very patient with having a museum available for displaying historical and geological material. Mary Hinderlie, village librarian, had also been patient but determined to have a library worthy of the faculty being assembled each year. The library and reading room were in the small room in the front of the Village Center, across from the snack bar. We wanted the library and museum to be a special place. One of Carroll's acquaintances owned a large wood-processing plant in Lilyhammer, Norway. Carroll contacted the owner, who agreed to donate laminated flooring for the library and museum. Since the company did a large volume of sales to the United States with materials shipped to Seattle, the donor had the shipping company provide free shipping to the Port of Seattle.

When it arrived at the port, we found out that, even though it was donated, we would have to pay an import fee based on the wholesale value. I contacted our insurance agent, Bernard Anderson, who worked with the shipping companies to see if he could negotiate around the import fee. I told him how the shipment had made it to Seattle without cost to Holden. He wasn't able to negotiate around the import fee, but he said his brokerage firm would pay the fee and transportation to the boat dock in Chelan. I contacted the Lake Chelan Boat Company and told them the story. I asked if they would be willing to ship the flooring uplake as their contribution, but they indicated that wouldn't be possible. The flooring was installed in the library and museum, but I think it has now been replaced. The laminated flooring from Lilyhammer, Norway, remained in place for at least twenty-five years.

The final phase of the Koinonia project was finishing the upstairs sleeping rooms. This project was advanced ahead of the original schedule because Carroll had invited Roland Bainton, Martin Luther scholar from Princeton University, to be on faculty. Dr. Bainton was scheduled to be in Japan for the first part of the summer for a series of speaking engagements. He agreed to come to Holden if we would provide housing and be willing to also host his family so they could be together in the village. Carroll promised them the new rooms in Koinonia, the part of the project that hadn't yet begun.

The project was completed, and Dr. Bainton and his family had a great reunion. Dr. Bainton never carried a camera but drew sketches and caricatures. When he arrived in the village, he offered to let us display his sketches. We hung clotheslines outside the dining hall and had an exquisite display of Bainton sketches. He continued to add to the display of Holden sketches and caricatures of many people in the village. If you weren't privileged to hear one of Roland Bainton's presentations in person, I suggest you go to the Holden audio archive and enjoy a rare audio experience.

Two groups not associated with the Lutheran Church were very instrumental in the early years. The Camp Farthest Out (CFO) was a nondenominational group with a Pentecostal leaning. The group came to Holden for two or three years in the month of August and generally attracted about two hundred registrants. They were definitely important to Holden in terms of providing revenue, but they also brought wonderful people, some of whom later came back year after year to participate in the Holden Village program. CFO brought a more emotional approach to religion rather than the intellectual or liturgical. We needed to communicate with the Holden staff to accept them as fellow travelers in the Christian tradition even though they took a different approach.

Each morning they conducted "Devotions in Motion," which was a combination of daily exercise combined with scripture and hymns. Healing services were part of their program, and they used evangelists rather than preachers. Ruth Carter Stapleton, sister of President Jimmy Carter, was at Holden Village one of the years as an evangelist with CFO.

The second group was the Air Force Spiritual Life Conference from McChord Air Force Base in Tacoma. They brought 250 people to Holden for a spiritual conference and relationship building. They made use of the Holden facility for two years and again were important to the revenue stream as well as introducing new people to Holden. The second year we suggested that they invite the army from Fort Lewis to join them, which they did. It was the first time the air force and the army had joined together in a spiritual life conference. The reason they didn't return a third year was their concern for physical safety. Since no road access was available to Holden, they maintained a medical team and medical vehicle at the Twenty-Five-Mile Creek dock, the end of the road on Lake Chelan, in case someone needed to be evacuated for any medical reason. Medical problems didn't occur either year, but their concern for not being in full control of the health and safety of their personnel ended their use of Holden.

Holden was taking on a life of its own. Although we were concerned about having each year repeating the previous year's flavor, we did recognize that some traditions were valuable for the welfare of community life.

CHAPTER 5

Holden's Program Develops

THE HOLDEN PROGRAM DIDN'T DEVELOP through a specific theory of communication or education, but rather out of a necessity to utilize close and fortunately prestigious friends of Carroll Hinderlie. Neither the Holden board nor Carroll assembled a program-planning committee. It was my observation that committee involvement by Carroll consisted of his listening to others share ideas, which he incorporated if he were already planning on doing it. The initial requirement for the program was to establish quality conversation, offering transparency and intellectual depth to encourage people to travel to Holden for a unique community experience and learning opportunity in the remote North Cascade Mountains. The miracle of the Holden Village program was its informal approach and timely, issue-oriented offerings.

Guests and staff responded to an opportunity to meet faculty in a small venue. It was an opportunity to listen, to question, and to agree or disagree with people such as Howard Hong, Fritz Norstad, Rosemary Rueter, Rudy Edmund, Paul Heyne, Martin Marty, and Roland Bainton. These individuals were just a few of the many quality faculty members involved with the Holden program. Holden came into existence when an increasing number of members in the church pews were eager to not only read and discuss spiritual or theological topics but also expand their knowledge dealing with science, music, art, and philosophy. Holden Village began at a time when people in the pews were wondering how the church could relate by positively impacting society as a partner and not as a separate entity in life. Most pastors and congregations weren't prepared to tie church and society together, but Holden provided an ideal arena for this challenge to be implemented.

Very few universities could provide the quality of teachers that were occasionally gathered together at Holden at any one time. I'm not attempting to provide an in-depth analysis of the Holden program, but I did have the opportunity to observe and experience the program as it developed over its initial twenty years. Guests would also share their impressions of the program and village with me. I was apparently a "safe" person who was associated with management but didn't have a reputation for emotional reactions or public reprisals.

My comments are in terms of how the program impacted me and my observation as to how the program impacted others. I had the unique opportunity to become well acquainted with Carroll as we worked closely during concurrent thirteen years as director and manager, respectively. The Holden program included more than worship, faculty, and lectures. The program also involved establishing and maintaining a community, which included the integration of volunteer staff, faculty members, guests, and a few paid individuals receiving stipends.

With Carroll as the director, the program was developed without a preplanned, written academic analysis, but rather through the experience and in the mind of Carroll. The success of the Holden program was in part due to Carroll inviting people whom he valued and whom he personally enjoyed and from whose thoughts he benefited. The program created a theological and intellectual climate encouraging the professional and academic aspects of the church to merge with the community of those sitting in the pews. It was an example of "the priesthood of all believers," a term promoted by Martin Luther advancing the concept that all people were able to be priests and not just the ordained.

The majority of the early faculty had little or no involvement with the Bible-camp movement in the church. In my opinion, Bible camps were advanced Sunday school meeting in the woods. Carroll was interested in developing a program that looked more like a college campus than a

Bible camp. However, each day began with matins and Bible study and ended with vespers. Lectures and discussions were scheduled through the day and into the evening.

The word began to spread concerning the opportunity to register at Holden and have the unique opportunity to interact with quality teachers and communicators, many of whom were shaping the church as well as parts of society. The church at large didn't offer opportunities for members in the pews to meet some of the great teachers and theologians except at sterile church conferences. Even the church conferences were controlled in terms of official participation. Besides the program opportunities, Holden also provided family and recreation opportunities that were frosting on the cake for those participating.

When Fritz Norstad first came to Holden he was teaching at Luther-Northwestern Seminary. The easiest way to describe Fritz is: he was quality—quality in how he treated others, quality in the words he used, quality in his approach to life, quality in the things he owned. One of the years he came on faculty he pulled a twenty-four-foot Danish cabin cruiser behind his Mercedes from Minneapolis and kept it at Refrigerator Harbor at Lucerne. I had the privilege of joining him for many fishing trips on Lake Chelan. I think he invited me because we became good friends, but I also realize that I had access to Holden vehicles and could provide transportation to the lake. I like to think it was the friendship factor that allowed me to be involved with Fritz.

Fritz loved whatever he did. Fishing was more than catching fish. It was also about conversation and fixing blueberry pancakes in the galley and just sitting quietly and enjoying the beauty of the lake in the early mornings. For the record, we always got back to the village by the time the workday officially began. On the other hand, my workday was officially 24-7. Fritz was highly respected by everyone. Fritz remained a close friend and a frequent participant at the village.

Once the word began circulating as to the quality of women and men on the Holden faculty, the program began to attract people from the pews to come and have a chance to listen to and even debate with some of the great church leaders in the country. One of the significant people to become involved this way was Leo Bustad. Leo had become acquainted with Fritz at a meeting in Pullman, and he didn't want to miss the opportunity to be in the village with Fritz.

The first couple of years, Holden offered a family week in mid-August. Fritz was on the faculty, so Leo and his family registered. At the same time, Carroll started a September week called the Lay Theological Gathering, and Leo also became a charter member of this group. The gathering appeared to me to be an opportunity for a few select people to get together, have good conversations, and eat the flatbread that Leo always brought along with Cougar Gold cheese from the Washington State University creamery. Leo himself was quickly added to the faculty, attracting many guests and becoming one of Holden's powerful supporters.

It is important to repeat that Holden Village came into existence at a time when people in the pews were hungry to be involved with reading theology, participating in theological conversation with their pastors, and not just accept a one-way exchange of thought. The Internet and instantaneous access to global communications didn't exist in 1963–1983. Holden became the pew-sitters' Google. It appeared to me that Carroll's approach to programming came from his own love for conversation, discussion, and debate. Carroll shared with me his experience with work camps in Europe after the war. These camps involved all ages and again combined physical activities as well as a worship discipline and study and discussions. It was also interesting that the one concern he expressed, based on his European experience, was the danger of single and widowed women dominating the camps and, according to Carroll, negatively impacting the future of the European work-camp tradition. I recall Carroll mentioning the single women and widow issue several times when more single or widowed women began to frequent Holden. Unlike the European experience, the single women and widows were an integral part of the volunteer staff effectiveness as well as frequent and supportive guests who contributed much to the life of the village.

Carroll always called life as he observed it and didn't hold back with his comments. This approach endeared him to many but also created potential conflicts with others. He definitely didn't make choices of faculty or subjects based on polls of what might sell, but chose faculty based on their ability to communicate and perhaps even encourage the church to take a new look at life and faith. He didn't hesitate to confront people if he felt they were wrong in terms of spiritual correctness. Carroll related one story of an encounter when he was on the Staten Island Ferry in New York City. He was standing on the car deck and heard several people expressing strong racial comments. He approached them and asked if he could take their picture because he wanted a picture of people who he knew were definitely going to hell. Fortunately, Carroll was too big to throw overboard.

The Holden program came together through excellent teachers that Carroll personally knew and respected. The subject matter wasn't as important as the personalities and communication skills of the teachers and the emotional conviction that the faculty person shared. Carroll brought in faculty who didn't have ego problems, even though many were world-class teachers and authors. They were more interested in helping others, exploring their questioning minds rather than trying to prove their own self-importance as teachers. The real genius of the Holden program was that it created a desire to learn and stimulate continued discussions. Holden faculty members loved to teach and discuss and share one-on-one on the trail or at the coffee break.

Carroll was interested in having Holden emphasize the *whole* person. He said the church too often operated in a manner that divided all aspects of the family into different parts. The church had the women's organizations, the men's organizations, the youth organizations, the pastors' organizations, etc. The approach that Holden would take was to bring back together the *whole* person in terms of the spiritual, the mental, and the physical. Holden would provide worship discipline. Holden would provide intellectual stimulation. Holden would provide physical activities through manual labor, volleyball, hiking, etc.

Carroll was well aware of the quality of teachers he brought to Holden, and he frequently scolded the volunteer staff for not taking advantage of the opportunity to learn from them. Teaching and discussions not only took place around the fireplace in Koinonia, but conversations also took place with faculty on hikes or even trips to Holden Lake to catch a trout. If you were fortunate enough to go on a hike with Rudy Edmund, you not only observed the art of fly-casting, but you also received a geology lesson on the trail or at the lake while eating lunch. This style of teaching and learning was perhaps what originally started in Greece when teacher and student were sitting under a tree or walking on a path or sharing a snack on a journey. The success of the program at any time could be measured by the number of conversations taking place at coffee break or while waiting in line for ice cream in the evening. Teaching and learning were almost a 24-7 opportunity.

Holden became a "folk university" in that it provided a uniquely qualified faculty offering high quality teaching and learning opportunities in a setting optimum for teaching and learning. There were no tests, and everyone was attending out of a shared desire to learn. Teachers taught out of their love for teaching.

Another important factor was that the community was continuous through the week, the month, and the year. Most people might arrive on a Saturday or a Sunday, but people arrived and departed each day of the week, so there was never a complete turnover of life in the village. Upon arrival, you were immediately a part of a living, breathing community. The faculty was handpicked, and you could be confident that information shared was based on much study and research, not just random thoughts or the reading of a favorite book. In the later years of my time at Holden, it was my feeling that the approach to the faculty changed, and in my opinion, that changed the impact of the program within the community.

The faculty also had a unique opportunity to teach in the true meaning of teaching. They weren't required to prepare lesson plans or notes. They could speak their informed and passionate thoughts and convictions and not worry about what they said as it related to the institution that employed them. For some adults it was the first opportunity to attend college-level classes. For most people sitting in the pews, it was the first opportunity to participate in theological lectures or discussions. In a real way, it was revolutionary for attendees in terms of reading and discussing theology. In the past it was only the pastor who had a library of theological books, and the pastor was the authority of all theological thought. That made it safe for the pastors. Now all of a sudden, people in the pews were coming out of Holden knowing the names of theologians, knowing theological terms, and in many cases have sat at the feet of and having had ice cream with the authors of the books that formerly only their pastors had had the opportunity to read.

The Aspen Institute in Aspen, Colorado, is a world-class program that was initiated in 1950. The Aspen Institute pays big bucks for it speakers, and it attracts the high rollers in politics, industry, and education. In a few instances in the 1970s, the Institute paid for teachers to come as far as Aspen, and then those same teachers—with their families—continued on to Holden. They would spend three or more weeks at Holden enjoying teaching, receiving nothing for travel or speaking but thoroughly enjoying the Holden experience that attracted young adults who would be future leaders and perhaps even future lecturers at Aspen.

Holden Village, without knowing it or flaunting its success, was providing training for emerging leaders and also helping some current leaders regain their humility after being elevated to pastor, professor, or bishop.

Carroll was always sensitive to the support of the national church bodies. I assume part of this sensitivity was based on his history in the church. As a maverick, he was admired, resented, and perhaps even feared. The way that the national church organizations could display their approval was through financial support. The American Lutheran Church (ALC) had agreed to provide $7,500 to Holden each year, the Lutheran Church in America provided $5,000 each year, and the Lutheran Church–Missouri Synod donated $2,500 each year. This financial support lasted only a few years before each of the groups indi-cated that they felt Holden Village was sufficiently established, and their support was no longer needed.

The contributions were from the youth departments, and The ALC wrote to Carroll indicating they had a difficult choice to make. Its youth department was still publishing *ONE* magazine, and it required a great-er subsidy. *ONE* wasn't considered to be a significant publication, but it appeared to have a powerful lobbying force in the headquarters. The youth department decided to eliminate the $7,500 for Holden Village and put it into the magazine. Carroll was so upset when he received that letter that he came into my office and literally shouted, "The church is going to find me dead on the street one of these days with a note pinned to my shirt saying, 'They supported a meaningless magazine instead of supporting the significant Holden ministry'!" Carroll was probably cor-rect about the magazine, but that didn't change the priority of The ALC youth department.

Once the national church groups were no longer financially sup-porting the village, it actually freed Holden to act more independently and not worry about meeting the approval of those in Minneapolis, St. Louis, or Philadelphia. After the initial anger over the elimination of the national support, we accepted this change as a positive move for Holden.

Worship life at Holden was critical to Carroll. It was the required discipline that everyone in the community would attend vespers in the evening. Vespers were initially conducted by one of the faculty members who had the ability to communicate, inspire, and keep vespers to within twenty minutes. If one of the leaders went beyond the time limit, Carroll would schedule himself for the next night and have a very short three-to-five-minute service and subtly, or not so subtly, make his point. Usually vespers involved a homily. The service was in reality an extension of the faculty lectures, but with a greater element of spirituality and personal witness. Every guest, and especially every staff member, was expected (required) to attend vespers. It was also my impression that for Carroll, the importance of worship was the discipline, the scriptures, and the ability to communicate not necessarily the atmosphere.

The worship wasn't based on establishing a visual or emotional atmosphere. It was my impression that Carroll would value worship even if music, candles or special lighting, wasn't central to the overall experience. The spoken word was the key.

Matins, in the morning, provided a worship opportunity in which staff members could lead. Wes Prieb was one of the regulars at matins, and everyone, especially the long-term staff, enjoyed what seemed to be the same matins in different window dressing with the same phraseology each and every time. Wes had a tendency to use the phrases of the television evangelist and the humor of the stand-up comedian. When not at Holden, Wes did watch a lot of TV. Fortunately, the Holy Spirit was with Wes during matins, because there always seemed to be a relevant message.

It was assumed that anyone who came to Holden would be aware of the worship discipline and abide by the rule. If someone didn't care to be involved with the worship discipline, Holden wasn't the proper place for him or her. We were told that some couples came to Holden even though one spouse didn't attend church. The couple came to vespers together, allowing the person who didn't attend church to still feel comfortable and not out of place. Holden wasn't attached to one theological approach, and Holden didn't proselytize.

The beauty of the Holden Village program was that it occurred in a unique community setting where faculty, staff, and guests had little option but be together much of the waking hours. Guests and faculty played pool together or bowled or even worked together on occasion when there was a community work opportunity. None of the living accommodations were what one would consider plush. The nature of life within the village tended to force everyone to common locations where conversations were easily initiated. Titles didn't exist; few people knew if one were a bishop, a pastor, a mechanic, a potter, or a volunteer staff member, all of who were likely struggling to find life's answers.

On one occasion, a man who happened to be a bishop from the Midwest shared at vespers that when he first arrived in Holden he was uncomfortable. In his district/synod, he was catered to, addressed as bishop, and chauffeured around. At Holden he was elevated to being a person in a community where even a bishop could have an in-depth conversation with a stranger. At first, the Holden experience was frightening for him, but then it became an opportunity to once again be free of title and position.

In what I would consider the golden years of the Holden community, the only titles in the village were guest, staff, and faculty. Even these three categories were difficult to identify. Carroll and I were the odd ones in the community with the titles of director and manager. From my experience, true community results when the vast majority of the gathered people have little or no identifiable difference in status or title as to how they fit into the community. During the twenty years I worked as manager, Holden had little semblance to a corporate organizational model. The offices that existed didn't even have identifications to separate them from the rest of the community. The main entrance to the office that Carroll and I shared still had the label "Dining Room Manager" from the mine days. We never saw the need to change the sign.

Some pastors were initially upset with Holden because the program brought new life and intellectual curiosity to the people in the pews, but this attitude was rather short-lived. Pastors themselves began to make use of Holden Village for their own personal enrichment. The ones who really benefited were those who left their title of pastor at Twenty-Five Mile Creek and arrived in Holden as members of a community where all delighted in joining the struggle to seek answers relating to individual identity and a purpose in life. Pastors also began to see Holden Village as a place of healing and would send people to Holden occasionally to provide the possibility of healing involving family or societal challenges.

In my estimation, Holden Village came to life at just the correct time in history. In the mid-1960s, financial capabilities of the middle class allowed young adults to volunteer their time as part of their educational and maturing process. College costs, as compared to middle-class income, allowed families to cover some or all of college expenditures without requiring students to work at paying jobs through the entire summer. This also influenced the availability of people for faculty positions. Some faculty could actually take two or three months off during the summer to volunteer time teaching at Holden, especially if the teaching opportunity also provided a unique opportunity for a family vacation. As with the operational staff, all faculty positions were 100-percent volunteer, with no financial help for travel or living expenses.

I recall one Holden board meeting when a board member raised the question concerning the possibility of offering stipends for faculty. Vern Rieke, board chairman, without any emotion in his voice said, "If you want to pay me anything, you need to pay me what I'm worth." At that time, in1971, Vern was being paid perhaps $3,000 per presentation outside of the classroom. He said he was thrilled to volunteer his time on the Holden faculty, but it was an insult to pay a faculty member less than his/her worth. The subject was never raised again, at least through 1983.

The other societal aspect that contributed to Holden's success was the evolution as well as the revolution within young adult segments of society in the 1960s and into the early 1970s. The Vietnam War was generating increasing opposition and protests on college campuses. College age youth were looking for meaning in places other than the home or church. The church wasn't attracting this age group because young adults were looking for new answers without the use of repeated spiritual phrases and programs imposed on the congregation by church headquarters. They refused to struggle with faith without the option to question faith. They didn't want to throw out creation, but they did want to explore the scientific basis for evolution. They wanted to hear multiple sides of a discussion and be able to argue and disagree and seriously debate its meaning. Young adults were looking for a safe place to say things and challenge concepts without being criticized or negatively labeled. They wanted to be able to challenge a teacher without being concerned as to its impact on their receiving their degrees. They wanted to be in a community that would allow them to have strong convictions with the option of changing their convictions with new and exciting information.

Without realizing its impact, Holden offered a safe arena for many young adults. No department at a church headquarters or Carroll's dynamic personality was solely responsible for what was happening at Holden. Sometimes, miracles just happen. However, Carroll was definitely important in the process. His preference was to have someone in most lectures to counter the presenter and insist on providing answers to questions when asked. When Carroll knew that a teacher with strong convictions was lecturing, he would frequently be in the balcony of Koinonia and would challenge any statements he considered arguable to make sure that no one in the audience was "brainwashed."

Perhaps one of the most important aspects of Carroll's leadership was his insistence that no one would dominate the discussion and no social or theological issue would form the total discussion within the village. Carroll knew the village community would always include a variety of thoughts and a broad spectrum of backgrounds and understandings of the gospel. He made sure that newly developed convictions were established through hearing and learning multiple options and not just the bias of one particular faculty member.

The gospel presents some points that weren't up for discussion, but so much of what the church deals with is based on human interpretation. It was my impression that Carroll intellectually knew the dynamics of a healthy community, and this was important as he observed the overall community of Holden Village. Even though Mary, Carroll's wife, generally stayed in the background, it's very likely that she was the more astute observer of life within the Holden Village community, and it's likely that she was as responsible as Carroll—or perhaps more responsible than Carroll—for the health of the community. It was my impression that Carroll had a difficult time shaping the community in any way that wasn't happening naturally. It might be that his insecurities in terms of acceptance and approval impacted how he personally related to the community. He too frequently waited until a perceived issue had fermented in his mind for some time, and then a stated change would come through an emotional outburst that many didn't understand.

Another factor in terms of the relationship between Carroll and the Holden Village program was that he was in residence in the community for only thirty-five to forty percent of each year. The period of the year when he was absent from the community—during the winter—might have been a more important time for the overall community development. It involved a smaller group that spent more time together, without the constant influx of new and short-term members, as was the case during the summer and early fall. It might have been more difficult and even stifled the growth of a healthy community if Carroll would have been present in the village throughout the year.

As the years progressed, Carroll wasn't personally acquainted with all the faculty selections prior to their arrival. People who Carroll trusted would make recommendations for new faculty, but even in those cases, new teachers were generally scheduled for shorter periods of time on trial bases. If new faculty didn't make an emotional connection with the guests and staff, or if Carroll didn't make a connection with them, they weren't invited back. Perhaps out of convenience rather than plan, a portion of the Holden faculty during the first ten or twelve years consisted of a small group that participated each summer. For many, involvement was for two-to-three months. Additional faculty came for shorter periods of time. This created a community of the known and loved. For many guests it was like coming home each year to their source of learning with faculty they knew and respected. The negative aspect of a faculty that repeated each year was that fewer faculty members became involved. Repeat faculty had the danger of becoming too emotionally or intellectually close to each other and potentially separating themselves from others in the community.

There was no doubt as to the importance of Holden having a faculty who were extremely knowledgeable in their field and willing to teach in the most effective way. It was my contention that Holden had a moral obligation to have presentations that guests could rely on as far as truthfulness with minimal personal bias or ego involved. This was also a new experience for many of the faculty. Too often they were accustomed to lecturing and assuming they were always right. No one would dare challenge their expressions of knowledge and opinion in their traditional classroom.

Hortie Christman, sixty-seven-year-old volunteer with an eighth grade education, would quietly say to a faculty member during a lecture that something they had said didn't seem correct. Hortie seemed to know when certain comments didn't pass the "smell test" of a logger who had time to think while working in nature. For many guests, Holden was a one-week university experience—no time to research what the faculty member said and challenge him or her in a week or two. Carroll was excellent at attempting to have two faculty members knowledgeable in similar fields present opposing concepts so guests could be exposed to various views. This wasn't always possible, but Carroll did all he could to make sure that multiple views were presented so discussion was generated, even if he presented the opposing view.

Carroll was a dynamic preacher. Anyone who heard him preach more than once would live with examples and stories that he used to provide powerful, touching, and/or humorous illustrations of the gospel messages. He always spoke and preached as if everyone in the audience knew everyone he knew and often mentioned those people in the sermon. Since I worked closely with Carroll for thirteen years, I became well acquainted with his history, his friends, and his enemies and could frequently provide the interpretation of a story or example Carroll used in a Bible study or sermon and help people understand what he said and why he said it. At times it was almost like Carroll was speaking in tongues and needed an interpreter. For me, Carroll was at his best when he was preaching. Preaching for Carroll didn't occur only in a church service setting. He was a different person when he was preaching as compared to when he might be dealing with other aspects of community dynamics.

Carroll had an excellent memory for scripture, poetry, and life experiences. Some people go through life and never remember any significant life stories. Carroll's entire life seemed to be one of interesting and significant stories. I never knew if all of the stories were factual, but over the years a significant number of the stories were more or less corroborated by others. I assumed that most of them were factual. It was difficult to win an argument with Carroll because of his powerful personality, depth of information, and intellect. This was especially true in the areas of his strength, such as Biblical studies and theology. He had a unique insight into the gospels and their relevance to life in the church and society.

In many ways, Carroll was perhaps similar to some of the Old Testament leaders. He had gifts that the church and individuals in the church needed but his personality was at times challenging. Carroll was a pastor had a title and a respected position as Holden Village director. He had a major impact on people, especially people who were struggling with their faith issues. His gospel examples and stories, his own life, and his insights into the scriptures were profound and helped many people break free within their own struggles. I find that today more than ever, I discover the powerful influence Carroll had on my life and my understanding of the scriptures and my relationship with God. For this I will forever be grateful.

I observed and participated when Carroll decided it was time to bend some silly church traditions such as not sharing communion with other Christians, more specifically not with the Missouri Synod. On a July 4th, Carroll grabbed Paul Heyne, Walt Bouman—and if I remember correctly—Bill Lazereth and me and suggested we go up behind Chalet 7 to share communion, without concern that we were members of different Lutheran synods. Following that act of ecclesiastical disobedience, Holden Village worship celebrated open communion. Life with Carroll was always exciting. I witnessed when Carroll "cast out demons" for a Holden guest. I observed and participated in baptism ceremonies in Railroad Creek.

Carroll had the habit of using his Sunday proclamation to communicate hidden messages to the guests, faculty, and staff as well as sharing God's word. Carroll was a great preacher, but if you really knew Carroll it became clear that he used the pulpit and/or the dining room podium to counter information from a lecture or to even publicly criticize a guest, faculty, or staff member concerning some personal feeling or private disagreement. It was communication without rebuttal. It wasn't one of Carroll's best traits. Most people didn't even know that it happened unless they were the recipients of his directed comments. I was convinced that when Carroll used the sermon or the podium to counter or lash out, the emotion for Carroll was then over. It wasn't always over for the recipient of the comment. A few people who were recipients of Carroll's emotional outbursts never returned to Holden again.

Carroll was sensitive concerning guest acceptance of the program, and he was also sensitive as to how the Holden board perceived its success. Carroll feared the board even though he handpicked the majority of the members initially. It became clear that his choices for the board of directors always admired Carroll's preaching and intellect, but that didn't mean they would always vote in favor of his requests. During one of the first program years, Carroll had invited Vern Rieke, board chairman, to be on faculty. That particular week only a few guests were in the village, and Carroll was concerned no one would show up for Vern's lecture. I was told to circulate to all of the work crews and tell them that all work should cease with all staff attending the lecture. The room was full of attentive listeners.

For Carroll, a quality program was the purpose of the village, but the program schedule was Memorial Day to the end of September. I don't think Carroll purposely didn't plan programs during the fall, winter, and spring, but I know that living at Holden wasn't easy for him. Soon after we started working together, Carroll told me he didn't like the mountains and felt claustrophobic living in the Railroad Creek Valley. Until 1970, whatever program or worship occurred in the late fall, winter, or spring fell into my unofficial job description. Although

I didn't keep an accurate record, over the twenty years as manager I may have preached almost as many Sunday sermons and led more vespers in the village than Carroll or any other village pastor. All of my sermons were during the months when no program or worship personnel were at Holden. Starting in 1970, more sabbatical families were in the winter community, providing more options for preaching and teaching.

The one place where, unfortunately, Holden mirrored the Lutheran Church was in terms of its identification with people of color. The Lutheran Church attracted only a small percentage of blacks. We did have African-Americans on the faculty and volunteer staff, but it was a very small percentage of the total faculty or staff. This situation resulted from our identification with the Lutheran Church and its membership rather than any racial issue. If Holden was at fault racially, it was the approach we took to promoting ourselves. Out of convenience, Holden promoted the faculty, staff, and guest involvement primarily through the Lutheran Church.

The Lutheran Church–Missouri Synod provided some options to involve more blacks on the faculty and staff. Will Herzfeld served on the program faculty for several summers. He was a close associate of Martin Luther King Jr. and later served as Bishop of the Association of Evangelical Lutheran Churches. It's my recollection that Holden was more involved with theological upheaval during the 1960s and 1970s rather than the struggle with civil rights as a societal issue. Holden did provide a safe haven for many teachers/theologians who struggled for acceptance especially from the Lutheran Church–Missouri Synod.

When Carroll was attending the University of Chicago, he became acquainted with Al Pitcher. Al later taught at the University of Chicago and was the coordinating director of Martin Luther King Jr.'s marches in Chicago in support of open housing. Al also served on the Holden faculty for several summers. Sarah Pitcher, Al's wife, is currently serving on the Holden board. Holden was fortunate to include other faculty who were involved with the civil rights movement.

The tape ministry was another area that grew over the years. I first started recording lectures in 1965. I personally purchased a reel-to-reel tape recorder in a pawnshop and used it to begin the tape ministry. I began recording lectures so workers, including myself, could listen to faculty offerings. Most of our work schedule didn't allow us to attend at the time the lectures were presented. It was apparent from the beginning that many significant people were going to be on the faculty, and we envisioned that many people would want to listen to lectures from other years. We also saw it as a way to have programming in the off-season when there was no faculty.

Dave and Mary Carlson were the first ones to formally organize and operate the tape ministry and establish an organized approach to both recording lectures as well as organizing them into a library format. Don and Dottie Rosenauer also provided input into what we called the tape ministry. In the mid 1970s, we established listening stations on the porches of the lodges so guests could enjoy listening to past lectures while enjoying the beauty of the surrounding area and enjoying all activities in the community. This occurred in the days of the cassette tapes. There was no digital recording at Holden at that time. Guests made good use of the listening stations, since it gave them an opportunity to hear faculty at other times of the year or listen to lectures that impacted their lives and emotions in pervious years.

Sig Schroeder later arrived and brought leadership to the tape ministry for a number of years, initially during the summer but eventually on a year-round basis. Sig became known as the tape ministry person, but he was just one of many involved over the years. He definitely added efficiency to what had been started and organized much earlier by others. We purchased duplicating equipment so the cassettes could be made available to guests through the store. It was Sig who initially requested use of the fireplace be discontinued in Koinonia because he felt the crackling of the fire made it difficult to get good recordings of the lectures. I loved Sig, but it is difficult for me to forgive him for his push to remove the fireplace hood. For me, the sound of crackling fires was an integral part of listening to a Holden tape. I personally felt that the fireplace was important to Koinonia, but after I left the hood was removed. The Koinonia fireplace was always a challenge, with the loss of heat up the chimney and occasionally lingering smoke in the room. The justification for removing the hood was a combination of energy efficiency and visual restriction from one side of the room to the other. Perhaps it wasn't Sig's fault alone.

When sabbatical families were in the village, it was easier to have some planned programs. When Carroll's son-in-law, John Graber, initiated the Life Style Enrichment program, it was the beginning of a more official winter program. A formal winter program was needed, but it was my observation that the specific Life Style Enrichment program was initiated, to a certain extent, to provide John a meaningful venture and job. John had been teaching for several years but, because of some health challenges, was without a job at the time. The winter activities had been increasing with a group home for dependent boys, public school, and more frequent sabbatical families. The Holden board was insistent that a more formal winter program be established. John Graber was available and definitely capable, and it also brought more of Carroll's family into the community, which for Carroll was helpful and perhaps even necessary.

After the first few years of working with Carroll, it was obvious to me that the support of his family was extremely important to him and his mental health. It was my observation that close family ties within the village were required for Carroll for his own sense of protection. It was a paradox, since he appeared to be so confident, so physically powerful, and yet he was so vulnerable. During many summers, Mary at least one of the Hinderlie children was in the village with Carroll. Although Tom Ahlstrom wasn't related to them, the Hinderlies appeared to be his immediate close family. Tom lived with them at times in Minneapolis, and whenever he was in the village, he lived in Chalet 9 with Carroll and Mary. There was no doubt that the Hinderlie children and Tom Ahlstrom enhanced the Holden community through their individual talents as well as for the physical and mental support they provided Carroll. Nepotism was alive and well, but it was also in some ways a gift to Holden, since Carroll may never have lasted thirteen years without this family protection and support. There was never any question that all of the Hinderlie children were exceptionally talented and enhanced the life and program within Holden.

Holden Village, especially in the 1960s and early 1970s, was an important refuge for certain teachers and even pastors who were struggling with their own faith issues or the doctrinal emphasis within their respective church organization. This was certainly true for the Missouri Synod at a time when freedom and truth were taking second place to what was considered doctrinal purity. Paul Heyne, who was a bit too liberal for the Missouri Synod, joined the Holden faculty and became an annual favorite. Paul was an ordained pastor and had a PhD in economics. He was a favorite of mine because of his knowledge and his moral convictions and understanding of the capitalistic system. He helped me understand that corporations aren't moral entities and their purpose is to make money for their stockholders, not accomplish morally sound actions. Julie Heyne, wife of Paul, was an accomplished artist, and their children literally grew up at Holden, which was true for several faculty families. Paul eventually accepted a teaching position at the University of Washington and at least during one year was listed as the favorite teacher of the year within the student body.

Norm Habel was an exile from a Missouri Lutheran seminary. He was a teacher and playwright. One of his plays was titled something like *Adam and Eve and the Elephant*. You can imagine what happened when the elephant was sitting on the hole where Adam and Eve were hiding from God in the Garden of Paradise. This was a bit graphic and too liberal for the seminary. It was considered sacrilege, and Norm was gone. *Adam and Eve and the Elephant* had a successful run of performances in the Holden Village Center. Norm was one faculty member who helped guests and staff celebrate the genius and love of God in a new way. He used humor to understand the miracle of what God was doing with the earth and humans. Norm helped many staff to lose their fear of questioning God and look for new understanding other than what came out of church headquarters.

Walter Bouman was another exiled seminary faculty member but found a new home at Capital University in Columbus, Ohio. Walt was one of the great teachers and theologians of the Lutheran Church. He not only brought life and excitement to Holden but also had a significant impact on the Lutheran Church as it was going through multiple years of tumult with theological debates and organizational fights. It wasn't unusual for several of the Holden faculty to leave Holden to attend one of the national church conventions and then return after being involved in major debates and decisions shaping the future of the church. They often shared and discussed some of these issues with the Holden community, receiving input and encouragement as they headed out to do battle. Walt could have been a Holden director, but my guess was that he loved teaching and was aware of difficulties involved with being in the community and the spiritual leader of Holden.

Rich and Liz Caemmerer were also frequent faculty participants. Rich wasn't an exile as such, but his father did end up leaving the Missouri Synod seminary and joining Seminex—the Seminary in Exile. Rich was head of the art department at Valparaiso University in Valparaiso, Indiana. He was a significant theologian in his own right but expressed his proclamation through his paintings. He also inherited from his father the powerful ability of verbally proclaiming God's relationship in the world. Rich spent a good portion of one summer painting the ceiling of the Village Center. He pulled a Michelangelo and even fell off the scaffold. Rich, wife Liz, and family spent several winters at Holden. During this time he discovered how productive he was as an artist, receiving creative energy and inspiration within a real community. He left Valparaiso University and bought the Grange Hall in Plain, Washington, outside of Leavenworth, and started the Grunewald Guild for instruction and production of art inspired through a community. The Grunewald Guild has existed for over twenty-five years and has inspired creative minds, encouraging those with a desire and need to express their spirituality through various forms of art.

Herb Brokering wasn't really an exile from anything, but he was a poet, author, and writer of hymns. Unfortunately even in the church, or perhaps especially in the church, a poet is often accepted with some hesitation and therefore is somewhat of an exile. Poets use words stimulating our emotions and words that require an understanding of life, society, and often the biblical narrative. We are generally trained to be literalists in what we write and hear. Poets use language that gives us a broad idea as to its meaning rather than being specific. Artists were also comfortable at Holden but not always understood or accepted. Holden was a good place for poets and artists, and Herb was on the faculty numerous times. I must admit that I also liked Herb because he had a family connection to my own. Herb's farther was a pastor of a church not too far from where my mother grew up. At a relatively early age, my mother became the director of nursing at a small hospital in Beatrice, Nebraska. It so happened that my mother assisted in the birth of Herb Brokering, which he reminded me about each time he came to Holden. Herb and I were almost brothers since my mother was also present at my birth.

The Holden Village program also made room for healing outside of the normal staff or village opportunities. In 1970, Holden Village became a Washington state group home for boys who were fourteen to seventeen years of age. A judge from Whitman County was enjoying Holden with his family and talked to us about the possibility of including a group home as part of the other Holden opportunities. He indicated that too much of his work involved young boys who became the responsibility of the state, but the only places to send them were large group homes of twenty to twenty-five boys where positive change was too-often minimal. He thought that a group home of five to eight boys would be ideal at Holden.

We moved forward to implement this program idea and officially operated a group home for seven years. It was my contention that even if we didn't totally change many of the boys, we did give them a unique opportunity to live in a community without law enforcement constantly checking with them concerning every problem in their community.

The state paid Holden based on the number of boys in the group home. Out of what the state paid us, we needed to provide for their living expenses and for one person who was officially their mentor. Since Holden in reality was subsidizing this program, I applied to the state for food through the USDA surplus food program. I was told that our group home was too small to qualify, since most of the surplus products were supplied in large containers. I pointed out that the state had come to us asking us to establish a group home and specifically to establish a small group home to maximize its effective-ness. The officials picked up on the incongruity of the surplus food rules and gladly added us to this program. Now we were receiving peanut butter in gallon cans along with pork and beans and even real butter.

The Holden group home program was terminated in 1977 due to new state requirements that the leader/counselor have a master's degree. There were great successes as well as failures with the group home. Some of the boys, now forty years later, live in the Wenatchee Valley and are productive citizens. Jim Allyn is the only one I have oc-casionally seen and talked with. Jim owned an electronic repair store and also invented an electronic testing device for the fruit industry. He is also perhaps the most active person in the local peace movement. Another one of he boys also went into electronics, and the last I heard was maintaining transmitting equipment for public radio and other stations in the area.

Unfortunately, other boys had more difficulty and at least one is in prison. At least one of the group-home boys was baptized while at Holden, but there was no attempt to proselytize them. They were members of the community and attended worship services. Perhaps the most significant healing for any of them was observing how other families interrelated, how strangers became friends, and how all of this could take place without any police supervision.

One of the additions resulting from the group home program was the Holden Village public school. The state required that we have an accredited public school if we were to start a group home. I made a trip to Chelan and discussed this requirement with Cecil West, superintendent of the Lake Chelan School District. Cecil was a member of the Chelan Lutheran Church and was acquainted with Holden and its program. To encourage Superintendent West, I indicated that we could supply a certificated teacher at no cost, since we already had a volunteer for the first year. Bev (Schultz) Cagle was on the volunteer staff and agreed to be our first teacher. Bev made it possible for the school to begin operating, which allowed Holden to begin the group home program. Through her generosity, she began the process of establishing a public school in the Holden community. The Holden school qualified as remote and necessary under state law and involved kindergarten through twelfth grade. Stehekin was also a remote and necessary school but offered instruction only through the eighth grade. Tom Flynn, member of the Holden Group Home, was the first high school student to graduate through the Holden Village School.

When plans were being made for the second school year, we were informed that the teachers' union required that if the Holden Village School were considered a classroom of the Chelan district, the teachers would need to go through the same hiring process as all other teachers and be paid on the same pay scale. This was in reality a good decision.

There were only two or three other remote and necessary schools in the state at that time. This designation allowed for funding based on three times the normal rate. For example, if the Chelan District received perhaps $3,000 per pupil for those attending in Chelan, the district would be paid $9,000 per student enrolled at Holden. The Chelan District actually got into serious trouble as a result of this arrangement. Through a state audit, it was discovered that the district had been spending some of this funding on the Chelan operation

The availability of the Holden school made it more convenient for college and university professors to come to Holden with their families to make use of the Holden community for their sabbatical years. This enlarged the winter community and also brought increased depth to community conversation, teaching, and worship opportunities. Many of these teachers helped with public school classes. Our daughter Kristy and son Jeff at times were the only students in their grades but at times had a PhD or someone with a master's degree teaching a third-grade geography class or a seventh-grade math class. In a very literal sense, the public school at Holden was a community education experience. When a school theater production was initiated, it involved many others in the community and not just those involved in the public school. It wasn't unusual to see students in the kitchen learning to make bread. Astronomy was a learning process with students gathered under the sky at night. Karen Strom was the official Holden astronomer.

At Holden, school didn't end at three-thirty but was more or less continuous. The students also had an opportunity to learn what being in a community was all about. Even some of the conflicts among community members became learning opportunities. In the restricted geographical setting, it was impossible to separate education from community function. I don't recall that Kristy or Jeff ever hesitated leaving for school in the morning, because it was always exciting. The day always involved learning from and working with community friends.

We discovered that several of the colleges utilized the month of January for off-campus learning opportunities. Through contacts at Pacific Lutheran University we came up with what we called the January Experience. One of the summer faculty members from PLU advertised a class during January to be held at Holden Village. The response was excellent, and this began the January Experience, which later involved other colleges that also offered the January off-campus education experience. This program helped the winter revenue stream for Holden as well as introduced more students to the Holden opportunities.

As the group-home program developed, we began receiving requests from parents who thought their high-school-aged students would benefit from the Holden-school experience. The decision was made to accept a very limited number of students to be in the village without their parents. One of the non–group home students was Paul, son of Camilla Wicks. Camilla had been a child prodigy violinist who made her solo debut at age seven in Long Beach, California. Now Camilla was living in a home on the south shore of Lake Chelan. She had originally come to Holden the previous winter through several contacts I had with the Wenatchee Symphony. We had invited them to Holden to share music with the community and enjoy a unique winter experience. During that visit Camilla talked to me about the possibility of having her son Paul attend school at Holden. It was Camilla's observation that Paul would respond more positively to the Holden School and the community than to the standard public school system. During the winter Paul lived at Holden; Camilla visited the village on numerous occasions and always offered mini-concerts for the community. Tears come to my eyes writing this as I remember Camilla playing Mozart or Sibelius in Koinonia as the wood fire crackled in the fireplace. Here was a person who played concerts around the world, even for royalty, and was now sharing her amazing ability around the Koinonia fireplace in this isolated community. At the time, I didn't fully realize that Camilla was this world-class violinist and teacher.

There were many examples of the impact Holden had on individuals and families. One of the most touching was that of Max and Eleanor Orlow. Max was a successful engineer at Boeing. He had a passion for mathematics. He and his family lived on Mercer Island and began coming to Holden for intellectual and spiritual growth. Eleanor was an energetic woman, always working on one project or another. One summer she put padding on most of the Village Center benches and many of the captain's chairs. She didn't hesitate to launch into a project even if a decision was still pending.

As a result of their time at Holden, Max decided to apply for a teaching position at St. Olaf College in the mathematics department.

He was accepted and resigned his position at Boeing. The family decided that in preparation for this major transition they would spend the summer at Holden on the volunteer staff and then head to Northfield. The Orlows owned the earliest model imported Volvo station wagon and decided to give it to the village. Max took the Volvo to a dealer in Bellevue for a tune-up. He had a small motorbike that he put in the back of the Volvo so he could ride it home. On his way home, something happened causing him to miss a turn, and he went over a steep embankment and was killed. Eleanor and the three girls decided to spend the summer at Holden as originally planned.

They spent considerable time peeling bark from the poles that were being prepared for the meeting room in Koinonia. Eleanor donated $3,500 toward the purchase of the second Snow Trac vehicle, and in memory of Max it was named "Maximus." Eleanor was later killed in a plane crash in Alaska on a flight to view the glaciers.

The group home, which led to the public-school program, which led to the expansion of sabbatical opportunities, all resulted from Holden being open to helping others in society. The village, in turn, was rewarded in many ways. The Holden program literally developed as needs and opportunities presented themselves.

John and Bobbie Maakestad came numerous times on faculty and then, with their family, stayed at least one year on sabbatical. John was on the St. Olaf art department faculty and lectured on art at Holden as well as produced many fantastic works of art. We purchased several of John's pieces and one specifically is still my favorite of all times. It's an ink drawing using individual lines with the resulting image a self-portrait of John standing on the ridge between Buckskin and Copper mountains, looking across at the hanging glacier on Mount Maud.

The importance of Holden faculty such as John and Bobbie was that they were more than faculty who lectured or interacted with the community.

They were also people who loved Holden and were willing to be a conscience for Holden to assist in maintaining a caring and loving community.

For one celebration of Christmas in July, John carved three wise men out of logs with a chainsaw. One wise man was a London banker, the second a clown, and I think the third was a baker. After the celebration I asked John if we could auction each one to raise money for a project. We held the auction in the dining hall after a meal. No one was bidding, so I bid hundred dollars on the London banker to get things going. I think Bill Pihl, Holden board member, purchased the clown. After the third wise man was purchased, we had raised over $1,200. I still have the London banker, although it could use a touch-up of the paint.

John wasn't a flamboyant artist but a quiet and thoughtful person with a mind that saw life in a unique and special way. Bobbie was more outgoing, with an infectious smile that communicated love and compassion and friendship. Bobbie was more likely to verbalize what both of them were thinking.

John and Mary Schramm arrived as Holden directors in the spring of 1978. They were chosen as directors following Fritz Norstad, who maintained the integrity of Holden after Carroll was replaced as director in 1977. Fritz and his wife, Gertrude, brought real healing to the Holden community, which was seriously divided at the end of Carroll's directorship. John and Mary brought a strong emphasis on peace and social justice. Carroll had created the climate for the professional and academic aspects of the church merging with the community of the laity. It was my observation that John and Mary were dedicated to encouraging the church and the laity to seek peace in the world and assure social justice for all. They also worked to minimize the perception of status differences within the Holden community. The faculty was renamed "teaching staff" and as such shared the community work, specifically kitchen / dining room cleanup duties. They also allowed or encouraged volunteer staff to make presentations and share lecture time with the teaching staff. It also appeared to me that, under John and Mary, the teaching staff would frequently include relatively young teachers with less experience and definitely more of an emphasis on the social issues in our society. I experienced an element of frustration with some subjects being presented with one-sided convictions and no option for alternate considerations. I personally looked forward to lectures that challenged my thoughts, but I also liked to have a good teacher lead me into new convictions rather than just say this idea is right without considering optional thoughts.

John and Mary were the first directors to come as a team to direct the community and teaching staff. They also worked on creating a community—especially with the volunteer staff—that would participate in decision-making through consensus. It was my observation that too many decisions were turned over to the community with too much time in discussion waiting for the group to reach consensus. I came to the decision that the consensus approach was a method to wait out the people who couldn't feel comfortable with the majority until, out of frustration, everyone finally agreed. I know this wasn't the intent, but it was too frequently my observation.

Someone should write an entire book concerning some of the Holden faculty such as Leo Bustad and Fritz Norstad. These men were unique not only because of their intellect and abilities, but also because they were recognized by people around the United States and actually around the world. One of Holden's frequent visitors told me that she would be happy just to sit and listen to Leo read the phone directory. Leo was also a very humble person and one who wouldn't impress you visually. He wasn't interested in impressing anyone. Both Leo and Fritz were significant human beings because they made others feel special in their presence. This is a gift given to a very few.

Prior to Leo getting acquainted with Holden, he was working as a research scientist at the Hanford nuclear project in Richland, Washington. He was a world-recognized scientist. Leo later became director of one of the laboratories at the University of California, Davis, and then became dean of the School of Veterinary Medicine at Washington State University, where he remained until he retired. The building that houses the veterinary school is appropriately named Bustad Hall. Leo was also a prisoner of war during World War II, so Leo and Carroll shared a life-changing experience, which brought them closer together.

A fellow member of Leo's Lutheran congregation in Richland was Dr. Bill Matheson. Bill was director of the Donald Douglas Research Laboratory. He made frequent trips to Holden but was never on faculty. However, it was in a conversation with Bill that the Science and Technology Committee became a reality. I was asking Bill about the concept of efficient heat transfer from the sauna to the dressing room. He indicated that they had been working on a heat-transfer device involving a vacuum tube. Bill expressed his regret that he didn't have time to come to Holden as a volunteer and work on some of these projects. I asked him if he thought it would work to engage technical people such as himself to meet occasionally and help solve infrastructure challenges with the facilities. They might come up with projects that would benefit Holden and provide additional educational opportunities for staff and guest. Bill suggested this concept would allow him, as well as other technical people he knew, to be involved. I proposed the idea to Carroll and asked Leo if he would be willing to chair such a committee. The Science and Technology Committee came to life.

The first members of the Science and Technology Committee were Bill, Leo, and Rudy Edmund. I was listed as an "ex officio" member. The other members initially added were friends or associates of Leo and Bill. Mark Adams was added because of his background as a chemist and his work in analyzing and testing. His son Russ also joined the committee. Leo brought in Al and Dorothy Halvorson. Al was involved with agriculture research at Washington State University and was very involved when we began working toward solutions dealing with dust from the tailings piles left from mining days. Leo also brought in Ray Skrinde and his son Jim. Ray worked at the management level of the US Corps of Engineers and was a recognized technical consultant dealing with dams and river flows. Pacific Lutheran University professor Bill Giddings and his family were frequent visitors at Holden. Bill, with his scientific background was also added to the committee.

The committee remained relatively small with a consistent membership in the early years. Gradually, as people expressed interest or when a guest with specific skills became known, the committee grew. Hugh Davis, Terrill Chang, Linda Hines, and Dave Larson were added, and by 1983 fifteen people were officially on the roster of the Science and Technology Committee.

Leo had many high-level friends and contacts within the scientific community across the country. He suggested we add a category of consultants who may not be able to attend many if any meetings, but who would be excellent contacts to obtain the latest and best technical information we might need on various projects. Dr. Roger McClellan, director of research administration with the Lovelace Foundation for Medical Education and Research, was a friend of Leo's whom he thought would be helpful in dealing with the tailings. Leo sent Roger a small sample of tailings and inquired as to the danger of blowing tailings for asthma or allergy sensitivities of guests in the village. The report came back that the actual health danger was minimal because the particle size was sufficiently large, but any larger concentration of dust could make it uncomfortable for those with asthma. The tailings dust was a definite irritant but not a health hazard.

The Holden Village program unofficially went beyond the scheduled lectures. Many of the projects that we initiated definitely fell into the category of educational opportunities. When I worked with the Science and Technology Committee, I frequently corresponded with Leo or other members whom I knew had specific technical skills or contacts. A few times, in response to inquiries, I would receive a package with scientific papers not yet released to the public but available from the director of a laboratory who was a close friend of Leo's. The committee wasn't involved with everything we did. Some projects were initiated because someone on the volunteer staff had experience or specific interest in certain areas. Since we started these projects to contribute to the operational challenges, we hadn't thought about their program implications. When guests started asking questions and requesting information, it was suggested I offer a program once or twice a week to share information, answer questions, and solicit ideas for other projects that we might consider.

It is interesting to note that at one point, the Science and Technology Committee became so active and proposed so many projects that the Holden board proposed an organizational change. I had been the management contact with the Science and Technology Committee, and I always had a lot of ideas to propose. The board requested that in the future, Science and Technology respond to requests from the board and not directly from the manager. I was asked to submit ideas to the board, and the board would determine what to submit to the

Science and Technology Committee. The committee generally met at Holden in the fall, and Leo always requested the opportunity for an evening session to outline what the committee was discussing and make sure the community got acquainted with the quality of people involved.

By the mid-1970s, science was losing some of its luster as the salvation for everything. About this time in history, DuPont stopped using the jingle, "Better Things for Better Living Through Chemistry." In 1977 the Science and Technology Committee was giving a report to the community when a group of volunteer staff and other young adult community members sat in the Koinonia balcony and jeered, disrupting the report. I was personally shocked that this disrespect would occur at Holden Village, especially when people such as Rudy and Leo were leaders of the committee as well as highly respected Holden faculty and members of the community.

My conclusion was that part of this reaction was the young-adult displeasure with any thought that science had answers to all of life's challenges. Perhaps the greater reason for the disrespect of the committee was a reaction against Carroll being replaced as director. The Science and Technology Committee had nothing do with this decision, but it was probably a reaction to the association of the committee with the board and even to me as manager. Those who disrupted the Science and Technology report included some of the staff members, at least one member of the Hinderlie family, and even the village pastor. The action of the Holden board concerning the removal of Carroll was a very traumatic event and impacted many in the community who acted almost irrationally because they couldn't accept Carroll's removal, no matter what the cause.

As the Holden Village program matured, there were many conversations and official board discussions about duplicating what had developed at Holden in other locations. It appeared to me that these discussions were initiated by those who were trying to convince themselves and others that Holden's location and isolated living weren't critical ingredients in forming this community. They wanted to explore if the Holden program and community could be duplicated and if the community was transferable. There was a serious attempt to find farm property within a hundred miles of Holden. The idea was to develop a Holden-type program with a community of volunteers operating a farm to produce food for Holden. That never materialized.

One idea involved using the small acreage Holden owned at Twenty-Five Mile Creek to create a small, Holden-type community that might also provide some produce and fresh fruits for the Holden kitchen and assist with Holden's communications and transportation requirements. The Twenty-Five Mile Creek program was known as the Tekoa Community, but the effort was short-lived. The Tekoa Community included a solar building, which was to be the center piece of an environmentally conscious community, but something was lacking. I think it's so difficult to create a community without a sense of healthy dependence on one another. The solar building now serves as the Holden Village Bed and Breakfast. The Tekoa Community was probably too dependent on a specific leader. My suggestion was that they engage a long-term resident monk to provide extended stability. I guess a monk wasn't available, and the Tekoa Community ended.

I personally believed that the remoteness of Holden and its inaccessibility combined with the worship discipline and program were important keys to creating this unique community. During mining days, Holden had been a town and also a real community. The Holden Mine community continued to meet for an annual picnic in Chelan for almost fifty years after the mine closed. Inaccessibility and remoteness aren't the prime requirements in the development of a community, but these factors help to speed the process. Many from the Holden Village community continue to return year after year to remain a part of the present and future community.

A community requires daily work that involves mutual benefit derived from accomplishing necessary tasks with an honest dependence on one another. A community based on contrived work is more likely to fail. Developing a community takes more than the gathering of people and a worship discipline. Any mutual challenge—including weather or communication or loneliness—contributes to binding the community together. The element of survival with everyone contributing to the necessities of living, combined with study and worship, is a powerful element of community building. The inaccessibility with no possibility for easy or frequent trips to enjoy other than shared community experiences creates a different atmosphere.

For community to develop, it's critical that all members have more or less equal opportunity to experience all activities. The more the Holden community created social delineations in terms of pay or housing or even title, the more challenging it was to maintain a true community. Perhaps the Holden Village community developed quickly because there had been the energy of a community in the valley the previous twenty-plus years. Like good wine, community is a combination of many ingredients. Like any wine, you can't guarantee quality just based on the ingredients.

A real community needs to have a feeling of freedom but within the confines that also provide safety, encouragement, and a feeling of value in terms of developing self-worth. George Utech made the observation that the three hour boat trip up Lake Chelan was like a baptism experience before entering Holden. Lake Chelan helped to deemphasize the past and open up the newness of a future for each traveler to Holden Village. I have always felt that all aspects of the Holden experience were critical, allowing the impact of the program to develop.

The inaccessibility required an effort to get to Holden. The simple accommodations didn't attract those interested in a resort experience. The eighty acres of tailings within a beautiful mountain valley visually reminded everyone that the good in life cannot be separated from the destruction around us, but communal living and gratitude could accommodate both. The lack of outside communications encouraged everyone in the community to converse with each other rather than conducting business or report day-to-day activities to family or friends wherever they lived. Fathers and mothers were hiking and fishing and learning crafts with sons and daughters. Questions and answers were being shared within families rather than expecting teachers in school to be substitute parents. The Holden program, perhaps accidently, provided an effective opportunity for families to enjoy freedom while at the same time being together to share the excitement of each new experience.

CHAPTER 6

Volunteer Staff—More
Than a Work Crew

IT IS MY OPINION THAT the Holden volunteer staff has never been recognized for its true significance as a Holden program and not just an operational necessity. Even though the volunteer staff was initiated as a way to cover the operational work of Holden Village, it was in reality much more than that. The volunteer program at Holden developed into an opportunity for many young adults—and retirees—to discover or rediscover the meaning of life and the miracle of experiencing community. Guests registering for a week were essentially auditing classes. The volunteer staff actually participated in a community university. Many volunteers discovered a new excitement for learning and found direction toward a particular vocation. The real value of the volunteer staff opportunities went way beyond covering the work of the Holden operation. If the staff had initially been paid or received a stipend, the experience would have been more like a minimum-wage job. As volunteers, the experience for many became more of an experience offering an opportunity to rediscover the meaning of life.

The first group of volunteers came into the village in 1961. They were known as the Forerunners. It's interesting that the Forerunners have, more or less, maintained their own separate identity over the years. The Forerunners came from throughout the United States and were involved in the major cleanup of Holden after the town site had sat abandoned for three or four years. I heard reports of nine thousand windowpanes

having been broken and needing replacing. The Forerunners were selected by and worked with Dr. Wilton Bergstrand and Gil and therefore
had an association with Holden that was, in some ways, separate from
the future of Holden's organizational structure. I have met a few of the
Forerunners but have very little knowledge of their daily activities, the
length of their stay, or their program. At least two of the Forerunners
returned to work on the volunteer staff. The Forerunners started the
tradition of the volunteer nature of the operational staff and must be
acknowledged for bringing the facility closer to an operational condition, including working with the crew installing the diesel-electric generators. The Forerunners were real pioneers since their life at Holden
was during the time when virtually no creature comforts were available.

The volunteer staff developed into a program of healing and encouragement for many young adults as well as numerous retirees. It's
ironic that the youth departments of the three national church organizations abandoned the concept of Holden being a program for young
adults, dropping their financial support. Yet the impact Holden has had
on literally thousands of young adults is almost overwhelming. It's true
that a program written at church headquarters and offered to young
adults registering at Holden would have had little chance of success.
The Lutheran Church organizations have never had a successful program for young adults, and to my knowledge they have never recognized
the need or attempted to have a program specifically for the retired.
Holden provided both for a limited number without any official program structure but on a very successful basis.

The summer of 1964 was my first opportunity as manager to experience the true impact of the Holden community. It was a joy but also
a major challenge, learning how to maximize work and program opportunities for the volunteer staff as well as dealing with operational
challenges. It was a new experience to design the applications to obtain
sufficient information, a reasonable indication of how a person might
adjust to an isolated, remote village, and how effective he or she might
be in a specific position. I soon learned that reference letters were next

to meaningless. I re-reviewed applications after volunteers had worked at the village to see how accurate the application information had been and made adjustments to the application form. I rarely, if ever, turned down volunteers who really needed Holden, but it was important to know prior to their arrival what to expect. We continued to require reference letters. It was helpful if we recognized the people writing the letters, who also acted as contact persons, other than family, if trouble with staff members developed.

The volunteer staff was an operational necessity to provide the work needed on a day-to-day basis. Holden's financial situation wouldn't allow workers to receive even a stipend. Volunteers received housing and meals, and they paid for travel and miscellaneous expenses including health insurance. Their pay was the opportunity to participate in an exciting educational and spiritual experience and live at the edge of the Glacier Peak Wilderness area only accessible by a forty-mile passenger ferry trip on Lake Chelan. Fortunately, the nature of society in the 1960's allowed college-age young adults and retired workers to consider this work and educational option.

In the beginning, staff assignments more or less followed society at the time. Women were assigned to the laundry, housekeeping, secretarial, children's program, and retail sales. That gradually changed over the years, not because of protests or a social awakening in the village, but through a new realization in society. Women started driving busses, picking up garbage, working as carpenters, handling the fire hoses, and being involved in mountain rescues. I never considered establishing a line item budget for the volunteer staff that might set a limit on the number we could accommodate. We didn't institute a study as to the most efficient number of volunteers to maximize the work and the revenue. Holden was always open to accepting one or two more if they needed Holden even more than Holden needed them. A community or the church shouldn't be divided in terms of age, or ability or intellect. A community is established when there are shared needs along with mutual gifts of labor to joyfully fill those needs.

The original work-program arrangement established by the youth departments didn't materialize as a viable program. It was decided following the summer of 1964 that Holden would take over organizing all aspects of the volunteer staff. Fortunately this approach worked very well. Word spread quickly that a great summer experience was available in the midst of the Cascade Mountains. Utilizing college students allowed the word to spread as Holden staff members retuned to their respective campuses and shared the excitement of their summer experiences with others. The faculty involved teachers from colleges, universities, and seminaries, and the teachers were also effective promoters of Holden's volunteer program.

The minimum work involvement for volunteer service was set at three weeks with no official maximum. Until the village opened year-round, very few volunteer opportunities were available past October. It didn't take long before we were receiving four hundred applications for the approximately two hundred volunteer positions needed each year. In the 1960s volunteerism in the country was very popular and possible, making it easier for Holden Village to develop quickly. Repeat staff were accepted the first couple of years, but we noticed returning staff had a desire to repeat the prior year's experience rather than allowing each year to be new. I got tired of being told, "We didn't do it that way last year." Since we were receiving more applications than needed, I decided to have a completely new staff each year without repeats.

It was a gift that over the years we had applications from volunteers who had specialty training in fields critical to the health and welfare of the Holden Community. Holden was especially fortunate to have registered nurses on our volunteer staff for much of the time and anytime there were medical doctors as registered guests they always volunteered to assist if medical expertise was required. The position of village nurse was one that we extended to a longer involvement if the person was available. Eventually we also added a stipend to this position since our remote location and the extended time to reach a professional medical facility required as much help as we could encourage.

Occasionally, exceptions were made to the no-repeat rule under special circumstances. When the village became a year-round operation, we stipulated a two-year maximum for the staff receiving a stipend. We felt that two years was a good Holden experience without generating an expectation that Holden could be a permanent place to live. Carroll and I were the exceptions since we had been hired by the Holden board. However, Carroll did work full time starting in the early spring of 1963 but never lived in the village year-round.

When I visited Holden during the fiftieth anniversary to share history stories, Kirsten Olsen introduced herself as the daughter of Steve and Rikke Olsen. Steve and Rikke met while on the volunteer staff in 1969. Steve was the head of the Hike Haus. Rikke worked in several areas, including assistant to Wes in the pool hall as well as the store and dining room. Steve and Rikke developed a close relationship right away, but Rikke was initially scheduled to work only three weeks. Kirsten reminded me that Rikke had written to me and asked if she could come back on staff to continue developing the relationship with Steve. Now, forty-three years after that request, I know the decision to make an exception was the correct one. Obviously, their relationship developed positively. Their daughter Kirsten, now a college instructor with an adventurous spirit like her father, joined the volunteer staff. Kirsten rode her motorcycle from Minnesota to Fields Point Landing, the up lake dock for The Lady of the Lake ferry.

Years ago, when I received the volunteer application from Steve Olsen, I noticed he was a member of the Iowa Mountaineers. To this day, I have a hard time understanding how Iowa could have an active group of Mountaineers. I thought if Steve was a qualified Iowa Mountaineer, he would be excellent directing our Hike Haus. Later that summer of 1969, I received an invitation to climb Mount Rainier and one additional space was available. I invited Steve to join us. We climbed Rainier via the Emmons Glacier route and reached the summit early in the morning of July 20. We left the summit and made it back to Seattle in time to turn on the TV at Ken and Gretchen Graybeal's home and watch Neil

Armstrong step out on the surface of the moon—two very memorable experiences all on the same day.

Ken Graybeal, our leader, had climbed Mount Rainier numerous times. Ken's wife, Gretchen, had been on the Holden volunteer staff some years earlier. In fact Gretchen and I had been classmates at Wartburg College in 1956. It turned out that Gretchen's parents also knew my parents when my father was a pastor in South Dakota, some years before my birth.

Since I was the first business manager hired by the Holden board my job description was developed as I observed what operational functions needed to be covered and what we could institute in order to develop a more effective and enjoyable community. Transportation from the Lucerne dock to Holden was, out of necessity, an added requirement of the Holden operation. The volunteer staff covered all functions with my being involved in coordinating all activities, making sure that the infrastructure operated in a safe and healthy way. At times there were jobs that I didn't feel comfortable turning over to volunteers because of some added potential danger. If we couldn't bring in trained technicians, I attempted to cover these jobs myself, even if not qualified.

The road was used by Holden Village under permit from the forest service, but Holden was the only user that was available to maintain the road. Either we maintained it or covered the expense of hiring a contractor to do the work. At one point the Washington State Patrol contacted me and indicated that we would be required to license all of the vehicles using the road. I wrote back and informed them that as soon as the State of Washington took over the maintenance of the road, including the snow removal, we would license our vehicles. They never responded or pursued the issue while I was manager.

The work of the staff covered all aspects of operating a small town in a remote location. Some functions were obvious in terms of providing an operational and especially a safe facility. Other community activities gradually developed as ideas surfaced that would enhance the celebration of life within Holden.

We had to maintain the potable water system as well as the system to provide fire control. Hoses were still in the firehouses from the mine operation but many brass nozzles had apparently been stolen. The sewage system was a major responsibility and a continuous challenge. Garbage pickup and disposal were a daily chore. We actually received a landfill permit from the forest service, and the state health department allowed us to bury solid waste in the tailings. We used a propane-fired incinerator for several years. We started a compost system that allowed us to produce organic material that we used on the tailings in our initial attempts to plant trees and grasses.

For many years the water system operated without any treatment. It was considered safe, and the water was tested on a regular basis. Federal law changed around 1970 and required all systems to be chlorinated when used in operations serving the general public. We fought this for a short time, emphasizing the impossibility of human contamination of our system because the water came down Copper Creek. The fact was, we couldn't claim the absence of animal contamination since deer, bear, and other animals roamed the area. We eventually added a homemade chlorination system but within a year installed a commercial system. Filtering of the water system was never required and never implemented at that time.

Over my twenty years, we operated with a fleet of used school buses and one surplus bus from the Hanford project in Richland. We purchased one new bus. In those years we weren't required to nor did we institute a process for obtaining commercial driving licenses for the bus drivers. From May through October the perishable freight was delivered by the passenger boat, and all nonperishable freight arrived on the weekly barge. From November through April there was no barge service and the passenger ferry operated three days each week.

Once the hydroelectric plant became operational, its maintenance and daily operation was assigned to a long-term volunteer so there was some continuity. Outside of lubricating several parts on the mechanical governors and perhaps adjusting the needle valve that controlled the water flow, the system was forgiving and reliable. There were several conditions that would cause the protective relays to shut down the system. If there was too much electrical demand in the village, the frequency would drop. Debris might temporarily divert water at the intake dam, or small debris might flow down the pipe and get stuck in the needle valve. Additionally, in the winter, certain icing conditions might divert the water or plug the needle valve.

During the day it was obvious when the power to the hydro went out. We used homemade alarms using a battery, relay, and an alarm that would provide a notice at night for the unlucky one assigned night duty, which was done on a rotating basis. At times I was the only one available to do the daily maintenance and operational checks of the hydro and re-start the system if it tripped due to overload or lack of water. The hydro operation was basically a sideline for one of the mavericks (volunteer maintenance staff) and not a full-time endeavor. The hydro was so for-giving and basically easy to maintain that it was ideal for Holden Village with its high turnover of the staff.

The only concern I had for those maintaining the hydro was the possibility of a runaway condition. When the hydro system was oper-ational, Henry Schwecke outlined the maintenance procedures and some safety instructions. The electrical end of the operation was pro-tected by relays. The mechanical function and the speed of the Pelton wheel were controlled by a mechanical governor. The governor kept the speed of the wheel and generator at the required rotation for sixty cycles. The governor controlled the speed by deflecting water from the nozzle away from the wheel. If the governor malfunctioned and allowed the wheel to have 100 percent of the water energizing it, it could poten-tially reach a runaway condition and the wheel would likely fly apart because of the centrifugal force. This came close to happening once. I ran to the hydro because I could hear the speed of the wheel increas-ing way beyond normal. I quickly entered the building and deflected the water away from the wheel. There was no time to think. I guess my only concern was how important the hydro was to the village operation.

Nothing flew apart. This was the only time we approached a runaway condition during my twenty years.

On one occasion during the winter, when the power went off due to ice at the diversion dam, I chose to snowshoe to the dam around midnight to clear the ice. It was foolish to do this by myself because of the dangers involved snowshoeing along the creek to the upper diversion dam but I suffered at times from dealing with a guilty conscience. I was the only paid person and felt embarrassed asking a volunteer to snowshoe to the dam with me in the middle of the night. These were also times when I knew I had a guardian angel.

There were several years when we had no one in the village to grade the roads. I learned the basic operation of our motor grader and did an acceptable job. Learning to grade roads should probably not begin on mountain roads. On one occasion I was grading, and the blade caught a deeply buried boulder in the road. The grader began skidding over the edge of the road where the bottom was perhaps two hundred feet below. I jumped out the door. Fortunately the grader caught a tree and didn't go down. We were able to pull the grader back on the road with no damage but resulting in considerable fright and embarrassment for the operator. During a couple of times, we had no one to operate our D6 Caterpillar. It was an old unit, and my greatest fear was starting and engaging the starter engine. Heavy equipment wasn't in my comfort zone, but again, my guardian angel saved me from disaster.

The refrigeration equipment was vital to the safe storage of meat and other food supplies. The compressors were old. We flew refrigeration technicians in several times to repair the units. We never did have a volunteer with any refrigeration experience. I would watch the technicians and ask questions and inquired if it would be safe for me to try to charge the units with Freon if necessary. The technician was sure I could do it but warned me that if I charged the wrong side of the compressor it would explode. I only charged the units a couple of times during the winter when it would be impossible to get the services of a refrigeration technician in time to save the food, and I'm here to write about it.

The promotion and selection of all of the volunteers was one of the most enjoyable parts of my responsibilities. I served as volunteer staff coordinator from 1965 until 1979, at which time Kay Fish was added as the first full-time staff coordinator, receiving a small stipend. During my fourteen years as staff coordinator, I selected all staff and made the work assignments based on their written applications. Personal interviews only took place when a longer-term employee was being selected. I filled many of the positions that received stipends with individuals who had been volunteers, so they were known entities. I assigned a lead volunteer to each work area. We operated the village similarly to a hotel, with housekeepers cleaning the rooms and making the beds prior to the guests' arrival. The dining room had waitresses to set, serve, and clean up after each meal.

We started a store in 1964. The registration office was originally in the schoolhouse, and the first store items we offered were sold as part of the registration duties. Initially, the store concept involved carrying the essentials for staff and guests during their stay to cover items they may have forgotten. With the remote location and no options to obtain basic items, it was a requirement that we try to anticipate what staff and guests might need. Film, batteries, and toiletries were the most important items. We moved the store and registration office to the hotel around 1967. The registration office also handled postal supplies and mail in the first years.

The store and post office eventually found a permanent home in the basement of the hotel. The post office operated under the auspices of the Chelan Post Office, zip code 98816. We inquired about Holden having its own post office with its own zip code so we could have one of our staff as a paid postmaster. The government wouldn't allow us to choose our own postmaster, and if we had someone move into the community as a government employee, he or she may not have fit into the other staffing of Holden Village. The idea of a Holden post office was too complicated, so we didn't pursue it seriously.

When the pottery shop became a reality the village potter made unique items and the store started to carry mugs and Holden plaques.

We also added weavings once we had looms. We carried sweatshirts to help guests stay warm and added the Holden symbol for a little public relations. All of the initial post cards were village and valley scene photographs I had taken in previous years. The store became a necessity for guest enjoyment and convenience, but also it became a significant revenue source. When I retired as manager in 1983, annual retail store sales exceeded $100,000.

A book section and thus the bookstore came into existence as early as 1967. Initially books were carried through requests from faculty members based on what they would be using during their lectures. Gradually more books were added as Mary Hinderlie provided titles that she knew would be significant to people coming to Holden as guests or staff. Books were extremely important in the life of Mary, and it was important for her to make sure that Holden, either through the library or through the bookstore, had a selection of books that could inspire and change the lives of those working at or visiting Holden Village. Mary made sure that the library and the bookstore were an integral part of the Holden Village program.

Holden Village was attracting many people who, because of their professional lives, didn't have the opportunity to read extensively or have easy access to theological or spiritual books. Coming to Holden for a week or more gave them the desired reading time. Dave Larson, a CPA, and his wife, Bev, were frequent Holden guests with their family. The Larson family was almost considered to be volunteer staff. In some ways, the Larsons were really responsible for what developed into the Holden bookstore. One summer, Dave gave me a check for $1,000. He said we should use the gift to buy books and all of the revenue generated from selling the books should be reinvested in more books to expand the offerings. Dave and Bev also gave an additional gift to purchase materials to make functional and attractive book display shelves. Dave loved to read, and he wanted a better selection of books when he visited Holden. The Holden board appointed Mary Hinderlie to be in charge of the library as well as select books for the bookstore. Lola

Deane, frequent Holden Village guest, volunteered to work with Mary on expanding the bookstore, allowing it to be the best little bookstore in a very small space in a very remote valley. The bookstore wasn't about making money but rather providing sources of inspiration and instruction for those who normally didn't have access to a wide variety of subjects and authors. Holden had a monopoly on retail sales in the Railroad Creek Valley.

Hiking was always a major form of recreation, and it was natural that we would add a Hike Haus with volunteer staff. The Hike Haus was originally in the basement of the hotel in the same location as the general store and bookstore. We later moved it to the west end of Lodge 6. Staff and guests could order lunches a day in advance and pick them up from the Hike Haus as they departed. Preparing Hike Haus lunches was originally a task of the kitchen. Overnight camp trips were popular with the staff, and we carried the essentials for them to enjoy this unique experience. We purchased a few fishing poles to rent and also sold fishing licenses in the store to give people a chance to enjoy trout fishing in Hart and Holden Lakes. Because Holden staff and guests were the prime users of the trails, we offered our services to the forest service to help maintain the trails, especially to open and clear the main trails in the spring.

We also worked with the forest service to open new trails. The Ten Mile Falls trail was popular since it was short and terminated at a beautiful falls. The forest service in the early 1990s made this an official trail and developed it to be handicap accessible. Ernie Zoerb, Holden volunteer, was an avid outdoorsman. He developed a trail East of Ten Mile Creek named Monkey Bear Falls Trail. The Forest Service added this trail to their official map. Perhaps the first trail into the valley was along the south side of Railroad Creek. It began at a junction of the Domke Lake trail. It had been abandoned for many years. Because we wanted to develop new trails out of Holden for the many repeat visitors, we worked with the forest service to reopen this trail. It had several difficult creek crossings, especially in the heavy runoff periods of the year.

The mavericks did the miscellaneous labor to keep the village functioning. They also worked on the hydro and other construction projects. Some of the other staff envied the mavericks because they were always working outside on a wide variety of tasks. We had volunteers assigned to lawns and landscaping. The lawns were beautifully maintained and mowed. These crews established flower beds along with hanging flower baskets. The deer and even the chipmunks were a constant challenge for anything that grew green leaves and produced seeds. During mining days, someone planted hops around several of the chalets. Perhaps they were imported for the purpose of producing homemade beer. Hops grew well and were one of the plants that the deer and ground squirrels didn't bother.

Purchasing plants and hauling them to the village was inconvenient and expensive, so we started to germinate our own plants in the basement of the hotel under fluorescent lights. At one point we were germinating over a thousand flower starts. It was a problem once the plants progressed to larger pots, needing natural light. We raised money to purchase a greenhouse. It wasn't really designed for heavy snow loads, but with additional bracing it lasted many years and expanded the opportunities for growing plants.

For me, the greenhouse was more than landscaping. In the winter, with the plants and the aroma of moist soil and the extra lighting we installed, the greenhouse became a therapeutic place for many people who desired the feel of life and nature. During the winter months, we most frequently lived with low cloud cover in the valley. The greenhouse in the winter was for many people their "zen" experience. We even had a couple of chairs in the greenhouse so people could sit and read or just enjoy thoughts of spring and summer. Maintaining a healthy community involves more than just shelter and food and worship.

We didn't initially consider the need for a children's program. It became evident, however, that with families involved, children's activities would be a necessity if both parents were to attend the morning lectures. Doris Edmund helped put together the concept for children's activities.

Doris was recognized as a national leader in the field of early childhood education. Jean Swihart worked with Doris to develop the initial ideas and activities for the children's program. Jean discovered that on the trail to Holden Lake one could easily find small snakes called Rubber Boas, and this was added as an activity for the children. The snakes were harmless, perhaps a foot long, but they acted like boas and would wrap themselves around a wrist and enjoy staying on the wrist until the children could show their parents and anyone else who would pay attention. We added the children's program to the list of positions on the volunteer staff once Doris worked out a more organized plan.

The crafts area gradually grew based on suggestions or donations of equipment. We initiated the pottery shop out of necessity to accommodate a choice for faculty. Carroll was trying to recruit faculty from other Lutheran backgrounds. He learned that Dr. Alfred Ewald, president of Wartburg Seminary, was an avid potter. Carroll contacted Dr. Ewald and asked him to be on faculty for the purpose of initiating a pottery program. Since we didn't yet have a pottery shop or any equipment, we set Dr. Ewald's arrival date as the date to have an operational shop available. Dr. Ewald did some beautiful work and started the tradition of having Holden-produced pottery in the store. Dr. Ewald made plaques based on the Holden "shield" that had been used for some early promotion. He combined a ceramic shield mounted in a piece of rough wood that came from the mine. At least one of these plaques is in the museum.

It wasn't long before we had an area for weaving, which we added when we received the gift of a loom. Holden had been offering card weaving, which was a great activity since guests could do card weaving during lectures and even take them home if not finished. The selection of crafts in the village was partially based on the ability to learn and finish a project within the usual guest visit of six or seven days.

The lapidary shop was the gift of Dorothy Bennett, a frequent guest. She was retired as an educational service director for an area north of Seattle. After her husband died, she decided to divest her life of all possessions other than what would fit into her car so she could be free to travel and free of the obligation to take care of "stuff." She had a complete lapidary shop and offered this prized object of passion to the village. We accepted on the condition that she come to the village each summer and teach lapidary. Dorothy gladly agreed. The arrival of her lapidary items was an indication of her ability to organize anything and everything. Each box was numbered and lettered. The number indicated the contents of the box and the letter indicated its location in the new shop. The basement of Chalet 1 was available, and the lapidary shop operated in that location for many years. The basement of Chalet 1 wasn't the greatest location, but Dorothy didn't mind and was delighted that so many people learned from her and gained knowledge in the field of lapidary. The only negative aspect of the lapidary shop was that the rocks around Holden didn't lend themselves to polishing, so rocks needed to be imported. Dorothy had a supply that lasted many years.

The snack bar was one of the first areas reactivated. Ice cream, soft drinks, and other snacks are a necessity when a community promotes celebration. Ice cream at Holden was never considered a junk food but a necessity in the daily diet. The busiest time for the snack bar was the period immediately following vespers. It seemed as if vespers stimulated the desire for ice cream as guests and staff rushed out of the Village Center to get in line at the snack bar, saying, "Amen," on the run.

The snack bar was also popular with those who weren't registered in the village but happened to be in the area. Railroad Creek Valley was a popular hiking and climbing area, and the forest service maintained a campground west of the village at the edge of the wilderness boundary. The Swiss loggers, a four-to-five-person commercial logging crew working in the area, were frequent patrons of the snack bar during the five months they were in the valley each year.

I always imagined the possibility of Holden adding a nightclub. Actually, the Holden nightclub was more like a coffee house. It just so happened that there was a room under the west end of the snack bar that was unused. It had been the repair room for the bowling pins during the mine operation, where they would repair, refinish, and lacquer the pins. We did a remodel using old boards from some mine buildings to build a serving area, some booths, and a small stage. We served pizza by the slice as well as soft drinks and peanuts. We encouraged the throwing of peanut shells on the floor for ambience. The area was called "The Lift." Al Swihart was a frequent entertainer with his repertoire of Robert Service poems. Many volunteer staff singers and guitar players always seemed to be available and interested in sharing their talent. It was an open stage invitation for local performers.

The volunteer staff attracted many young adults, probably out of their desire for a unique mountain and wilderness experience rather than any intent of joining an exciting liberal arts education opportunity along with an unusual spiritual journey. The young adults in the 1960s were emerging from an emphasis in the church on Bible camp. I always saw Bible camp as a forced spiritual and social emotional experience. Bible camp might have been interesting and fun, but college students were looking for a new direction. What the church offered was ineffective or not available. Holden provided a new and exciting opportunity for young adults. Even though the mountains and the work opportunities initially attracted the young adults, what occurred for many was a revelation as to the excitement of worship and insights into how real education can take place. The Holden program brought teachers who loved to teach and explore new concepts without fear of being reprimanded or embarrassed for expressing their thoughts. The volunteers discovered opportunities for new relationships that had never occurred prior to their Holden experience.

Holden was literally a life-changing experience for many as they went from Holden "to ventures unknown," often returning to school with new enthusiasm, pursuing a new interest, or entering professions that interested them through their Holden Village experience. For the first time, many became acquainted with teachers whom they considered "human" and respected and admired. Education and learning excited them in a new way and challenged them to respond to their newly discovered passions. One of the experiences for many volunteers was their involvement with a community that also valued their ideas and thoughts. Age and intelligence didn't determine a person's worth in the community. The way the Holden community operated brought together those working with their hands as well as those working with their minds. There appeared to be a new respect and understanding for the meaning of community.

I wish I could list names of all the volunteers. Unfortunately, a complete list of volunteers may not exist. Over the twenty years I was involved, Ron Vignec became for me the personification of what Holden and the volunteer staff was all about. In a real sense, Ron brought true meaning to the concept of discovering a new opportunity but never forgetting the humility of understanding what love, forgiveness, and acceptance really mean. If Holden Village didn't accomplish anything else during its fifty-plus years of existence, it at least had a part in the journey of Ron Vignec, who has, over the years, so positively impacted many lives. Ron also had a ministry through his life that was based on true service, love, and compassion and didn't involve building church monuments or working into a large and prosperous congregation that would have given him the basis for a larger pension. I don't know how much Holden influenced Ron's ministry, but Holden can be thankful that Ron's journey came through this community.

Carroll was on a promotional trip and first met Ron in New York City in the spring of 1965, where he was being raised in the home of his first-generation Russian grandparents. Carroll apparently saw something in Ron and felt that Ron and Holden would be a match. As I recall, Holden Village covered the travel expenses for Ron's trip to Holden. Ron spent the summer and early fall on the staff. The Village wasn't open in the winter at the time, so I was making preparations to move the office back to Seattle for the winter. I had rented a small apartment in the University District and had already paid for the first and final months' rent. Ron decided to move to Seattle since he had developed a close friendship with Nancy Olson from Mercer Island whom he'd met at Holden during the summer. I suggested that Ron take over my apartment in the U District, and I contributed the first and last months' rent to help Ron get started. I lived in the basement of my brother's house in Seattle in the Wallingford district that winter.

Ron got a job washing dishes in a small, greasy spoon restaurant in the U District. He later attended Luther and Wagner Colleges and then went on to Lutheran Seminary in St. Paul. During his seminary years, he came back to Holden to serve his internship with Fullness of God congregation. Some years later he accepted a position as Pacific Lutheran University campus pastor and at the same time began the Salishan Eastside Lutheran Mission in Tacoma. Salishan was at the time the largest public housing development west of the Mississippi River. Ron didn't see a hopeless housing project but rather an opportunity to learn from the residents how to regain hope and how it would be possible to develop a community. Combining his work at Salishan with Pacific Lutheran University, Ron called his involvement the University at Salishan.

I know that Holden played only a small part in his life, but I have a feeling that the freedom he experienced at Holden to explore the gospel in a unique way as well as observe the power of change that can occur within a community probably had an impact on his life and ministry. Ron never forgot that sharing the gospel involved celebrating the value of each person within a community. While working on these memoirs, I received word that Ron died on November 10, 2013. Kathleen Merryman, writer for the *Tacoma Weekly* newspaper began her remembrance of Ron in a very touching way. Merryman wrote, "Pastor Ron Pierre Vignec, Poet of the Eastside, Bringer of Peace to the troubled, Forager of Food for the hungry, Speaker of Truth to power, Sharer of Burdens with the hopeless, and Santa Claus to those who choose to believe, has died."

Holden was fortunate that the significant journey Ron traveled through in his life included impacting Holden Village. Ron's life must be a reminder to the Holden community that the real significance of Holden Village is out in the world and not exclusively in the isolated Railroad Creek Valley.

Another memorable volunteer staff member was Doug "Leo" Hanbury. Leo, in some ways, represented the special nature of the Holden ministry and the freedom we had to enjoy a diversity of personalities. Leo was graduating from St. Olaf College in 1971 and sent an application to be on the staff. I specifically recall that his application was handwritten with marginal legibility. On the final page of the application, he noted that he was a "champion" typist and could out-type the IBM Selectric typewriter, the ultimate in typing technology at that time. This was my first clue that Leo might be a unique person. If he was such a good typist, why hadn't he typed his application?

I don't recall where I assigned Leo based on his application, but when he arrived in the village it was obvious that a new assignment would be necessary. Bill Pihl, a Holden board member, was in the village, donating his time to plant trees. He offered to have Leo work with him for a day and let me know where best we could place him. Bill reported back that he didn't feel there was any position Leo could easily fill. We assigned Leo to washing pots and pans in the kitchen, and he did an excellent job. He was assured of job security.

When Leo arrived in the village he informed me that he would need a private room. Volunteer staff didn't get private rooms, and it was more likely that there would be two and sometimes three staff in one sleeping room. However, Leo had a convincing argument. Leo needed to sleep with the lights on so demons wouldn't bother him. Fortunately we weren't paying for electricity. After perhaps six weeks, Leo asked if he could have a session to address the entire village. This we normally wouldn't consider, but out of consideration for Leo we indicated that he could have his session in the Village Center at ten o'clock in at night, after all of the regular activities were finished. The Village Center was completely full, and Leo talked for an hour, sharing thoughts concerning his experience with demons. A breakthrough for him had occurred in the last week, and the demons had disappeared. He no longer needed to sleep with the lights on.

Leo continued to be an excellent washer of pots and pans and was a delight to have in the village because of his uniqueness. He loved listening to music and knew all of the DJs and popular singers. When Leo first arrived, he walked around with his portable radio on his shoulder, looking for locations where a station with music would come in. His favorite locations were sitting next to the hot water pipes for the radiators in the dining room. I suggested to Leo that he would make a top-notch DJ or a TV weatherman. I don't know what he ended up doing with his life. The last I heard, he was typing thesis documents for graduate students at the University of Iowa.

Leo entertained us many winter evenings by bringing out a large map of the United States and having us name a city, any city large or small, and he would—without looking—tell us what highways served the city. He had a perfect record. Leo later joined the Lifestyle Enrichment program. Leo proved that Holden was open to all and Holden could be blessed and enriched through the involvement of all shades of uniqueness. I hope Leo found his perfect niche in society. I still think he would make a unique and entertaining TV weatherman. I still smile when thinking about Leo and the gifts he brought to Holden Village.

Another gift to Holden Village was Verlon Brown, a volunteer staff person from Kansas City. At least until 1983, Verlon was the only person of color we had on the volunteer staff. Verlon's application indicated he was legally blind, although he was mobile and could get around on his own. He was quiet but friendly and had an infectious sense of humor. He became the Holden stand-up comic once he felt comfortable in the community. He gave matins one morning—his famous "cornflakes" meditation about being raised by his grandmother. It had a real impact, and Verlon became a village celebrity. It was obvious he could easily become a stand-up comedian, and many of his meditations are available online in the Holden Village audio archive. Verlon went on to seminary and was ordained, returning to Holden as village pastor some years after I retired. The last I heard, he was involved part-time with a church in Seattle and also doing social work.

Another aspect of the Holden program was the opening for new volunteer work opportunities for retired people. Holden was lucky to come to life at just the correct time when many retired individuals and couples, for the first time, were leaving full-time employment with adequate retirement income to travel and to volunteer. People who had worked and gained skills for a lifetime were now seeking opportunities where they could use their skills but in a new way, impacting society by giving back and helping the next generation. Involving the retired wasn't a calculated program developed out of studying the demographics. It was a part of the volunteer staff program that naturally occurred because Holden needed volunteers with talent and an increasing number of retired were available without the need for compensation. Looking back on the miracle of the volunteer program, it was the brains of the retired coupled with the energy and brawn of the young adults. It turned out that in many cases, the energy of the retired as well as the determination to complete a job went well beyond anything the young adults could offer.

The other aspect of the retired and young adult interaction was what occurred in terms of personal relationships. It was a beautiful experience to observe. It even happened to our family in terms of our very young son, Jeff. Omar Cline was a retired human resources manager for a large corporation in Salt Lake City. He had recently been divorced and was looking for a new opportunity to bring meaning to his life. A friend encouraged Omar to go to Holden. Omar had never heard of Holden but was willing to go for a visit. Holden became his home and family for several years. My son Jeff and Omar became best of friends. Jeff was probably two or three years of age, and Omar was in his late sixties. Every evening after dinner, Jeff would run over to Omar and hop on his lap for *Beany Sings*. Omar had a box in his room in the hotel filled with little toys and miscellaneous nuts and bolts, hinges and wires. I would, at times, need to remind Jeff and Omar it was time for vespers.

At first I was jealous of Omar, because Jeff and I didn't seem to have that same relationship. Then it occurred to me that Jeff was in need of a grandfather figure and Omar needed a surrogate grandson for mutual growth and enrichment at this stage in their respective lives. I was able to switch from jealousy to extreme gratitude when I gained a new insight in to how a real community worked.

All of these experiences illustrated what real community is all about. It isn't just worshiping together. In fact it's my opinion that the Holden community developed perhaps in spite of—rather than because of—worship. Worship provided a unique opportunity to hear from Carroll, who was an unusually gifted preacher of the gospel, and also hear from staff and faculty who shared their individual spirituality. For me, much of the proclamation in the village occurred during conversation while working or during coffee break. The worship that really hit home for me was hearing and observing how individual lives were being impacted and changed, not necessarily through formal worship, counseling, or intense studying. Rather, an experience of developing a God relationship occurred by having time to observe the miracle of new friendships, the healing of a listening ear, or even the mysteries of nature impacting personal lives as each one of us struggled to understand our relevance in life. The value of the Holden congregation and worship in the village was to make sure nothing spiritual or social got in the way of allowing God-given friendships and community from occurring naturally.

Establishing an atmosphere for worship wasn't as important as finding an avenue that opened a life to explore the new. The Holden community worshiping by the river, or on Chalet Hill, or in the gymnasium with dim lights and candles, was definitely interesting, but for me it was simply hearing how the gospel impacted a life when it was least expected. Vespers would frequently dovetail with the experiences of daily friendships, work, and even the problems, coming together to bring new meaning to life and love. For me, the real impact of Holden was how mysterious life is and even the unlikely gift of a mining town or the willingness of teachers to volunteer their time or the staff person who was rebelling against almost everything but still volunteering for menial work. How everyone could come together and celebrate life in a remote village and then experience breakthroughs without any form of communication to be able to share with family or friends in places far away was most unusual. Experiencing the mystery of life and faith became commonplace. We all have individual ways to access our personal spiritual depths.

The unique experience of how young adults related to the retired was touching and wonderfully observable. Numerous times a relationship would develop between a young adult staff member and one of the retired couples or individuals. What we were experiencing was the initiating of surrogate grandparents, surrogate grandchildren, and I think in some cases surrogate parents. No one was under pressure to develop any relationships. They could meet and then reject each other and later develop strong bonds. Occasionally, parents literally begged me to take sons and daughters on staff because they felt they were losing them and sometimes felt their children were losing spiritual faith. We never turned down a request to help someone over the twenty years I was manager. I don't know if those parents regained the relationships they wanted from their children or if the Holden experience returned their children to the family fold, but I can assure you that in most cases their children were closer to being complete persons when they left Holden.

When I was involved, the volunteer staff wasn't tightly organized. Each area more or less worked as an autonomous unit. Whoever was the lead person might come up with activities that would draw the group together, and they would also keep track of any problems that might develop in terms of personality conflicts, etc. This system seemed to work rather well as it minimized any feeling of a strong top-down management. This style might have resulted from my age. I was twenty-four years old when I first became manager, which was close to the same age as many of the young adults coming on staff and much younger than the retired. We instituted a weekly staff meeting for an hour prior to vespers. The meetings were primarily to share information and hear from staff about situations needing attention. It was also an opportunity for staff to share ideas about how to make the staff experience more enjoyable and productive. It was the time to express gratitude to those who would be leaving and to introduce new staff members. The staff meetings were the only occasion that the volunteer staff ever met as a group separate from guests.

The volunteer staff also attracted some individuals from Europe. As word of Holden spread through various publications and visitors, increased numbers of requests arrived from Europe, especially from Germany and the Scandinavian countries.

In 1968, Ides Eberbach, a young lady from Hamburg, Germany, spent time on the staff in late summer and fall. She was what we would call a program associate and administrative assistant for a large Lutheran church in Hamburg. The reason I remember her was that she loved to hike, and in the fall, after a hike to Holden Lake, she brought back a large bag of mushrooms. I personally couldn't safely identify wild mushrooms, and when she suggested that the kitchen fix them for the evening meal I was definitely apprehensive. I remember asking Ides if German mushrooms were the same as US mushrooms. Her mushrooms were a great addition to the meal, and the addition of Holden Lake mushrooms was repeated several times.

Since Holden was open to so many people without questioning their faith or even their abilities, the village was often blessed with the surprise of how valuable and special people were if allowed to be themselves in a community that celebrated uniqueness. Holden was blessed by many unique people who may not have made the cut if the application process had been designed for perfect fits. The volunteer staff wasn't without tensions and disagreements. As with any group of people, there were the unofficial leaders who often set the attitude and pace of the staff. It begs remembering that this all started in the early 1960s when there were riots on the campuses, with sit-ins and buildings being occupied to force action by school administrators.

The volunteer staff didn't organize in terms of a union concept, but we actually had a threat of a strike at one point over what I thought was an insignificant issue. Rock 'n' roll music was emerging, and groups like to listen to loud music together. Holden didn't offer any opportunity for this to occur. We did have the beginnings of the tape library that had playback equipment with earphones. We were sensitive to guests enjoying peace and quiet in the village and didn't allow music to be amplified.

A young couple who were graduate students at Washington State University became the leaders of the effort to force "management" to provide a place for staff to listen to loud music. We finally agreed on a room in the schoolhouse that would be made available to the staff. As I recall, once we established the opportunity for staff to listen to music, it was infrequently used after the first week. Even though the issue of authority in the village wasn't evident, in the 1960s and even the early 1970s there was a resistance to authority. The smoking of marijuana came up not only among the staff but also the faculty. The agreement for participation with the faculty and staff indicated that marijuana wasn't allowed. On occasion marijuana was confiscated and flushed down the toilet, but overall it was considered a minor problem.

One of the ongoing challenges was encouraging the volunteers to at least occasionally break away from their staff friends and eat meals with guests. I knew personally that it wasn't always easy, and I also needed to discipline myself to eat meals with new arrivals. The major problem with long-term staff members and incoming guests occurred each spring. The winter community was rather stable. It was easy for the small community to become possessive of their personal time and the assumed ownership of the village itself. I had a set speech that I offered at the first staff meeting in May, reminding staff that it was only because of the paying guests and their generosity with their gifts that the rest of us were able to enjoy the village, especially during the winter months. It sometimes took two meetings to make sure the staff understood that the guests, who would be arriving in larger numbers, weren't interfering with our unique life but were the ones we needed to thank for making it all possible.

Occasionally I would receive letters from people who lived along the lake or in Chelan reporting a problem with staff. Some local people were still uncertain as to what was going on at Holden with its religious emphasis and sometimes strange-looking young adults traveling up and down the lake. With the remote location without communications, it was easy for rumors to be generated. One winter I was informed we had a serious problem not only with the use of marijuana but also drug sales in the village. I hadn't seen evidence of this but made a trip to talk with the Chelan County sheriff and get his advice. He suggested the sheriff's department send a young couple who had worked undercover with his department and were about the same age as many of our volunteers. They would join the volunteer staff and determine if a problem existed. The couple along with their infant child joined the staff. After two weeks they met with me and indicated that no serious problem existed and we shouldn't worry about the minimal marijuana use that existed. It's only in the past several years that I have shared this story. For many years no one knew this had occurred. I heard several years later that the husband, who continued his undercover work with the sheriff's department, was killed in a surveillance situation.

During the spring that Fritz Norstad served as interim director, we experienced another episode of marijuana use. Discipline was always a challenge. We never knew how the community would react and what problems discipline of a larger group might have on the entire community. Fritz was a wise administrator. He announced after vespers that he was disappointed that there were those in the community who had elected to disregard the rule about use of marijuana. Fritz didn't name anyone involved; he merely asked those who had used marijuana to decide for themselves to be on the bus and leave the village the next morning. This amounted to self-deportation. He asked that they remain out of the village for at least thirty days so they had sufficient time to think about what it meant to be a member of a community. Those leaving were welcome to return if they wanted to rejoin the community. Twelve staff went downlake the next day. I think only three or four people returned after thirty days. This approach allowed each person to decide if he or she should leave, and it didn't create any feeling in the community that anyone had been treated improperly.

There are so many great stories concerning volunteers, who literally created the atmosphere that allowed the village to impact so many people. I cannot name all of them, and I apologize that I will refer to only a very few. The stories I'm sharing involve volunteers who had some special impact on me or became a symbol of the miracle of the volunteer staff.

Fern Olson, from Spokane, Washington, was one of the special volunteers. She was in her sixties when she began offering her many services and talents. Fern was a widow and had sufficient financial means to spend four to five months at Holden each year for perhaps eight or nine years. She was the unofficial chauffeur for Carroll when he was traveling around the Northwest seeking funds and increasing village registrations. Fern never received any compensation from Holden for the thousands of miles she drove. Whatever Fern did for Holden was pure gift. During the months she spent in the village she was in charge of housekeeping and laundry, making sure the rooms were clean and beds properly made. She was also one of the unofficial hostesses to guests as they arrived. Chalet 8 was her chalet for the years she served Holden. Fern was also a significant financial contributor and introduced others from the Spokane area to Holden, encouraging their financial support. Her home in Spokane became a minihotel for some faculty and staff over the years. Fern was one of the many people who literally allowed Holden to develop into a significant national retreat center. She volunteered but she wasn't recruited. You can't find people like Fern or Hortie or Al or the many others who, in a sense, just appeared, and it became obvious that they should stay as long as possible.

Hortie Christman in my estimation was the ultimate volunteer. Hortie and Mary Christman were significant in defining Holden Village as a loving and compassionate community. Hortie was everyone's grandfather

and the village engineer, barber and philosopher. I had a degree in engineering, but he was the real engineer who had a mind that solved problems and created new adventures. He was the one who figured out how
to extract a fifteen-thousand-gallon tank from the mine level by floating
the tank out of its hole, rolling it on the flatbed truck in just the exact
position so we could roll it off into a predug hole next to the diesel generator building, and have the tank in the exact position so that the fill
spout and vent pipe were precisely vertical. Holden had no equipment to
lift a tank and make the final adjustment. The only thing we had was the
flatbed truck and Hortie. He was officially the village plumber, builder
of the river sauna, and project manager and engineer to get the prefabri-
cated thirty-six-inch beams across the creek for the vehicle bridge.

Hortie had been a logger and at one time a barber in Chelan.
He became the official barber and cut hair for the staff, for a few
visiting bishops and university professors from St. Olaf, Augustana,
Princeton, and Harvard. I think he also did a trim on a former governor and perhaps a former senator. Having Hortie trim your hair was
a sign of pride, and many guests and staff made it a priority to have a
"Hortie cut."

Hortie was a tall, lanky man and, to me, had a mind with some similarities to Abraham Lincoln's. Hortie's formal education ended after the
eighth grade, when he went off to work. At Holden, he would attend
lectures when possible and invariably ask the question that would cause
the teacher to rethink or again try to explain what didn't seem to make
sense. He knew that we don't need to understand everything about life
to celebrate life and live with a spirit of thankfulness. Hortie became
known as the village philosopher and offered the famous quote, "If you
understood Holden, you would spoil it." His comments often pricked
the ego of the teacher, but he was soft-spoken and always kind, and never said anything to hurt.

Hortie could be seen frequently sitting on the rock wall or under the
tree on a bench talking with one of the staff or guests. He became the
village counselor not by education or training but through compassion

and love. Those who gathered around him ranged in age from ten to eighty. Everyone loved Hortie.

When we were getting ready to put the new bridge across Railroad Creek, Hortie told me one afternoon that I shouldn't tell anyone where he was because he wanted to go to the bridge to sit and think. He worked things out in his mind and then was ready to act. He was one of three or four people whom I have known that I thought God should let live for eternity. Obviously my priorities didn't materialize.

Al Swihart was a very special person for me. Al arrived merely as the husband of Jean Swihart but quickly became a central character within the community. Earlier in his life, he had been the manager of a large Elks Lodge, and during a national convention, he and Jean were featured on the classic TV program, *Truth or Consequences*. Occasionally, we would show the 16-mm film of this program in the Village Center.

Their daughter, Bonnie, recently gave me a DVD of the program for my personal enjoyment and remembrance.

Al became the operator of the electric golf cart and was therefore popular with the youth. They all wanted rides with Al if our dog Bernie wasn't already his passenger. One of Al's jobs was counseling with the multitude of ground squirrels. Holden purchased two live traps, and it was Al's job to catch the ground squirrels, transport them down the road, and let them loose. Shortly after the relocation project was initiated, he requested a high-level meeting to discuss what he observed was the quick return of the banished squirrels. He suggested adding a small dot of red paint to the head of the squirrels while in the cage so we could document if they were actually returning to their easy source of food. Then Al reported that the group he took to Ten Mile was back in the village almost before he returned in the electric cart.

Al was also known as the "cherry man." We would receive large quantities of Bing cherries as donations from orchard owners. The kitchen would use many for meals, and Al would package the rest of the cherries and sell them to guests as a "subcontractor" of the snack bar. He was also a great conversationalist and had the ability to talk with all ages.

He was my frequent boat copilot on my many trips downlake for business trips to Wenatchee. Al was still owner of a food service in Oklahoma City and felt the need to keep in contact with the manager they had hired while at Holden. He also loved to stop at the Entiat Fruit stand to purchase whatever was in season. He had a passion for marinated artichoke hearts and would purchase a case of these at least once a month. We generally consumed one or two jars of the artichokes during a trip to Chelan. We had our trips downlake planned so we could be at Smitty's Pancake House in Wenatchee at nine in the morning, necessitating a departure from Holden by six in the morning.

Al also loved to fish the beaver ponds on the way to Hart Lake. He didn't mind walking out into the shallow ponds using whatever methods were effective to catch the fish. He wasn't a fishing connoisseur and didn't require any expensive equipment, but he was a happy and success-ful fisherman. He would have people lined up to accompany him on a fishing excursion.

Al was always an entertainer, so any trip with him was pure joy. One time I recall a seventy-year-old guest who had been the executive assistant to the president of SeaFirst Bank ask me if I could convince Al to take her ninety-year-old mother on a hike to Hart Lake. Al was some-what apprehensive but agreed to go as far as the ballpark, the area used by the miners for recreation, to see how she would do. He reported to me when they left and told me to be prepared for a rescue operation. When they returned four hours later from Hart Lake, Al confessed he had had a difficult time keeping up with his new ninety-year-young hik-ing partner.

Al had a repertoire of jokes and stories, although a few of the jokes needed to be censored at Holden. He was a dashing figure; his daily wardrobe was red coveralls, but on occasion he would dress up and give an indication how handsome he must have been in his younger years. Al grew up in the days of vaudeville and had participated in some vaude-ville talent shows when he was young. His specialty was the recitation of Robert Service poems. He knew most of these poems by memory and became best known for sharing the poem, "The Cremation of Sam Magee." Following Al's death, Jean presented me with his well-worn copy of the complete poems of Robert Service. I have since turned over this treasurer to my son Jeff. He will be the keeper of these memories.

Holden was most fortunate that Al Swihart shared part of his life with us. You can't plan for gifts such as Al's, and you just need to let them happen. I probably spent more time with Al than any other person in the village besides my direct family. Anytime I went downlake in my boat, God may have been my copilot but Al Swihart was most often the one to sit in the copilot's seat.

One of the unique and talented couples sharing its time at Holden was Ernie and Pearl Zoerb. Pearl was full of patience as well as talent. For many years, she was the bookkeeper and counter of the Holden money.

She never once complained about her working hours or office conditions. In those days we used whatever rooms were available for the various offices. She never seemed to mind the many people coming into the office that she shared. Many people just wanted to visit with her. Pearl was everyone's friend and, for many, the perfect grandmother. Ernie Zoerb was a retired pastor and had served as a military chaplain, but his love—other than Pearl—was the outdoors. He sometimes embarrassed Pearl by what he would say or how he would act, but she would smile and say nothing. Ernie was an accomplished identifier of birds, plants, and animals. He loved to hike and developed—and I think named—the trail to Monkey Bear Falls. I can't remember how Ernie became the operator of the sawmill, but for six or seven years he was the manager of the village lumber operation. During this time we accomplished many of the construction projects at Holden using our own milled lumber. The waste from the sawmill added to the winter firewood supply.

Ernie, for some, was a crotchety old man. He verbalized life like he saw it, and he didn't spare colorful words to explain his position. He didn't have patience for the lazy or for those who didn't like to spend time outdoors. Some of his language may have come from his military experience. I always saw him as a loving, dedicated community member who loved to work—as long as the work was outdoors. He took people on hikes and would watch for those in the community who were too shy to ask to be involved. Ernie helped to create the powerful, loving community experience of Holden.

At one point in our working partnership, Carroll designated me the "prior" of Holden Village. According to definitions, a prior is a monastic superior, usually lower in rank than an abbot. I guess Carroll was the abbot, who held the highest rank in Holden's monastic chain of command. The prior was to perform the duties of his office entirely according to the will and under the direction of the abbot. Holden Village wasn't a monastery and didn't adhere to monastic practices, but it was another example of "make-believe" that often increased joy to each day of work.

I don't know if conducting noon prayers was in the job description for a prior, but Carroll asked me to conduct noon prayers. I would ring the bell at twelve noon and lead prayers. In good weather we would meet under the trees, in a small meeting room when the outdoors wasn't practical. The noon prayers also became the source of sharing some national and international news. This wasn't intentional, but I have always been a news junkie. I listened to as much news as was possible with the limited communications available to us. I frequently prayed for a person or an event at noon prayers that then became the topic of discussion. Noon prayer was very meaningful for me. It never involved a large group, but it became a discipline of the community and meaningful even for those not attending.

I think Carroll liked the concept of discipline, at least in theory. Carroll himself wasn't a disciplined person. His main discipline was spontaneity. At times I got the impression that he fantasized about Holden being a monastic community, but probably with him having the freedom to move in and out of any discipline involved. Carroll didn't give me a lot of direction in the operation of the village, and perhaps it was best that way. We had frequent conversations, primarily as he was walking through my office. I had a small office, and often the conversations would last the four or five steps it took for him to reach the outside door. I don't recall that we ever had an office meeting, but we did have many great conversations.

Mary Hinderlie was never listed as the co director of Holden as occurs now, but she was definitely a critical part of Carroll's impact. Mary in some ways became the mother of the volunteer staff and monitored the staff pulse, being especially aware of those who gave the appearance of needing someone to talk with and receive guidance and encouragement.

On April 7, 2003, I learned that Mary died, and the best way I could deal with this news was to sit down and write the following thoughts:

Mary Hinderlie died today. Mary was and is a saint in the very real sense. I first met Mary in the summer of 1963. This was the year Carroll became the director of Holden. It wasn't an easy summer for Carroll and Mary as they needed to deal with their own lifestyle transition into Holden, but also they needed patience to have the community of Holden make the transition from Gil Berg and his style to that of Carroll and his very different style. Carroll had an imposing personality with a special gift to preach and teach.

Mary was often in the shadow of Carroll, but Mary was generally the one who smoothed the ruffles after Carroll tore through a situation. Mary had a smile that healed all hurts. One felt comforted and at home in the presence of Mary. Mary wouldn't dominate or wouldn't be aggressive, but she was always ready to add her comments. Even when corrections were needed, Mary would rather make a comment that would subtly correct an error that someone else had made without pointing to someone as obviously wrong.

Mary was small in stature but very large in terms of the comforting power that surrounded her presence.

I don't remember Mary ever getting angry, at least not in public. I do remember that especially in the early years, Mary suffered from allergies and perhaps asthma. The blowing tailings in the valley didn't help her condition, but she wore her mask and was never bitter or didn't appear to display a martyr's attitude for having to follow Carroll to this remote wilderness setting.

Carroll would frequently talk about their experiences in prison camp during World War II. I remember hearing about their first child, Maren, being born in prison camp and some of the fears and difficult times they all experienced. I don't remember ever hearing Mary blaming anyone or complaining about these experiences.

Mary was the one who kept the family together and provided a calming effect to the intense emotions that surrounded Carroll. It appeared to me that Mary traded her professional future for accepting or preferring or tolerating her role as wife, mother, mediator, and spirit of love with a healing spirit. She grew up in the days when wives and mothers accepted their station in life as mother to their children and as working partners for their husbands.

Even though Mary had great mental and emotional strengths, she also appeared to be powerless in dealing with some of Carroll's weaknesses that no doubt caused much grief and suffering. Mary Hinderlie was a special person, and I'm sure that she is still smiling and comforting those she meets in heaven.

Holden from its beginning honored the value of women in life and community. However, I think it's also true that when Holden began in 1963, it was a time when women were appreciated but still left in the leadership shadows, primarily involved where women normally served. The Development Council was the first committee Holden Village established, and finally one woman became involved because she was an interior decorator. The wives of the Development Council members would sometimes participate by bringing treats. Their input was valued, but they were never listed as members of the committee. Holden changed as society changed, but to be honest, I don't think that Holden provided any leadership push in terms of promoting women as leaders in operational or theological areas prior to society gradually making the shift.

Mary was definitely a leader but also appeared to be willing to stay in the shadows of Carroll even though many recognized her as the more significant intellect and theologian. Since Carroll promoted me to the position of unofficial prior of Holden, and the title has never been revoked, I'll declare Mary Hinderlie as patron saint of the volunteer staff.

CHAPTER 7

The Upper Lake
Chelan Community

IN ORDER TO UNDERSTAND THE story of Holden Village, it's necessary to become acquainted with some of the neighbors in the upper Lake Chelan region. They weren't directly involved with Holden Village but had a profound impact on me. Part of the uniqueness of Holden Village was the gift of being accepted as a geographical member of the remote, sparsely populated, upper lake community. The spectacular scenery surrounding the charming town site of Holden Village, the relaxing ride up Lake Chelan, and the worship life were all special, but to me the real impact was the amazing variety of people who gathered to work, teach, learn, or just visit. The community that shaped Holden Village was more than the parcel of land leased from the forest service and more than the people directly associated with Holden.

Holden doesn't have close neighbors as one normally thinks of neighbors. When in a wilderness area, neighbors cover a much larger geographical area. Many of these people I met initially on the commercial boat since this was the mode of transportation for the majority of the people living and traveling on Lake Chelan. On subsequent boat trips, I enjoyed many hours of conversation. I learned quickly that those living for years in remote areas often enjoyed solitude and weren't always interested in visiting. It became part of the initiation process of remote living to recognize the clues of those wanting to visit and those wishing to remain within their own thoughts during the three-hour boat ride.

Our neighbors along the shores of Lake Chelan were from Domke Lake, Lucerne, Stehekin, Fish Creek, Meadow Creek, and any other stops the boat made to deliver people, mail, and groceries. The winter trips were the time to meet and develop friendships. The impact of neighbors involved knowing their history and understanding their power of survival. Wilderness living requires appreciating the solitude, being aware of dangers before they become a threat, and celebrating the many gifts of nature as they occur in the moment.

I'm introducing a few people I considered my neighbors since they played a part in the Holden history I lived. These neighbors may not be frequently mentioned, but for me they represented the heroes and inspiration as I felt an increasing part of the upper lake area. They were important because of the years they lived in this spectacular, remote reality of what we dream the world should be. They all had personal stories of a life that only a few are privileged to experience. Living year-round in a remote area without communications brings people together in a community of survival as well as solitude.

Humility is a strong trait for those who survive, and it's important to understand you are not in control of the power of your surroundings. Those who humbly celebrated their vulnerability in the wilderness survived. Those who claimed dominance over nature soon left or died. For these people this lifestyle wasn't an experience of months or a few years, but rather forty or fifty years or even a lifetime.

Esther and Ray Courtney were the patriarchs of the area. They lived nine miles up the road from Stehekin landing. They owned sufficient acreage, inherited as a homestead that Ray's parents acquired initially. Ray and Esther had a ranch and packhorse business. They were well known throughout the West and by countless people in other portions of the country. The Courtney family was featured in a *National Geographic* issue around 1961, an issue that featured authentic mountain living. Their family and their life story were featured in numerous outdoor and hiking magazines, and Ray and Esther were almost worshiped by some as the ultimate conservationists and environmentalists. They were featured in *The Alps of the Stehekin*, the Sierra Club movie.

Everyone loved the Courtneys, and their repeat business kept them booked each year. I had the privilege of joining them on one trip that was called their Fall Color Hiking Trip. They set up camp at Cottonwood Campground, a campground at the end of the road in the Stehekin valley, allowing us day hikes to Horseshoe Basin, Trapper Lake, and Cascade Pass. In the evenings they would have great meals prepared and tents ready for a good night's sleep. Conversations were most enjoyable.

Ray never understood why people were so interested in meeting him, but he was an icon for mountaineers and hikers in the North Cascades. Both Esther and Ray were very humble, but many people traveled uplake just to meet them and, if at all possible, see their log cabin. Ray became the guru of the wilderness with many people dreaming of living the life Esther and Ray experienced daily. Ray built their three-story log home. The bottom logs were thirty inches in diameter. The stairs to the second floor were hewn out of one log. The dining table was one log slab. Ray had engineered a small hydroelectric system that provided sufficient electricity for a few light bulbs and help with the hot water supply. Heat was provided by the wood stove and cookstove, burning wood cut from the surrounding land. I stayed with the Courtney family in their home on at least two occasions in the winter, and it was a privilege just to be with them.

Ray had been in World War II with, I think, the Tenth Mountain Division. He was an excellent skier. Although the Courtneys would initially pack for hunting parties in the Stehekin Valley, by the early 1960s they decided to eliminate hunting parties from their business. They chose to pack exclusively for those wanting to go into the wilderness to enjoy the beauty of the surroundings and the solitude and purity of the undisturbed. Even though eliminating hunting parties reduced their revenue, they decided that they would add new fall hiking opportunities rather than pack for hunters who too frequently were interested in drinking and displaying an unfortunate disrespect for nature.

During the winter months, without income from the packing business, Ray would supplement the family income by splicing cable for chair lifts at ski areas. He would receive emergency calls via the boat company or the sheriff's department that a ski area in Alaska, California, Colorado, or Montana needed him immediately. He would fly out of Stehekin by floatplane and be at a ski area in less than twenty-four hours.

He loved his horses and was respected by everyone for his gentle approach to life and his love of his animals. Ray was tall, probably six foot four. He always wore his weathered cowboy hat. He was a powerful man, but I never witnessed him using his strength except to help someone or some animal.

His brother Curt also lived in the Stehekin Valley until the National Park Service took ownership and control. Curt and his wife owned the restaurant at Stehekin landing until the park service purchased the facilities. She was featured in *National Geographic* for the quality of her homemade pies, especially her Washington nut pie. Curt operated heavy equipment and once told me that he helped build the road into Holden from Lucerne. He also worked in the Holden Mine in the early years. He was a big and powerful man, heavier than Ray. Curt was proud of the fact that, while living at Holden and working for Howe Sound, he didn't miss a feeding in the dining hall. The Holden dining hall served five meals per day with the last one being served at ten o'clock at night. He told me that he would set his alarm so he would make the ten-o'clock feeding.

As the National Park Service took control of the area, life and work changed for the Courtneys. They were limited in terms of the total number of horses and people they could accommodate in any one party. These rules potentially reduced the marginal revenue from the business and made it more difficult to continue packing in the area. They began what they called pack and hike trips involving fewer horses. They were set up so that the people would hike with day packs, and packhorses carried food, tents, and personal gear.

Ray and Esther had a large family. Tom, the oldest son, owned a floatplane for a while and operated a commercial charter business on the lake for a number of years. Another son became a mechanic and heavy equipment operator and did a lot of the excavation work for private individuals and the park service. One son died in the lake from a recreational accident. Peggy, their daughter, became a folk singer and song writer. She sang professionally in the area with various bands. Another son started the Stehekin Valley Ranch, which has become a successful operation with lodging and meals. Another son and his wife started a successful bakery and eatery. The Courtney sons still operate or have a hand in many of the commercial activities in the Stehekin Valley. I became best acquainted with Cliff, I think the youngest son, who was on the opposite spectrum of political thought from me, but I always valued his opinion and appreciated the opportunity for personal conversations with him.

Ray died in 1983 resulting from an accident in the area around Hilgard Pass above the Tenmile Creek canyon. One of his sons ran down to Holden to report the accident and I called the Chelan County Sheriff to send a helicopter and medical assistance. Ray sacrificed his life trying to help a horse that had slipped off the trail. Esther and her sons continued with the family business for many years. Two of Ray and Esther's grandsons took flight instruction at Wings of Wenatchee, and our son Jeff had the privilege of being their flight instructor.

Living up Lake Chelan was a unique experience. So much pioneering history was still alive in the 1960s, and it was actually possible to meet many of the people who were the characters and the residents of this unique and remote undeveloped section of the country.

Paul Bergman was another one of the very special people I had the privilege to know. Paul must have been sixty-five-plus when I first met him. He had a small photography shop in Stehekin and had lived in the area for many years. He had a collection of photos that recorded the history of the wilderness and the animal friends he met and admired in the mountains.

Paul had gown up in Switzerland. His father was a university professor. Paul told me that he always assumed that he would be going to the university, but he really wasn't that interested in academics. He was more interested in using his hands for crafts and art. As a young boy he would delight in visiting the cobbler in the village and help make shoes. His father discovered his enjoyment of working in the cobbler shop and banned further visits. Paul did well in school, including the university, but his prime motivation in getting good grades was the all-expense-paid trip around other parts of Europe that was given to the student who had the highest grades. He received this reward several of the years he studied at the university.

Paul came to the United States as a young adult. His desire was to live off the land in the wilderness. He went to Canada one spring to begin his new adventure. He shared with me the fact that if it hadn't been for the compassion and kindness of the people of the First Nation, the real habitants of the area, he would have died. The people of the First Nations helped him build a log house and taught him to live off the land by hunting and trapping. They made sure he had food to eat and wood to keep warm so he survived the winter.

At some point Paul decided to pursue the field of photography and attended a school in Chicago. His specialty was the hand tinting of black-and-white photographs that was popular before the advent of color photography. That remained a specialty throughout Paul's career.

Paul shared with me some highlights of his life, painting a picture of a very interesting journey. In his young adult days, he was a strikingly handsome figure. The photographs he shared made it clear that he might have been mistaken for an Errol Flynn. I think he was in Coeur d'Alene, Idaho, when he fell in love with a young woman. At the same time, the daughter of the local banker fell in love with Paul. She was very persuasive and determined to marry Paul. The banker's daughter won. They were married and had a child. Some years later they divorced. He indicated to me that he frequently wondered what happened to the other young woman whom he really loved and never forgot.

At some point after the divorce, he moved to Stehekin and remained there until his death. He lived in a simple cabin within walking distance of the boat landing. His cabin was sufficiently large to house his photographic darkroom as well as his collection of zither music on vinyl records. He lived by himself the rest of his life. Even though he had many friends who loved him dearly, to me he always appeared to be lonely.

Holden always had a great Thanksgiving celebration, but generally there were few guests. It primarily involved the Holden community. One year I decided to invite some of our neighbors who had no families. This included Paul, Oscar Getty, and Gordon Stuart. Paul was the only one able to join us. When he arrived in the village, I met him and helped carry his luggage to his room in Koinonia. When we got to his room, he asked me to close the door and said he wanted to ask me a question. He approached me and said, "Why did you invite me to join you for Thanksgiving?"

I was somewhat taken aback by the question but answered, "Because we like you and thought you would enjoy celebrating Thanksgiving with the Holden family."

Tears came to his eyes, and he replied, "No one has ever given me something without wanting more in return."

Paul had a great time the next few days and thoroughly enjoyed sharing some of his life stories with many young staff members around the fireplace. We became good friends, and at one point Paul approached me about moving to Holden Village to live. However, he'd had his larynx removed and also had problems with his legs that required medical care. Holden wasn't set up to become a care facility. Although it would have been great to have had Paul as a member of the community, it wasn't practical to seriously consider this possibility. Paul was one of the special people who helped Holden become part of the larger upper lake community.

Oscar and Mona Getty were really the pioneers of Railroad Creek Valley. They were the only ones, besides Holden Village, to actually own property in the valley or, for that matter, on the south shore of Lake Chelan between Twenty-Five Mile Creek and Stehekin. Oscar first arrived in the valley around 1918. He left for a time during World War I and then returned and gained ownership of a mining claim and a mill site at the mouth of Railroad Creek. He never developed the mine claim, but he did sufficient work to obtain patented claims to three or four acres of land. The mining law of 1872 was generous in allowing mining claims to become patented land for the sake of encouraging exploration.

As the early mining activity in the valley developed, Oscar became the primary packer of men and materials before the road was established. Before Holden Mine was seriously developed, the Crown Point mine, near Lyman Lake and approximately nine west of the future Holden mine, with a molybdenum deposit was developed. One story floating around was about when this mine was being developed and sections of narrow gauge rail were shipped uplake to establish rail tracks for ore cars in the mine. Oscar had the task of transporting the rails to Lyman Lake by packhorse. According to the story, the rails were too long to strap to horses. He decided to heat the rails and bend them in a shape that could be carried by the packhorses. When he got them to Layman Lake he again heated them and returned them to a useable shape. I don't know if I believe this story, but one time I asked Oscar if this actually occurred. He just smiled and asked if I would have had a better idea. He never did tell me if the story was true.

Until the Howe Sound Company established the road, Oscar had a monopoly on the business of hauling people and material into the valley. After the road was complete and the mine opened, Oscar turned his entrepreneurial activities into building small cabins on his private property at Lucerne and renting them to Holden mine workers and their families. During the operational years of Holden Mine, Oscar returned to offering commercial pack trips into the Lyman Lake area as well as other portions of the mountains surrounding the Railroad Creek Valley.

I had several people tell me stories of trips their families had with Oscar. They were two-week trips, and Oscar would do all of the cooking as well as organize the packing. He would take chickens for fresh eggs. He would also walk a cow up the trail for fresh milk. Oscar was famous for his "glacier ice cream" made from fresh cream, eggs, and ice chipped from the Lyman Glacier to freeze the ice cream. Oscar didn't tell me this story, but I did hear about Oscar's famous pack trips from some people still living in Chelan at the time. They confirmed the story, especially the glacier ice cream. My first visit to the Lyman Glacier was in February 1965. It was still an impressive mass of ice at that time. I have heard recently that the Lyman Glacier has essentially disappeared. I haven't visited Lyman Lake since 1982.

When the mine closed, Howe Sound kept a security person on the site through the summer and fall of 1957. Prior to snow closing the roads, the security person left. Before the roads opened in 1958, Howe Sound hired Oscar to more or less be the security person. I would never consider Oscar to be a security-guard type of person, but he did live at Lucerne and did have a car, and he was probably available at low cost. After the first summer, security was minimized. The Lucerne Resort, developed during the Holden mine operation began advertising that visitors could go to the resort, hire the taxi, and go to Holden, "the ghost mine town," to collect souvenirs. The Lucerne Resort had cabins to rent but also had a tavern and restaurant that help supply sustenance required by hungry and thirsty miners. During the summers of 1959 and 1960, many items were taken from Holden and ended up furnishing many of the cabins up and down the lake. Beds and bedding along with captain's chairs and some dining and kitchen equipment disappeared. When Holden Village became a reality in 1961, Oscar and his wife Mona became good neighbors and were always helpful to everyone coming and going up the valley.

In 1966, Holden began a year-round operation and we became regular visitors to the Getty cabin, especially in winter months. Until the new forest service dock was built in 1970–1972, the commercial boat would dock in front of Oscar's cabin during the winter. As the lake level went down, the boat would nose onto the rocks, unloading freight and people down a steep gangplank. All luggage and freight were carried over the rocks to the vehicles in front of Oscar's cabin.

Mona didn't spend as much time at Lucerne. I don't know how long they had been married, but I think the length of their marriage was facilitated by their spending a lot of time away from each other. Mona was kind but also headstrong. A schoolteacher, she had taught in Alaska and was accustomed to isolation and spending much time on her own. She was from Conconully, Washington, and would stay at her place in Conconully when not at Lucerne.

I enjoyed Oscar and his willingness to share stories. I considered him a real friend, although when I first met him I was twenty-four years old and he was probably sixty. Oscar was short of stature, about my size. He generally wore a ranch-style red-plaid coat. One day I noticed that when the boat was about to arrive he took off his new plaid coat and put on a threadbare coat and an old hat before walking down to the dock. I asked him about this procedure, and he said that the tourists on the boat liked to take pictures of a mountain man in old clothes. One summer when we were celebrating our Christmas in July, Oscar even put on a Santa hat that we gave him so he would be in costume. He was always kind to everyone. He didn't initiate a lot of conversations but was always friendly. He provided an important point of contact for Holden, especially in the early years when we were gaining knowledge and learning how to survive in this remote area.

Oscar believed in "witching" for water. Water witching is a method of using a live 'Y' branch from a tree or shrub or even metal rods to detect water that might be under ground. One sunny spring day while waiting for the boat, he began talking about witching for water. I told him that I didn't totally dismiss the validity of witching for water, but I didn't understand its scientific basis. Oscar said that to get the feel of witching, it's sometimes necessary to hold the hand of an experienced technician. The next thing I knew Oscar went over and cut a fresh Y branch from a bush with emerging growth. Soon I was holding one hand on the switch, the other hand clutching Oscar's hand. I felt the "power," but I have never since felt it on my own. I'm glad no one saw Oscar and me holding hands that day. It might have been misunderstood.

Oscar had a low-key personality and dimples when he smiled. He generally had a corncob pipe in his mouth—occasionally lit. He was generous in letting us wait for the arrival of the boat in his cabin during the winter months. He always had a pot of "Oscar coffee" on the wood stove. He had what I would call a seven-day coffee recipe. Each Monday he began by dumping out the old and starting with fresh grounds. Each subsequent day he would add additional coffee grounds and new water when needed. By Friday, the coffee was getting a little strong. Monday morning the process started anew.

Oscar coffee predated Starbucks by many years, and his brew never made it to the big time. However, Oscar coffee was the stimulus for many great conversations and the opportunity to warm the innards. Oscar would frequently make cookies or some type of munchies to enjoy with the coffee. One time he made a mistake and added salt instead of sugar to the receipt. Rather than throwing the cookies away, he used them to test his visitors through the week to see if they were honest when they tasted them or if they would act as if everything was OK.

From November until April, Fridays were special days at Lucerne. It was the season for the "Friday Club." The club had a restricted membership, but while we were waiting for the boat, we were listed as unofficial members. Friday Club always met in Oscar's cabin and began by listening to Paul Harvey on KPQ AM radio, broadcast out of Wenatchee. Club conversation was rather conservative, and I never discussed politics or religion with the group. I understood I was an honorary guest and also realized I could never win an argument in their presence. Occasionally they would make comments about church and religion to see if I would take the bait, but they were always friendly and welcoming.

Oscar was the host of the Friday Club and the other members were Gordon Stuart from Domke Lake and Dinsmore Bigger from across the lake at Moore Point. Gordon would snowshoe down from Domke, and Dinsmore (known as Dinty) would row across the lake and tie his rowboat to various rocks as the lake receded during winter. Dinty was one of the former owners of Moore Point Resort at Fish Creek and was caretaker of the property when I knew him. According to many in the area, Moore Point Resort was the only successful resort on upper Lake Chelan in the early days. Dinty worked at Holden Mine when it was being built. He was a certified welder and also welded the hydro penstock at Lucerne. During the time Holden Village was building its hydro, we hired Dinty to do some welding for the project.

Besides listening to Paul Harvey, every Friday Club included a fifth of whiskey. When the bottle was drained, the club meeting was officially concluded. Gordon and Dinty always stayed overnight. As the official host, Oscar did all of the cooking. He was also a good baker. Many humorous stories came out of the Friday Club. Since Dinty rowed across the lake and since the effects of the whiskey often lingered over to Saturday morning, Oscar would look out the window to make sure that Dinty was navigating the lake OK on his return home.

One Saturday morning Oscar did his check of Dinty. He couldn't see him on the lake, so decided to go down to the shore to check. When he got to the place where Dinty tied up his boat, he noticed the boat was still there but couldn't see Dinty. When he got to the boat, he found Dinty asleep in the bottom. No harm done, just a short delay in the trip home.

Both Gordon and Dinty had dogs. When everyone got into Oscar's small living room with two wet dogs whose hair was singed by the hot wood stove, along with perspiring men who infrequently bathed or showered or laundered their clothes in the winter, together with coffee that had been brewing all week, it was almost more than the olfactory senses could tolerate.

Oscar was a wise and witty character. He was frugal, and it was my guess that he had accumulated reasonable wealth over the years. After the mine closed and he lost the income involved from cabin rentals, he began to purchase land through sheriff's sales. He received the *Wenatchee World* and would watch for the sale notices. He bid on land that he never saw. He told me sometimes it paid off and sometimes it didn't.

One spring we were sitting on a log in front of his cabin, enjoying the warmth of the sun. He said, "Werner, I need your advice." I replied that I would be happy to help if I could. He proceeded to tell me about some of his real estate acquisitions. He would frequently bid on property sight unseen by sending in a check and not even going to the public sales. He ended up with a considerable portfolio. In some cases he lucked out, acquiring relatively valuable land at very little cost.

One purchase involved fifteen acres of property. He didn't realize at the time of the purchase that it was located at the bottom of a Bureau of Land Management earth dam. Several years after the purchase, the earth dam began leaking, and the irrigation company was obligated to purchase his property because of the damage that was caused. The profit realized by Oscar was considerable. He never actively tried to sell any of the property but waited until someone contacted him. That generally meant that they were more interested in purchasing the property than he was interested in selling, a situation which maximized his opportunity for profit. After about an hour of listening to all the real estate stories, the boat was in sight. He got up and thanked me for my help. I didn't offer any opinion, and in fact, Oscar did all of the talking, but I guess he felt I helped him simply by listening to him.

During one of the winters when we had limited snow transportation available, a group of youth and adults came after Christmas. We could take only about fifteen or twenty people per trip because of the capacity limits of the snow vehicles, so we needed to make several trips to get everyone to Holden. The trips were very slow because of the amount of snow. Before we could transport the entire group, we were down to one Snow Trac due to mechanical problems. Oscar had invited the people waiting at Lucerne into his cabin to stay warm. He also fixed them snacks. The last group of people ended up sleeping in his cabin until the next morning. Oscar fixed them a "trail" breakfast of bacon and eggs. They had a great experience, and for some of the youth, it was the highlight of their trip.

Oscar had an ongoing conflict with the forest service. The forest service at one point asked him to paint his cabin so the appearance from the lake was more presentable. Out of spite, Oscar painted the cabin a bright yellow rather than the requested forest-service brown. The forest service tried to purchase his private property numerous times, but because of his feelings toward them, he wouldn't even entertain a serious discussion on the subject. When he knew that his life was getting closer to the point where he may not be in control of his property, he came up with a plan that he hoped would keep his property out of the hands of the forest service forever.

He and Mona had two children. Neither was living in the area. According to Oscar, the son and daughter could never agree on anything. He left the property to his son and daughter, indicating in the will that the property couldn't be sold unless they both agreed 100 percent to the terms of the sale. He felt that this provision would keep the property safe for many years.

In the late 1970s, both Oscar's and Mona's health deteriorated. They purchased a small house in Chelan, and Mona spent most of the time before her death in Chelan. Oscar also spent more and more time in Chelan and finally moved there full-time before his death in 1978. It was the end of an era for Holden and for all of the uplake community. Oscar had leased his Lucerne property to the Lake Chelan Boat club. Members rented the cabins and fixed them up for their use when traveling uplake. The Getty estate still owns the three acres in Lucerne.

Gordon Stuart had a cleft lip, and it was sometimes difficult to understand his speech. This made it difficult for him to feel at ease socially, and he tended to avoid people unless he invited their friendship. The story I heard indicated that Gordon was the son of a career military father. Because of his cleft lip, he was often hidden during social functions within their home. He left his family as soon as possible and eventually began working for the forest service. He was a brilliant man of the woods. People often considered him to be a hermit at Domke Lake. If he was a hermit, he was also a very smart, capable, and well-read person who received the *Wall Street Journal* among several other newspapers.

A regular visitor at Domke Lake was Stan Bryant, an investment counselor from Wenatchee. Stan and Gordon became close friends, and Stan helped Gordon make some good investments. Gordon had a sharp mind and quick wit. He carried all of his supplies, including mail, on his back during at least six months out of every year. When the trail was clear of snow, his horses did the work.

Gordon was a true mountain man. He lived most of his life in his small cabin on the shore of Domke Lake. The lake is a three-mile hike and a thousand-feet elevation gain above Lucerne. I was told that when the forest service began replacing personnel with college graduates, Gordon lost his job and refused to be transferred out of the area. He decided to move up to Domke Lake. A. L. Cool was the lone resident at Domke Lake at the time but was getting old and apparently accepted Gordon to share the area as long as they didn't live too close to each other.

"Pop" Cool had lived at the lake for some forty years. Gordon moved into the small cabin originally built by Cool and basically took advanced graduate courses in living and surviving in the wilderness by observing Cool. They shared Domke Lake for seventeen years. Cool died when his new cabin burned down, at which point Gordon took over as the only human inhabitant at Domke Lake.

Gordon lived there for over forty years total, many of them alone. He operated the Emerald Park Resort, originally started by Pop Cool, which included two hand-built cabins made from hand-split cedar slabs and was located across the lake from his cabin on the south shore. He rented rowboats and outboard motorboats for fisherman and for those renting cabins.

Gordon generally had one dog, and he preferred Weimaraners. His cabin was perhaps sixty square feet. He had a covered wood storage area outside of the cabin, and on the outside wall displayed an extensive array of animal horns, antlers, and feet from various wild animals that he shot or trapped over the years. He also had an excellent root cellar that kept his homegrown vegetables eatable for some months. The root cellar also allowed him to share cold beer with friends. Gordon always had a great garden with the soil supplemented from his horse manure. He had a small gas pump that allowed him to pump water form the lake for his garden and domestic use.

I don't think that Gordon had a large yearly income, but he didn't have high overhead and his capital investments were more in terms of time than costly materials. What he did earn could be saved or invested. The rustic cabins on the south shore of the lake were wonderful wilderness cabins. You could see through the cracks, and the mice and chipmunks could move in and out at will, but the ambiance was perfect. Wood stoves provided sufficient heat for late spring, summer, and early fall use. Gordon provided the cooking utensils and made the beds prior to arrival with flannel sheets for added comfort. Each party using the cabins was responsible for sweeping the floors and replenishing the wood supply. Most of Gordon's guests flew in by floatplane with Lake Chelan Airways.

We tried to keep in contact with Gordon each winter, especially in the early years, and we would try to schedule a snowshoe trip to Domke Lake. One winter we packed fried chicken and a fresh pie, which helped cement our relationship with Gordon. He was an excellent chess player and delighted in beating just about everyone who was willing to challenge him.

For a number of years prior to his death, Gordon would take a spring trip to Las Vegas. It was the only time I saw him more or less "dress up." He told me that he would buy his round-trip ticket to and from Las Vegas ahead of time so he knew that he could always get home. He would also take a specific amount of money and wouldn't lose beyond a given amount.

Gordon began having problems with arthritis and more difficulty in getting around. This was serious for him since his whole life revolved around being mobile. He talked to me one day about "hiring a girl." I wasn't sure what he was talking about, but he explained that he wasn't able to do the work of cleaning the cabins, washing the sheets, and taking care of the boat rentals. When we understood what the job would involve, we let some of the Holden volunteer staff women know about the job possibilities. Over the next few years, a number of "Gordon's girls" came from the staff at Holden.

Gordon started mentioning that before he died he wanted to live in a real house. Sid Burns was the forest ranger at Lucerne and was helping Gordon more and more as Gordon's mobility decreased. Sid offered to build him a hand-hewn log cabin, but for Gordon this wasn't a "real house." He ended up ordering a Pan-Abode house kit. The house parts were delivered to Lucerne by barge. Then, Gordon contracted a helicopter to make seventy trips between the Lucerne dock and Domke Lake to deliver the house parts. A contractor assembled it rather quickly. Gordon lived in the Pan-Abode home for about six months before he died. At least he was able to live in a "real house" before his death.

In his will he was very generous to some of the special people who made his life enjoyable. The Domke Lake home, outbuildings, cabins for rent, boats, and basically his business went to Sid Burns, who continued to operate Emerald Park Resort after Gordon's death.

In 1986 Sandy Nelson Bryant published *Mountain Air: The Life Of Gordon Stuart, Mountain Man of the North Cascades,* an interesting book about Gordon and some history of the Lucerne and Stehekin area. Sandy came to Holden as a volunteer worker in 1982 and became "Gordon's girl number 16." The group of young women that Gordon hired over the years developed friendships and a close bond based on sharing this unique experience. They gathered one or more times for reunions to meet and share "Gordon stories." Gordon treated his girls very well, and it's my understanding that in his will, each girl received a generous bequest.

By 1990, Oscar, Gordon, and Dinty had all died, leaving the upper Lake Chelan area without its authentic pioneers. I know they never regretted living in a rather remote area without many of the comforts of life. As long as they could get KPQ radio, and as long as the boat delivered their food, whiskey, and occasional mail, they were happy pioneers.

Sid Burns was the newest and youngest resident of Lucerne. He arrived as the Lucerne ranger working for the forest service. At first he was a seasonal employee and occupant of the ranger station. He loved the area, and even though he was paid only on a seasonal basis, he received authorization from the forest service to live in the ranger station year-round. Sid was a real friend of Holden's and most helpful in every way possible. He became acquainted with Gordon and more or less became his understudy. Following Gordon's death, Sid left the forest service and moved to Domke Lake, continuing the tradition of operating Emerald Park Resort there. Sid married one of Gordon's "girls," and they had two beautiful children. The children were homeschooled for their first years. Then Sid and his family rented a home in Stehekin for several years so the girls could be in a "regular" school.

Sid was a thoughtful and compassionate person, whether he was dealing with humans or animals. He was also an artist as a wood worker, especially using an axe. Sid was definitely on the far right of politics, but I always looked forward to our conversations. Perhaps it was the fact that KPQ was the only radio station available to much of the uplake community that those who lived in the remote area developed a strong far right or libertarian political understanding.

For several winters, Sid ran a trap line for mink or other fur bearing animals on Railroad Creek from the wilderness boundary to Lucerne. He would come through the village on snowshoes, checking his traps through the season. He was a good mountain man with excellent survival skills and a healthy respect for the many positive aspects of nature. He also respected the dangers of the weather, snow conditions, and animals, especially the cougars in the valley.

Sid was always very kind to Holden, the staff, and guests, and he appreciated opportunities to participate in some of the Holden activities. He was an excellent representative of the forest service but also became a real friend and advocate of the Holden Village community.

These unique individuals were important to the life of the Railroad Creek valley and contributed authenticity to the larger community that was so important to Holden Village. They also provided knowledge for survival in this remote location in which the experience of living day to day was more important that book knowledge. Honesty and humor are sometimes more important than lectures and even worship.

CHAPTER 8

A Community with
Two Seasons

LABOR DAY BECAME A MAJOR time of transition during the earliest years of the Holden community. The population declined from perhaps 150 down to thirty following the bus departure on Labor Day. Even the majority of the volunteer staff left, with most heading back to school. The program Carroll established normally ran from early June until Labor Day. Before and after those dates we were on our own for program and worship. The small community that remained often experienced a feeling of elation and excitement, even though we all knew that the revenue needed for the continued operation required paying guests. The feeling was similar to that after a large family gathering when everyone goes home, bringing relief with lingering sadness. Occasionally we had larger groups such as a conference of Northwest pastors scheduled for later in September. The extra staff needed for those days was easily recruited by sending out a letter to our mailing list of those living in Washington State.

The first winter Holden was operational occurred in 1966–1967. Five of us lived in Chalet 1, the only building remaining open. The hydro was running, so we were rather comfortable with adequate electricity for heat as well as light. The village purchased its first Swedish Snow Trac, a six-passenger vehicle, during the summer of 1966, making travel to and from the lake convenient and mostly comfortable. A Snow Trac was

181

powered by a Volkswagen 1600cc air-cooled engine. We built a sled with fiberglass-covered plywood runners. The steering system on the Snow Trac wasn't well designed to pull a sled, but it worked. Luggage, freight, and even passengers rode the sled.

Communication in and out of Holden was always a challenge, even during mining days. It was my understanding that the mine had had phone communication via the power lines into the Howe Sound office in Chelan. Calls could then be routed from the Chelan office onto regular phone lines. When the power lines were deactivated, this option for communications disappeared.

When we decided that we would do a trial run of operating the village during the winter, it was evident that we needed some form of emergency communications. I contacted the Chelan County Sheriff's

Department and inquired about setting up radio communications with their Wenatchee dispatch. Ruben Rose, known as Rosy, was the deputy sheriff. He brought a technician to the village to test the radio signals. No signal was possible directly between Holden and Wenatchee, but they did discover that a signal was possible between Holden and Stehekin. This would require that emergency messages from Holden be relayed from Stehekin to Wenatchee. Holden purchased a radio, and we received authorization from the sheriff's department and the FCC to use their frequency for emergencies. Rosy was a great friend of Holden. I looked to him as more of a father figure for those of us at Holden than a deputy sheriff. His smile, his kindness, and his enjoyment in helping us was a unique example of the ideal approach to serving others through our law enforcement.

The winter of 1966–1967, the Chelan County Sheriff's radio and also a citizens band (CB) radio was located in the dining room of Chalet 1 and at times served as entertainment. The CB radios didn't function in the valley, but during the winter we would get a skipped radio signal from the mountains of Arkansas. The signal would last less than an hour, but it was great to listen to the chatter of fellow "mountain people." The communication with Arkansas was listening only. On Saturday nights we could also listen to the sheriff's department communications as they dealt with the normal weekend problems on the road. Without TV and with the same five people in the same house from November to May, every bit of entertainment was appreciated.

Harry Buckner, Stehekin postmaster and also proprietor of the general store, was our contact with the outside world. Harry, of course, didn't live at the store, so the radio communications were covered only perhaps eight hours each day in the summer and four to six hours Monday, Wednesday, and Friday in the winter. An alarm system was installed, so if we had an emergency we could activate the alarm if no one answered the radio. We counted on someone in Stehekin to hear the alarm that indicated an emergency at Holden. The system wasn't perfect but provided the best coverage we could arrange at the time.

With such a small group living in the village that first winter, there was very little disturbance of the surrounding snow, with the exception of a snowshoe path to the hydro and a path less traveled to the dinning hall for food supplies. By March, the sun had risen above Buckskin Mountain, therefore shining all the way to the valley floor. The beauty of the winter scene was much better than any fantasy or imaginative painting. Early one afternoon I heard a helicopter, went out, and watched it head toward Lyman Lake which was approximately eleven miles west of Holden and the location of an annual snow depth survey. It was flying at about four thousand feet. I got the idea that it would be great to have the pilot stop in for coffee on his return trip. It would be helpful to have someone join us with a few new stories. After four months together without radio, TV, or newspapers, the conversations can become routine and less frequent.

We made our way to the dining hall and got a couple of institutional-size packages of cherry JELL-O. We wrote "coffee" with it in very large red letters on the ground, which showed up well against the pure white snow. We waited for the helicopter knowing that it would likely return within an hour. It flew back over the village, and we were afraid that he was going to continue on downvalley. All of a sudden, the helicopter made a turn and began its descent, landing in the open area to the east of the school house, directly over the "coffee" sign. We didn't have a lot of company that winter, so it was exciting to have the pilot literally drop in for coffee and stimulate new conversation.

During the shortest days of winter, it was dark by four thirty in the afternoon. The winter nights were beautiful and generally peaceful, but for me the anxiety of how to deal with an emergency was always in the back of my mind. Being isolated by a forty-mile boat trip, depending on snow vehicles to reach the lake, and depending on someone in Stehekin to hear the emergency alarm at night didn't provide a reliable emergency plan. If a message could reach the sheriff's office in Wenatchee, they would send a helicopter, but nighttime trips in the mountains with frequent snow storms minimized those chances.

Terry Sateren was one of the members of that initial winter community. He first visited Holden in 1963 and again in 1964 with a theater group from Augsburg College in Minneapolis. He later returned as a volunteer. He spent many summers and a few winters in the village. Terry found a real home at Holden. He was so talented Holden could have used him forever. We finally encouraged him to move on, though, because Holden couldn't really offer him a future. Terry would have been welcome to stay, but he also understood that there was more to life than Holden Village. He was multitalented, not necessarily by training but rather with natural intelligence. There was hardly a job that he couldn't do or at least figure out. He became the lineman for the electrical distribution system and also provided daily operational work with the hydro. Terry was also an artist and initiated art-welding activities. He created the *Dancing Servant* sculpture that became a symbol for Holden. He had grown up in an artistic family. His father was Leland Sateren, long time chair of the music department at Augsburg College as well as the director of the Augsburg Choir.

Since it was our first winter, we didn't know if we could count on food delivery. We decided to store a winter supply of eggs, potatoes, and meat. We planned on powdered milk and didn't anticipate receiving any fresh vegetables unless someone from the winter community made a trip downlake or an occasional guest, aware of our plight, arrived with fresh lettuce. We discovered later that it was a simple matter of sending a shopping list down on the boat, and they would deliver the request to one of the two Chelan grocery stores. We could have had fresh milk and fresh salad ingredients throughout the winter. The first winter was definitely a learning experience.

Before Carroll left the village in the fall of 1966, he sat me down and outlined some suggestions about living together in a small group in an isolated situation. The main point of advice was his request that each Friday afternoon, the three or four, or five, of us should sit down as a group and basically have a time of sharing. You need to keep in mind that the three, four, or five of us ate three meals a day together, did the cooking and dishwashing together, and then sat together in the living room in the evening, reading by the fireplace. We followed Carroll's advice the first week and met together on Friday afternoon. We looked at each other, and no one had anything to say. Carroll's suggestion to keep the lines of communications open was valid, but we were sharing and conversing much of each day. At this point I don't recall any conflicts within the small community.

Even after the population during the fall, winter, and spring increased, with more programming offered, life in the community was much different from June through August than September through May. It was really two different communities. The frequency of the passenger ferry and the mail delivery and pickup at Lucerne was reduced to three days each week.. The boat schedule in many ways dictated life in the village.

During the fall seasons of 1966 and 1967 there were few staff and only an occasional guest. We did however have hunters come through for the "high hunt." The entire Railroad Creek Valley was listed in the high hunt, but we seldom saw deer except around Holden Lake or higher elevation areas. Since hunters were dependent on our bus transportation and the boat transportation, there was always a problem keeping their game cooled. We made a deal with them. They exchanged fresh venison liver for the privilege of hanging their cleaned venison carcasses in our walk-in coolers. They were generally glad to leave the venison liver with us so we enjoyed numerous meals with fresh liver each fall.

For some reason, Wes was always the one to fry the liver. He never did any of the cooking except venison liver, which was his specialty. The other wild meat we ate was bear and, on one occasion, beaver. Joe Walmer, our mechanic and maintenance specialist for several years, was a hunter. A two-hundred-pound bear lasted a long time for the small community. The bear in the valley had an excellent taste. Most of the bears' food came from berries, bugs, and honey, but not fish.

The most unusual wild meat we tried was a hindquarter of beaver, a gift from Gordon, who had trapped beaver at Domke Lake. He was authorized to trap a certain number of beaver each year to help control the population that was gradually damming the outlet of the lake and increasing the lake level. A higher lake level would negatively impact the natural spawning of trout. We had an Alaska cookbook that fortunately had a section on cooking beaver. The hindquarter was boiled for four to five hours and then roasted for another couple of hours. It was OK. It tasted like beef heart, but I couldn't get over the mental aspects of eating beaver. Boiling beaver meat for several hours didn't create a pleasant aroma. We were grateful to Gordon for thinking of us, but we didn't ask to be put on his list for future gifts of beaver.

We soon moved winter activities to Koinonia, which provided more guest housing and a small kitchen. The area around the fireplace became the dining room, with folding tables set up for each meal. It wasn't convenient, but it worked. Koinonia was heated with wood, and volunteers rotated duties to keep the furnace stoked. We also added a second Swedish Snow Trac to accommodate increased guest and staff traffic. We considered purchasing a used heavy-duty snowblower to keep the road open, but the initial cost and the cost of maintaining the equipment wasn't feasible. A snowblower would work only if the village had a dozer to help remove snowslides. The two Snow Tracs, with the later additions of two Canadian Bombardier twelve-passenger snow taxis, provided the winter transportation, at least through 1983.

Since the valley floor was without sunshine from mid-October until mid-February because of Buckskin Mountain and the low angle of the sun it became easy to understand how some civilizations worshiped the sun. We couldn't wait each spring for the sun to shine in the valley and designated February 14 as Sun Over Buckskin Day. February 14 also coincided with Hortie and Mary Christman's wedding anniversary, so it was declared an annual Holden holiday. Most of the February 14s I remember gave us clear skies and bright sun. Some years it was sufficiently warm to have barbecues and outdoor picnics. The Holden community was always up to celebrating another holiday.

As the size of the winter community grew, so did our attempt to have at least limited programming. Worship was a daily discipline. I would preach and serve communion if no pastor was available. Dr. Clarence Solberg was bishop of the North Pacific District of the American Lutheran Church. He was aware that I, not an ordained pastor, was serving communion. During one summer visit, Dr. Solberg had a conversation with Carroll and mentioned that he was concerned that I was offering communion without proper authorization. Carroll didn't argue with him, and Dr. Solberg didn't request that anything be changed. For me this was an example of how the church organization needed to do its thing. Dr. Solberg apparently understood that perhaps the rule should be reconsidered in this unusual circumstance.

We used recorded tapes from the summer for some winter program opportunities. We also started to have movie nights and rented 16-mm films to show about once each month. We rented some of the films but also discovered that the public library had free films. Before moving to Holden, I had lived in Seattle and enjoyed attending the compline service at St. Mark's Episcopal Cathedral. The compline service is traditionally the final church service of the day in the Christian tradition of canonical hours and occurred at nine o'clock each Sunday night at St. Marks Cathederal. During the winter it was known as the "skiers' service." Many young adults would ski during the day and attend compline at night. KING-FM also broadcast the service. We couldn't pick up the direct broadcast at Holden, but I wrote to KING Broadcasting and asked if they could send us a tape each week. They agreed to do this, and for at least one winter we enjoyed weekly recordings of the St. Mark's compline service. KING Broadcasting did request that we provide the blank cassette tapes, which I thought was a bit too frugal on their part. In 1993, I began working with Harriet Bullitt, former owner of KING Broadcasting, and I was tempted to tease her about KING's frugality.

The winter at Holden was often magical in terms of scenery and recreation. However, an isolated community is more than scenery and recreation. I had a genuine concern with the winter community, especially in the early years. The winter community was rather stable with minimum numbers of new arrivals. Confining people who had perhaps been raised in conservative religious families could potentially develop into a community with tunnel vision and limited desire to consider new approaches to life and spirituality. The conversation could be manipulated by one or two people expressing strong opinions, especially when dealing with controversial subjects. It's what I referred to as informational incest.

In every winter community, there would be identifiable leaders of the community thought process, whether it related to worship, social issues, or world concerns. Without much input in terms of radio or TV, it was easy and even dangerous to allow thinking in the community to be focused in only one direction without new thoughts and concepts generated by outside influence. As the winter community grew and when sabbatical teachers were present, the dangers were minimized, and it was great to have a wide variety of thoughts to stimulate the community discussion.

One December morning, with fresh snow on the ground, someone ran into the dinning hall to report seeing Sasquatch footprints. Everyone headed out to inspect these large footprints up around the hospital. The community was abuzz with doubt, speculation, and excitement. Later that morning someone in the woodshop discovered plywood cutouts of large feet. We didn't know who was involved. I announced at the noon meal that I had placed a radio call to the Northwest Sasquatch Information Clearing house. They would be sending someone to the village to inspect and document our discovery. One of the youth in the village claimed he found Sasquatch hair in one of the footprints. The announcement of someone coming to verify the discovery was sufficient for Dale, our mechanic, to sheepishly admit that he had devised the prank. I hadn't actually contacted anyone, but it helped uncover the clever prankster. This event illustrated the community's delight in creating its own events to bring energy and imagination for all to enjoy.

I've mentioned my interest in the TV program *Northern Exposure*. The Holden Sasquatch event could have easily been incorporated into that series. Without TV and only limited movies and radio, the community literally needed to initiate its own events to stimulate creative juices for mental health and conversation. The Sasquatch event dominated conversation in the village for a few days.

Not everything conducive to creating community was a result of advanced planning. In fact, many of the fun and exciting experiences weren't planned. In May 1971, Gene Starcher made arrangements to live in the old schoolhouse at Lucerne originally used when miners and families were also living at Lucerne. Gene was fabricating jewelry that his business partner, April Jorgensen, designed. We got well acquainted with Gene and would invite him to the village for visits and to do his laundry. In January 1973, he sent word that his electrical generator had died and asked about setting up shop at Holden. Gene was a very talented individual, not only producing quality jewelry but with anything mechanical or electrical. He was a delight to have in the community. He brought a new perspective and was an example of the importance of diversity of thought for everyone to maintain positive mental health. He was one of the individuals who provided some checks and balances to thinking and conversation. He continued to live at Holden until September 1973. He later established his successful jewelry business, Goldsmith Lucerne, in Chelan.

I'm also thankful to Gene for the gift of a bit of uplake "history," a rocking chair that he had obtained—I think legally—from the old Moore Point Resort site. A portion of the Moore Point Resort complex burned sometime in the late 1950s. According to stories I heard, it had been the most successful of the uplake resorts. Dinty Bigger was originally one of the owners then served as caretaker of the remaining facility, continuing to live at Moore Point into the 1980s. He maintained the facility's hydro plant, running it on waterpower from Fish Creek.

During the summer, Dinty kept the swimming pool operating and heated. I think it was 1966 that I took a few staff over to Moore Point to swim in the pool, located right on the shore of Lake Chelan. Moore Point had a most amazing setting for a pool. The Health Department eventually ordered the pool closed, because it wasn't being maintained as required. The forest service purchased the property and removed the remaining buildings, pool, and hydro plant, converting the site into picnic and camping spaces. After the forest service purchased the property, people having access to it by private boat removed some of the remaining relics. I think this is how my rocking chair changed ownership.

One Christmas we were preparing for the arrival of thirty guests. Four days prior to their arrival, the main waterline froze. Water stopped running in early evening. Most of the waterline was underground. We had installed a two-inch bypass line from the hydro penstock to the village waterline via a fire hydrant on the lower mine level. Unfortunately, part of that line was exposed. I remembered Hortie telling me that when galvanized pipe freezes, it's most likely to initially freeze at a fitting such as an elbow. I can't remember if we didn't have a designated plumber at that time or if I didn't want to ask a volunteer to sit outside in fifteen-degree temperatures, trying to thaw a pipe at an unknown location. I got the propane torch and headed to the lower mine level. A two-inch galvanized pipe with water in it is very, very difficult to warm with a handheld propane torch. I sat in the snow for an extended period of time and was ready to give up and perhaps even evacuate the village when I finally heard the water break through, and water began flowing into the village.

During another winter, the hydro went off-line. Every time we activated the breaker, the power kicked off. We couldn't find the problem. I sent a message to the Chelan County PUD in Wenatchee asking for help. They immediately flew a lineman uplake. We picked him up at Lucerne. Once he was in the village, it took him only about thirty minutes to find an insulator on a cross arm that had cracked. The power line was shorting to ground.

The PUD didn't charge for sending help to Holden and on numerous occasions helped the village. I would write to the PUD with questions or would visit with them in Wenatchee. We also purchased surplus transformers and other line supplies from the PUD. They were updating their transmission system, and many of the items they were removing were what we were still using at Holden. They were always generous with suggestions and even some engineering work. Since Holden wasn't on the PUD system, they had no responsibility or obligation to assist us. Holden was the only electrical system in Chelan County not connected to the Chelan County PUD system.

One winter the community tried a Solitude Day. It was, of course, on a nonboat day. Nothing was planned during the day. The kitchen would put out do-it-yourself eating options. The idea was that even conversation in public would be minimized or eliminated. Solitude Day would end with vespers. I was never convinced that this was beneficial. When I was working I felt more comfortable in my office with unlimited activities staring me in the face. Facing solitude was uncomfortable since for me, Solitude Day broke my comfortable routine. However, most in the community appreciated Solitude Day.

Community meetings were sometimes a challenge in terms of accomplishing an end result. After John and Mary Schramm arrived as directors, they instituted the concept of greater involvement by the entire community in decision-making. Decision by consensus was becoming more avant-garde. Theoretically it was a great concept. In a practical sense, in my opinion, it had flaws. A few of the famously long community meetings became legendary. Potato Day was the subject of one meeting. Potato Day was originally initiated to allow all members of the community to make a contribution to Hospitality House in Wenatchee. Most people were on a volunteer basis. When an offering was taken at church, many volunteer community participants didn't have money to share. We came up with the idea of serving only potatoes one noon a week, and the money saved with that meal was given to Hospitality House. We were able to arrange a gift of free potatoes for the winter from one of the farmers in eastern Washington. The use of the free potatoes resulted in a lunch that had practically no direct cost to Holden.

The Potato Day discussion was multifaceted. Should potato day only serve potatoes? Should we allow butter with the potatoes? If not butter, then what about salt and pepper? Should we make guests coming into the village participate? The discussions went on and on. One of the community meeting discussions went until eleven at night and was then adjourned until the next night, when it was resumed. This definitely set a record for the length of a community meeting. Even though the discussions seemed endless, it did allow everyone to participate in the decision-making process. Some of the frustrations that surfaced in these discussions were often a cover for some other feelings that were more difficult to express. To this day, I still question the positive impact of the consensus approach.

Wintertime made it possible to enjoy wonderful winter recreation activities. During the mine operation, the Winston community had set up a rope tow above and to the west of the home site. It was my understanding that Jim Sullivan, a mine worker, had been responsible for organizing the ski operation. Jim later became manager of the Stevens Pass ski area not far from Holden Village as the crow flies. We were also interested in a rope tow. I read the Snoqualmie Pass ski area, approximately fifty miles from Seattle. was replacing one of their tows. Webb Moffett was owner of the Snoqualmie operation. I contacted him to see if he would consider donating the rope tow to Holden Village. He invited me to meet him at Snoqualmie Pass to discuss the possibility. It turned out that the tow used a 440-volt motor, which wasn't compatible with our electrical system without some major costs.

Snowshoeing was one of the first forms of transportation and for some a recreational enjoyment. Cross-country skiing was unlimited. One of the first winters, someone donated a four-person toboggan. We established a track down Chalet Hill but found that a toboggan was too dangerous. It was retired after a not-too-serious accident. Inner tubes were ideal and relatively safe. It was a great recreation for children as well as adults. When the snow conditions were ideal, we added banked curves to the slide for an extra thrill.

Our average snowfall was 320 inches a year. The most we recorded was 585 inches. On occasion we would receive a snowfall of up to four inches per hour. The heaviest snowfall at Holden was during the mining days, around 1956, and measured approximately 620 inches. Pictures of Holden with people walking out of second floor windows appeared in *Life* magazine.

The weather could change quickly. Occasionally we would have a Chinook wind, a meteorological phenomenon bringing strong winds and warm temperatures to mountain valleys. Temperatures would rise to fifty degrees in January. One time when we were enjoying a Chinook with fifty degree temperatures, I called Stehekin and indicated the nice spring weather we were enjoying. Their temperatures hadn't been above twenty degrees while we had fifty degrees. The most dangerous time for avalanches was when rain followed a heavy snowfall.

I read some material on avalanches to try and learn a little about their origins and the nature of avalanche conditions. I knew that we were in a dangerous valley, and I also knew that I didn't have sufficient knowledge to help others in the winter community know the potential dangers involved. I wrote to the forest service district ranger to ask if they could provide some educational tools. As a result of this contact, I was invited to attend the first forest service National Avalanche training school held at Crystal Mountain. I had a pair of downhill skis but had used them only once on Stevens Pass and felt fortunate to have survived. Some skiing was going to occur during the avalanche training so I notified the forest service that I would like to attend but that I wasn't an experienced skier. They assured me that some others attending were also inexperienced.

The first day of instruction in the lodge was all bookwork and discussions. I met Ed LaChapelle, University of Washington expert on glaciers, who also provided training on the chemistry and physics of snow and avalanche safety. Several years later, Ed was invited to be on the Holden Village faculty. Later, his son Randy joined the volunteer staff, got involved with art welding, and went on to become an accomplished artist.

The second day of the training would be in the backcountry. We were transported by the ski lift to the top of the mountain and then walked on skis into an area off limits to even expert skiers. That gave me some concern. The first event was using live explosive charges to dislodge loose snow. We all wore avalanche cords. Each of us would have a chance to ignite and throw a live explosive charge. The student next to me ignited his charge and began throwing the charge, but the burning fuse caught in his avalanche cord. The wicks were thirty-second wicks. The instructor calmly took his knife, cut the cord, and threw the charge. I don't even recall if I went through the process. We did several other training exercises and then were told we would return to the lodge. We would, of course, be skiing down a part of Crystal Mountain that was off-limits even to the experts. I had some concern. Obviously I made it, and that is all I'm gong to say. I attended a second avalanche school in Reno, Nevada, but elected not to participate in the mountain portion of the training.

One of the main training tools we used at Holden for several winters was a 16-mm, one-hour movie made by the BBC and filmed mostly in Switzerland. It did a good job of creating an element of fear that can be effective. Most of the people at Holden during the winter respected traffic on the city streets but had literally no knowledge about the dangers of avalanches. The English narrator in his deep voice kept repeating, "Those who live in the shadow of a mountain will one day die in the shadow of the mountain."

A series of avalanche paths existed between Holden and Five-Mile Creek. Depending on the temperatures and moisture conditions, snowslides would occur, cutting off road access. Usually there would be only one and possibly two slides at any one time. There was never any warning until making the trip to or from Lucerne. Missing a boat day wasn't unusual. One year the conditions were ideal for snowslides. The Holden community was isolated for seven days. We sent word via the radio that we were OK but not able to reach Lucerne. Holden in those early years didn't attempt to keep the roads open during the winter. We had two six-passenger Snow Tracs and also two of the twelve-passenger Bombardiers. When a snowslide occurred, our only option was to ramp the snow on either side of the slide and flatten the top so the snow vehicles could go over the slide. We did all of this work with shovels and human muscle.

In the early days of the winter operation, we parked one of our old buses at Lucerne. We put a wood stove in the bus and had some emergency supplies, such as blankets and food, in case the transports weren't able to meet the boat because of avalanches. John, Karen, and Kevin Rieke ended up sleeping in the bus one night and then ended up taking the boat back downlake the next day. That winter of 1970–1971 proved to be the most difficult. It was mid-January, and we had had significant snowfalls in the preceding weeks. It warmed slightly and began to rain. We measured about seven inches of rain over a several-day period. Every avalanche chute seemed to clear itself.

Fortunately we had a group of twenty students from St. Olaf College during the month of January for their break between first and second semesters. As soon as we were aware of the avalanches, we sent staff and guests down the road to begin shoveling slides. We had no heavy equipment at the time. The only option was to dig by hand. After several hours, the group came back and indicated that they had shoveled over one slide but then came upon another. They needed reinforcements.

It was a full seven days before we reached Lucerne and could resume normal transportation of passengers and freight. There was no problem with running out of food. We had a food supply stored that could last for three to four weeks. We also had radio contact with Stehekin, so they knew we were OK but that we wouldn't be able meet the boat. That seven-day period was the longest that Holden was cut off from the outside world since the mining company had built the road and begun the year-round operation. An experience such as this created more anxiety for some, but overall people felt safe, well cared for, and comfortable. The situation was, of course, the subject of ongoing conversations and topics for matins and vespers during the week.

Fritz Norstad won the award for the most innovative experience while being stranded by a snowslide on the road. Fritz was returning to Holden with ten other passengers when they were stranded on the return trip from Lucerne. The snowslide was located around Six Mile Creek, approximately four miles from Holden and had occurred following the trip to Lucerne earlier in the morning. Without communications there was no way to call for help. The driver started walking up to the village. Fritz was the type of person who, if at all possible, would make a celebration out of a potentially negative experience. Knowing that they might be stranded for two or three hours, Fritz retrieved a chafing dish from his luggage. He had just purchased it as a gift for his wife, Gertrude. The freight also included a shipment of eggs and other food items. With the Sterno-powered chafing dish, he whipped up scrambled eggs and used a few other food options to serve a delightful lunch for the stranded group. It was a sunny day, and when rescuers arrived to help shovel the snowslide, the stranded group was almost disappointed that their experience was coming to a conclusion. Only Fritz could initiate this type of experience.

In the winter, I made occasional trips downlake for business or meetings, or we as a family made trips for medical appointments or shopping. We most frequently stayed at Scotty's Motel in Wenatchee. Hank and Christine Thor owned and operated Scotty's and were great friends to Holden travelers, always the ultimate hosts for our times away from home. I greatly admired Hank since he was a glider pilot and actually had a design patent on a glider that is still being built. Having helpful friends while we were downlake was important. Being away from home always presented some challenges. Hank and Christine were always willing to help in any way possible. Scotty's Motel still exists but under different ownership and with a different name. Christine died some years ago, and Hank now lives in Leavenworth.

The Chelan County PUD had authorization to conduct a snow survey each winter at Cloudy Pass. For years Ray Courtney conducted the survey via snowshoe with the data used to determine probable water volume that would be filling Lake Chelan. The PUD had a license to control the level of Lake Chelan for power production. I think the PUD was interested in eliminating the snowshoe trips into Cloudy Pass and set up electronic measuring and transmitting devices, but this was problematic due to the wilderness area designation. The forest service agreed to conduct an avalanche survey of Railroad Creek Valley, which concluded that the entire valley was basically a series of avalanche chutes.

As a result of this study, the forest service agreed to discontinue the human-conducted annual snow survey at Lyman Lake and allow installation of electronic equipment that would transmit the data by satellite to a receiving station in Montana. The agreement also allowed the PUD to do a series of manual survey trips via helicopter. Because the snowshoe survey trips were discontinued, the forest service required the PUD to remove the log cabin at Lyman Lake that had been used for the winter snow surveys but also important to hikers for winter excursions. I've been told that the logbook containing the names of visitors to the cabin was placed in the archives at the University of Washington.

I made two snowshoe trips to Lyman Lake before the cabin was removed. The first trip was in January of 1965. I was invited to join two members of the Portland, Oregon, Sierra Club. We snowshoed from Lucerne to Holden the first day and the next day traveled from Holden to Lyman Lake. The Lyman Lake log cabin was tall, with a high-pitched roof. A pole was attached to the peak of the roof with a shovel wired to the pole. The roof of the cabin was visible as a bump in the snow. We took the shovel and shoveled down to the door, then shoveled a part of the roof to connect the stovepipe so we could light a fire in the wood stove.

We spent three days snowshoeing around Lyman Lake, over Lyman Glacier to Phelps Pass, and up to Cloudy Pass. We had clear, blue sky the entire trip. The cabin was comfortable. When the temperatures in the cabin reached forty to fifty degrees, the mice woke up and enjoyed running all over everything. It's estimated that the mice population in the area decreased after the cabin was removed. The Lyman Glacier has all but disappeared.

Almost every year, the Holden board would want to review the winter activity to see if we were justified in staying open. The winter operation was expensive to maintain. In the early years of operation we were approached by a group in Hawaii suggesting we take over the operation of their retreat center. The idea involved operating Holden from May through October each year, closing down the Holden facility, and then going to Hawaii and operating that retreat November through April. It definitely had some appeal, but the idea never materialized. I finally prepared a report for the board indicating that keeping Holden open in the winter was the most efficient.

We could maintain a more stable staff and also have time in the winter to do maintenance and facility improvement not possible when the village was full in the summer. Financially it made sense, even though the winter operation wasn't likely to generate sufficient guest revenue to cover expenses. The board finally agreed that a year-round operation would become permanent as long as we could offer a program to the winter community.

CHAPTER 9

The Experience of Living at Holden Village

HOLDEN VILLAGE WASN'T THE FIRST small community I enjoyed. DeWitt, Nebraska, where I grew up, was slightly larger than Holden in the summer but was still small in population and somewhat isolated in the farm fields south of Lincoln. My graduating class totaled seventeen. Out of necessity I had experience with band, chorus, and drama and lettered in three sports all four years. Growing up as the son of a pastor, I had some knowledge and experience understanding pastors and attending church meetings—mostly without having had a choice. Missionaries stayed in our home for mission festivals, and church leaders would occasionally visit. I listened to many discussions concerning life and problems in the church and was acquainted with the blessings of a church community. I also observed the challenges and politics that are always present. Church-related work seems to be more about grace and forgiveness and less about saints.

I don't recall if my initial Holden experience, the weekend of September 30, 1961, was as a paying guest or if the village was opened without cost for those who registered for the dedication of the diesel-electric generators. I had no responsibilities that weekend and plenty of time to walk around and visit with the thirty guests. The short time we spent in the village was primarily looking around the mine, walking a short distance up the trail to Hart Lake, and exploring the village itself. It wasn't until I joined the volunteer staff in 1963 that I had the opportunity to experience Holden as a participant in the operational community.

As a volunteer the summer of 1963, I felt more like an observer than a shaper of the community. Because of the tensions at Holden during this summer, it may not have been a valid experience. Yet I later discovered that Holden was never free of tensions and struggles. Holden never has been nor ever will be a Shangri-La. Even the beauty of the valley was compromised by the mining operation—a good reminder that pure beauty rarely exists in nature or in humanity. We must keep in mind that if the Howe Sound Mining Company hadn't dug the heart out of Copper Mountain and spread eighty acres of tailings along the banks of beautiful Railroad Creek, Holden Village, as a retreat center, would never have existed. The transition away from the natural continues with the remediation work designed to reduce the pollution resulting from mining activity of more than sixty years ago.

Without a doubt, the people who formed the staff/faculty and those who arrived as paying guests together formed a special community, creating life-changing experiences. Some of these unique people were short-term visitors and others spent numerous years in the community. Many families made almost annual trips to Holden Village and became valuable members contributing to the health of the community as well as paying guests allowing Holden to continue its operation.

One of the special families that had a deep connection with Holden was Howard and Loretta Gylling and their children, Sandy and James. The Gyllings were instrumental in the life and work of Holden year-round, but perhaps their greatest impact on the village and its guests occurred during their winter visits. The Gyllings were also special personal friends of mine.

I first met Howard and Loretta in December of 1966. They were the first paying guests to register in the winter. Howard was a CPA in Seattle. He and Loretta belonged to Glendale Lutheran Church in Burien. My specific memory of their arrival was that Howard was a bit overdressed for the occasion. When serving in the military, Howard had been assigned to the Arctic temperature-testing facility. Upon arriving at Holden, he was wearing his cold-weather gear, which was designed for minus-fifty degrees. The day they arrived, we were having a winter heat wave with clear blue skies and forty-plus-degree temperatures.

Howard and Loretta were perhaps the most generous people I ever knew. Their life was devoted to helping others. At least until 1983, the Gyllings were the most generous financial contributors to Holden Village. Howard became the accountant for Holden and volunteered many hours of work in addition to being hired to do the annual village inventory and year-end accounting. Holden was dependent on gifts. For any large gifts to be possible, an annual audit was needed. This was difficult because of the very nature of the Holden operation, but Howard found a way to do a valid audit within those limitations.

Starting in 1968, Howard, Loretta, Sandy, and James started their tradition of celebrating their family Christmases with the Holden community. This tradition continued past my retirement in 1983. As a part of this tradition, Loretta baked special cookies and other treats to take to Holden each Christmas. These cookies and other bakery items were made with real butter, real cream, and real love. Each year, Loretta baked ten thousand cookies, five thousand candy treats, and seventy-five loaves of sweet cakes. This tradition lasted for nineteen years. These were gifts to the Holden community and were generally consumed during the weeks of the Christmas / New Year holidays. As you might guess, Loretta was lovingly known as the "cookie lady."

Even though Holden Village was very remote, Santa Claus arrived each Christmas. Howard Gylling disappeared on Christmas Eve, reappearing as Santa Claus to distribute gifts for the children. Many of these gifts Howard and Loretta brought to be shared with the children, including the boys in our group home who didn't have immediate family at Holden. Both of our children loved Howard, but when he appeared as Santa, Kristy was petrified. It was impossible to get a picture of Kristy sitting on Santa's lap. In fact, when Kristy began to hear the bells on the Santa suit, she would run into the Koinonia library and hide. I just found out that one of Kristy's daughters also had a fear of Santa. Possibly, Santa anxiety is hereditary.

Karen Strom was one of the great gifts to Holden. She was initially introduced to Holden through the Young Adult Stehekin program, making the trip with a group from Minneapolis. Even though I didn't consider the Young Adult Stehekin program a success, I was forever grateful that this program introduced Karen to Holden Village. Her father was in the diplomatic service, and she had grown up around the world. She graduated from Luther College and did graduate work at the University of Minnesota. Karen had a brilliant mind and was a great problem solver. She was the Holden registrar for ten years and brought professionalism and efficiency to this critical area. Unfortunately, during the years Karen worked in the village, Holden was in the precomputer era. My estimate is that she played and won more Scrabble games at Holden than any other person in the history of Holden Village.

Karen was an important member of the Holden community in so many ways. Her intellect and her openness to all involved helped create the community that brought guests back year after year. She was important as a registrar, but perhaps even more so as a community member with all of her other gifts. She became the Holden astronomer, taking groups out many evenings to share information about the stars and planets visible in the exceptional night skies. Holden offered an unusual location for observing the night sky since there were limited exterior lights around the village, providing conditions ideal for observation. Northern lights didn't occur frequently, but one fall we enjoyed a most spectacular display, with multiple-color lights dancing at least 180 degrees around the sky. Since northern lights were seldom seen at Holden, that unique display created an experience of mild fear for me personally over this unusual display, even as I celebrated the spectacular beauty.

When Karen retired from Holden, she purchased a home in Leavenworth and immediately found a job with a company in East Wenatchee that utilized her analytical mind and computer skills.

Dorothy Caro, a retired jewel of a person from Spokane, was in her sixties when she first came to Holden. She returned year after year to help with some of the tedious work involved in sending out mailings, which was our main source of gifts. Dorothy loved everyone, and everyone loved Dorothy. She enjoyed the Holden community, and I think Holden provided something very special for her, as she lived alone when not at Holden. She represented many of the retired volunteers who did the work that young adults thought uninteresting and boring. The first twenty-plus years for Holden were precomputer years. Dorothy did some of the critical work that is now done by pressing "enter" on a keyboard. She was invaluable in launching the Holden Village healing community.

Mechanics were always a special gift to the life and well-being of the Holden community. All skills were vital to the operation, but maintaining transportation was a community safety as well as operational necessity. During my tenure, we operated primarily with used equipment. Some buses were fifteen-to-twenty years old. We purchased our initial snow vehicles new. In addition to our two Swedish Snow Tracs, a new Thiokol Spryte served both as a work and transportation vehicle. The last snow vehicles we purchased were the two used twelve-passenger Bombardier B-12 snow buses. During one of the early winters of operation we were down to one Snow Trac, and that unit wasn't starting. We didn't have a full-time mechanic at the time, but one of our retired volunteers, a backyard mechanic, was willing to take a look. The Snow Trac had a simple Volkswagen engine. The volunteer did an inspection and discovered the rotor in the distributor had cracked. There was no chance to order a new rotor, but we did have super glue. Within an hour, the Snow Trac was running, and we ordered a new rotor by mail. Fortunately, the repaired rotor lasted until the new one arrived.

All of the mechanics were miracle workers. Don Wagner wasn't only our full-time mechanic but also an inventor and innovator. He was a great worker and would do anything for Holden and the community even though at times he appeared a bit grumpy. He was an example of someone who didn't feel comfortable with all of the Holden Village expressed theology, but he was a great community member. Don loved to create something new from the old and discarded. Because the mine scrap was literally worth its weight in gold, Holden Village was an ideal location for his creativity. We had been splitting our firewood by hand when Don decided that a hydraulic wood splitter would bring more delight to the process. I think one of his hydraulic wood splitters is still in operation. He also fabricated wood stoves and even a rotating-tub compost system. It was dangerous for me to begin a conversation with the words, "Do you think it would be possible to..."

A Don Wagner creation even more significant than the hydraulic wood splitter came to be known as the Holden Embrace. Wally Johnson was one of our great volunteers from the ranks of the retired. He and his wife had been volunteering for several summers when one summer the effects of Amyotrophic Lateral Sclerosis (Lou Gehrig's disease) began taking their toll on Wally. ALS impacted Wally's shoulders, and Don began imagining a brace that could take the weight off Wally's shoulders and eliminate some of his pain. The Holden Embrace was born. The Holden Embrace was, I'm sure, the only medical device ever conceived and fabricated in the Holden Village maintenance garage. Several women on the volunteer staff made Velcro cuffs to allow stability and ease of application. The Holden Embrace gave Wally perhaps a year or more of enjoyable life.

The Johnson family, with the approval of Don, patented the Embrace, with proceeds to go to ALS research. I never did hear if the Holden Embrace was ever manufactured, but the important point was that Wally experienced the joy of life made possible through the compassion and ingenuity of the Holden Village staff.

The miracle of Holden Village allowed items such as the Holden Embrace to be created without seeking authority or committees discussing implications of liability issues or worrying about time spent on non-Holden work. Musical instruments were often fabricated, or furniture made, or poems written, or pictures painted through the freedom and innovation so prevalent in the Holden community. The use of materials was seldom a concern since Holden Mine had left a junkyard, we cut our own lumber, and lots of "stuff" was around, just waiting to be reinvented.

We seldom advertised for volunteers with specific skills. When people arrived in the village and mentioned they had technical skills, word quickly got to me. On occasion, a pastor would write and indicate that a certain person might be helpful to Holden. Ben Matter was an electrician with the Seattle public school system. He and his family were representative of the many great people who made themselves available for a week or more over many years. The Matters also illustrated that helping Holden went from one generation to the next. Joel, Ben's son, joined the volunteer staff and shared his skill with computers. Once we became acquainted with these people, we kept a list of specialists we could call on short notice and would most generally respond without question.

Artists, craftspersons, and musicians also did much to create the Holden community. The exciting factor was that many people, whether staff or paying guests, discovered they could become potters, weavers, or poets without beginning at Learning 101.

During the summer of 1965, George Utech was Holden's poet in residence. George had written the text for several new hymns in the Lutheran Book of Worship. He also worked with Arnie Flatten on construction of the altar that has been a part of worship in the Village Center for almost fifty years. Arnie, art professor at St. Olaf College, was asked to design an altar that would generate the feel of the mine and valley. He spent time walking around the mine area, finding some railroad ties and the beams used to shore up the mine shaft. The remnants of the mine operation frequently became the source of materials for both construction and art projects.

Arnie and George designed and constructed the altar so the pieces fit together without the use of nails or other attachments. Because the altar was exceedingly heavy, it was placed on a raised, movable platform. It could to be moved to accommodate varying worship experiences as well as to allow the Village Center to be used for basketball and other recreation opportunities.

During my tenth year working as manager, Carroll and Mary arranged for me to receive a small, preliminary carving that Arnie designed for Lutheran Brotherhood when he was commissioned to do a ten-foot wall carving for the insurance company's headquarters lobby in Minneapolis. I gave the carving to Faith Lutheran Church in Leavenworth when we moved to Tucson in 2013.

During that summer, I talked to George about recording a series of sounds that were unique to Holden. We recorded the various sounds on a reel-to-reel recorder and then arranged to meet in the fall to edit a soundtrack for a $33^1/_3$-RPM record. I traveled to Lutsen, Minnesota, where George and his wife were living in a small rented home. During the week we spent together, we edited the soundtrack and wrote the script for what was then titled *The Sounds of Holden*. We produced the records and sold them in the Holden Village store; we also gave some to those who were supporting the village. *The Sounds of Holden* didn't make the "platinum" designation for sales, but it was a memorable project. The record was professionally narrated and had sounds of Beany playing the chimes, the dinner bell, *Beany Sings*, and excerpts from various lectures and sermons. There is at least one copy of the record in the museum. I still have a copy that our son digitized onto a CD. George completed his career as student chaplain at Texas Lutheran University.

Life at Holden was almost a make-believe existence. I considered it more of an experiment in socialism than the kind of life that we normally live. Everything was provided, including food, entertainment, care for the body, as well as care for the soul. I took the approach in my job as manager to maintain the operational aspects of Holden in a way that didn't dominate life in the village. I saw my responsibility as allowing the program and creative nature of the faculty and staff to dominate. This was possible only if everything allowing the village to operate and survive was basically hidden underneath all of the other activities, with people not aware of all the aspects needed for day-to-day existence. Stressing the operational aspects of community life would, in my estimation, decrease the freedom of staff and guests to offer and receive the maximum of learning and inspiration.

It all goes back to the tension between Carroll and Gil Berg—Holden existed for the program, not the facility operation. There is a definite advantage to consolidating community functions with the fewest number of people. Every time you add a department head, that person feels an obligation to make his or her area significant. Costs and complexities increase quickly.

We even minimized signage, attempting to make operational aspects invisible. We tried to minimize operational announcements at meals and posted announcements on the insides of doors of toilet stalls. Sitting on the toilet provides time to read announcements and perhaps even read them several times. This concept of minimizing the awareness of the operational activity didn't come through a formal discussion or decision, but rather an observation of how important the life and program of the community was as it related to the impact on all community members. The staff had no uniforms or identification. For many it was difficult to tell who was a guest, who was on the volunteer staff, or who was in the community as faculty.

It was great to see that many guests or faculty liked to participate in some of the manual labor involved with the operational activities. The Holden community seemed more alive when the complexities of the operation weren't made an observable part of community life. I recall becoming upset with a particular fire chief who wanted to create realism during fire drills by using real smoke. I finally told him that he would be the best fire chief if the guests in the village weren't aware of how seriously we took our firefighting preparations.

The Holden Village community began life as a mirror image of what existed in Lutheran Church demographically. Holden was open and inviting to all, and once a person stepped onto the Lucerne dock, everyone was basically an equal. Holden received all manner of professional people, bishops, senators, former governors, legislators, wealthy entrepreneurs, university professors, noted authors, famous musicians, and even one who scaled Mount Everest. I don't recall any of them receiving special attention or even inflated introductions. Holden had a quality that equalized all residents. If anyone was recognized and put on a pedestal, it was the one who could solve a problem with the hydro or perhaps the one who ordered a new flavor of ice cream for the snack bar.

Holden, from a societal consideration, in many ways more or less duplicated what one would experience in Wenatchee or Seattle or Minneapolis. Perhaps the main difference was that at Holden Village, worship was more of a spiritual experience than an organizational experience. Holden wasn't identified with a specific religious group but rather emphasized its openness to all people. I always identified Holden as a nonprofit corporation in Washington state that had close ties with but not ownership by the Lutheran Church. Faculty, staff, and those from the pews felt free to express thoughts or ask sensitive question that may not have been easily verbalized in Wenatchee, Seattle, or Minneapolis.

Holden owned property associated with the mine as a result of the gift from the Howe Sound Mining Company but the buildings gifted to Holden Village were located on land under a special use permit from the US Forest Service and therefore the forest service impacted the daily life and activities of the community. It was a somewhat strange relationship but one that benefited everyone involved. The forest service had the power of the government on its side, but we had the power of remoteness and willingness to deal with a facility on government property. Forest service officials knew it would be an expensive headache for them if we hadn't moved in to reinvent a mining town. We also proved that our operational interests in maintaining and improving the environment matched, or at times exceeded, the plan of the forest service for multi-ple-use of public lands.

Twice during the years I managed Holden, the Chelan Ranger District was closed as a result of extensive forest fires in the area. The first fire wasn't that close to Railroad Creek Valley. The decision to close the Wenatchee National Forest was based on a lack of manpower in case more fires were to ignite. The forest service allowed the guests who were in the village to remain until their normal times to leave, but no new guests were allowed to enter. The closing was over Labor Day, which also coincided with the high hunt season for deer. The two closures of this part of the forest lasted less than two weeks. One of the registration staff went downlake and called those who were registered to inform them of the closure. Those who were on the road didn't get the message until they arrived in Chelan. It was definitely an inconvenience.

The second closure occurred just as Lutheran bishops from through-out the United States were arriving to honor Bishop Fred Schoitz upon his retirement. This closure was more problematic. It was 1970, and we were still working at getting information about the Holden ministry out to the entire church. Having all of the bishops enjoy the village would have been most helpful. I made a trip to Chelan to meet with the district ranger. The closure requirements were more stringent this time. Guests in the village would be required to leave, and no one would be allowed to go to the village. I negotiated (pleaded) with the district ranger, who finally allowed us to designate the bishops as staff. Staff members were allowed to stay to protect our property. I informed the bishops that they were considered Holden staff for the duration of their stay. The bishop from Ohio was upset with this arrangement. He stated it was dishonest and demanded that they have a recorded vote whether to stay or leave. Only one bishop voted to leave.

In 1977 I wrote a document titled "Proposal for Village Operation Under Wenatchee National Forest Closure" and submitted it to the forest service. The proposal outlined an operational plan that, under certain circumstances, would allow Holden Village to have guests stay through their registration periods and guests that had advanced registration enter Holden. The intent of this proposal was primarily for those circumstances where Holden Village wasn't in imminent danger. The proposal was accepted by the forest service but was never implemented during my remaining years at Holden.

From the start, the Holden facility was basically operational, with the exception of a source of electrical power. Activating the infrastructure included community involvement. Transportation between Lucerne and Holden, a viable food service, a reliable water source, as well as a way to deal with sewer and garbage, were the necessities. Other, less important, challenges but ones that were critical we dealt with as they surfaced. Whether it was new flavors of ice cream for the snack bar or specific books for the bookstore, guests and staff were very free to make suggestions. We had suggestions concerning new celebrations or games that children and adults could play.

One summer we had a suggestion box for ideas on how to deal with the tailings. One guest suggested that everyone leaving Holden take one gallon of tailings home with them. This suggestion was actually listed in one of the Holden newsletters. For two summers, numerous people did take tailings home with them. No one ever calculated how long it would take to remove the tailings by this method, but my estimation was that the next ice age would occur before the tailings would disappear.

Paul Fahning, whom I think was a Presbyterian, visited Holden frequently. He was a deep thinker. During one coffee break, he announced that Holden should make Golden Holden Sermon Timers, using tailings as the timing sand. This would help eliminate the tailings and would also provide a practical device to control the length of sermons. The timers, of course, would be designed to measure twenty minutes. That idea never reached the production stage.

Carroll was the one who requested adding a Jacuzzi therapy pool. Carroll and I had attended a meeting in Seattle and stayed at the Royal Inn, which had a large, indoor Jacuzzi. When we got back to the village, Carroll was convinced that Holden needed a Jacuzzi, and I started investigating the possibility. Therapy pools were just coming into popularity in the late 1960s. I visited Central Washington Water on my next trip to Wenatchee. They were listed as a Jacuzzi dealer, but I discovered they had no plans available for a therapy pool. They could sell us the jets, floor drains, pump, and heater, but it was up to us to do the design.

The next time I was in Seattle, I again stayed at the Royal Inn and visited the therapy pool. I measured the pool, including the height of the seats, by noting the level of the water on my body. The design of the Holden Jacuzzi was born. Fern Olson made some contacts with members of her Spokane congregation to request gifts for purchasing the equipment and doing the construction. Licensed electricians living close by, Ben and Claude Case, volunteered to do the electrical work on the project when the construction occurred. The motel in downtown Seattle is still in operation, but the last time I was in that location I noted the name was the Loyal Inn. It still has a therapy pool.

The first years I managed Holden were both meaningful and an exciting experience, but they also intensified my personal loneliness. I never found it easy to date. Although initially I was close to the age of many of the volunteers, it was uncomfortable attempting to develop a close relationship with those who I had selected to be on staff and then was directing in terms of daily work. And I never have been able to detect when a woman was interested in me. I did get well acquainted with one volunteer the summer of 1966. Judy Meek had been a student at Lutheran Bible Institute and earlier that spring had attended a presentation I made to encourage LBI students to consider volunteer opportunities at Holden. Judy joined the staff in June, and we were married on Labor Day. It's a very different and somewhat difficult experience dating within a small isolated community and also dating a volunteer who theoretically I supervised. Holden fortunately didn't have any rules covering office or village romances. Privacy was a challenge. We couldn't even go for a ride in a car and park in a secluded area. Following our honeymoon, we took up residence in Chalet 1 which then initiated the year around Holden Village operation.

The wedding was in the Village Center and, of course, everyone at Holden was invited. This wedding was the first wedding during the Holden Village era. The wedding was a part of the Sunday morning service with my father officiating. In the early years, the Sunday Eucharist was in the morning. It was later changed to evening so those arriving could begin the week with the Eucharist. It was interesting to see how many in the community became involved in helping with the decorations and wedding plans.

I wasn't looking forward to traveling by bus to Lucerne after the wedding dinner or riding down Lake Chelan on the *Lady of the Lake* as a newlywed. For a couple of years we had a very unreliable crank telephone in the village with a single wire strung on trees that went from Holden to Lucerne and continuing on to Chelan. I decided to try to make a call to see if I could charter Cascade Helicopter out of Cashmere to pick us up on the upper mine level after our wedding dinner and fly us to Twenty-Five Mile Creek where our car was parked. The phone line seldom worked. I had no idea if the arrangements had actually been made until I heard the helicopter approach the village. We were packed and ready to go, just in case. Bill Wells was the pilot. We would later become fellow members at Faith Lutheran Church in Leavenworth. We flew over the village on our way down the valley, and I threw the bride's bouquet out of the helicopter door. I don't recall if someone caught the bouquet or if it landed in a tree.

In the spring of 1967, I received notice from the Selective Service Department that I was to report for my physical prior to induction into the military. I had received a deferment when enrolled at Purdue University in the School of Aeronautical Engineering. I began employment with The Boeing Company in 1961 and again had a draft deferment since Boeing was considered a critical industry. My employment with Holden wasn't considered critical to the security of the United States and at twenty-seven, I was about to be drafted. I thought my employment with Holden might be short-lived.

I reported to the induction office on the waterfront in Seattle and discovered that there were a lot of others who had also been deferred for various reasons. All of us lined up in our undies for the required physical. Following the physical, we reported to a meeting room and were told to pack our bags and be ready to ship out in a few days. After being dismissed, I immediately walked to an air force recruiting office on Second Avenue and ask about enlisting. I assumed that with my engineering degree, I would have a chance to use my education. I was told that I was too old to enlist. That was the first time I had been told I was too old for anything—definitely a new phase in my life. I headed back to Holden and prepared to receive my draft notice. I never heard from them again, and I never inquired why I hadn't been selected. If the letter arrives at this point, I'll offer it to the Holden museum.

It is my feeling that of our twenty years together, Judy and I had seventeen or even eighteen years of wonderful married life (I can't speak for Judy), including conceiving our children at Holden and with much delight and thankfulness watching Kristy, born in 1970, and Jeffrey, born in 1973, spend their initial years of development within the Holden community. The last two or three years of our marriage didn't seem to work and led to a divorce in 1987. At Holden, I had managerial responsibilities 24-7 for twenty years. Judy, in some ways, matured into adulthood at Holden. She was nineteen when we became engaged and twenty when we married. I was twenty-seven. Living at Holden didn't allow Judy to finish her college degree. I have been asked if our marriage was dependent on our living within the Holden community. Did moving away from Holden in 1983 cause the breakdown of the relationship? I don't think so, but one never knows. Divorce is always a shared activity and occurs as a result of shared difficulties.

For me, being married was much more enjoyable than being single at Holden. Holden can be a lonely place, even with all of the people and all of the activities. Loneliness is more than being without a partner. Loneliness can be intensified at a place such as Holden. You are constantly observing others who appear to have direction in their lives and seem to develop relationships more easily. I felt that being the manager created a separation in terms of potential close friendships between the volunteer staff and me.

It was the old problem of being a boss or supervisor and trying to relate to the staff during periods of work as well as during the general life in the community. As manager, I dealt with operational challenges or statements from Carroll that could be upsetting. It was a blessing to have a family supporting me through the uncertainties, tensions, and disappointments involved with living and working in a rather tight and confined community.

It was a surreal experience for our daughter Kristy and son Jeff to grow up at Holden. They were both born in the Chelan hospital and arrived at Holden at ages seven days and six days old respectively. They both enjoyed and benefited from unlimited surrogate grandparents, brothers, and sisters. Child care was never a problem when Judy and I left the village for a couple of days. People were on a waiting list to stay in our chalet and take care of Kristy and Jeff. As our children became more independent, they became somewhat involved with the children's program. Since the children's program was designed for a weekly turn-over of participants, it tended to be repetitive. Our children usually didn't participate for more than a couple of weeks each summer. The exception was if something special was being planned, such as a party or a community celebration.

Jeff had a childhood paradise with unlimited opportunities for adventure. If he wasn't playing in the thousands of acres of forest behind the chalets, he might be at the vehicle shop observing Terry Sanderson, the mechanic, who always seemed to have something for him to take apart and reassemble. We, as parents, had rules; we realized that the surrounding area had lots of potential dangers for any and all children in the village. One day Jeff might be sitting on the D6 Caterpillar, pretending to rearrange the tailings, and another day sitting in the Bombardier snow vehicle, pretending to drive to Lucerne. When Jeff returned to the house with yellow powder on his clothes, we knew he had been exploring the tailings.

Kristy grew up relating to college-age young women rather than those her own age. Perhaps the greatest problem was the difficulty of developing long-term friendships with the frequent turnover of guests and staff. The one major exception for Kristy involved a very close friendship with Randine, the daughter of Brooks and Diane Andersen, who were at Holden for a family sabbatical. Kristy was approaching two years old while Randine was perhaps eleven. It was very touching for me to see the depth of their friendship. When Randine left with her family, I was amazed to observe Kristy's sadness based on the intensity of this friendship and the realization that even at this very early age, she could feel the depth of a friendship that was now ending. Her tears indicated how special this friendship had been. Randine shared with me many years later that she was so sad after leaving the Holden community and the special friendship with Kristy that she didn't eat for a week. This illustrated for me the problem of raising a family at Holden. With the frequent turnover of residents, relationships generally lasted weeks or months, not years. It was perhaps similar to military families moving from base to base, but at Holden, we stayed put while everyone else moved.

When Kristy and Jeff were sufficiently old enough to have personal interaction with others in the village, it was closer to a complete experience for me and not just based on my employment. It was more interesting to be identified as the father of Kristy or Jeff than being identified as the manager. As a family, we made it a point to eat the evening meal together with the community in the dinning hall. Kristy and Jeff frequently ate breakfast in our chalet. They most frequently ate the noon meal with their friends in the dining hall. On occasion, our family would eat a meal in our chalet, but probably ninety-nine percent of the time we were a part of the community. Attendance at vespers was a given and if we didn't see our children after dinner, we always saw them at vespers. Kristy and Jeff had a lot of freedom, and I never experienced anxiety over their enjoyment of this freedom. They generally knew where to find me. I didn't always know where to find them. I do believe that it was convenient and effective, raising children in an exciting and trusting community

I don't know if it really takes a community to raise a child. I can tell you that when children are raised in a community such as Holden Village, it can have a profound impact. There is no way to tell how Kristy and Jeff would have matured if we hadn't been at Holden for the early part of their lives, but I can tell you that both of our children did benefit a great deal by being raised at Holden. It's my conviction that Kristy and Jeff developed within a unique chance to observe life in a community. Children are more likely to learn from observation than from verbal instruction. Holden provided an unusual opportunity for our children to observe people relate to each other and value these relationships, especially as it related to cross-generational experiences. They observed people celebrate life through activities that were new each day. They observed people suffering the struggles of future decisions and often expressing their struggles through words during a matins service or through conversations with friends. They observed how people worked together to deal with emergencies. They observed adults crying, laughing, expressing anger, and offering and accepting forgiveness.

The greatest anxiety I experienced occurred during those early years as a parent was when our daughter Kristy, age two, had a high fever. This was, of course, during the night and, of course, in the winter. All of these conditions intensified the feeling of helplessness. If we were living anyplace else, we could have gone to an emergency room or called 911. At Holden we relied on our resident nurse to help us through the anxiety.

Kristy and Jeff also had a unique opportunity to observe their father at work, an experience not frequently possible for many children. None of these experiences of observation occurred via the television. They didn't watch a TV reality show but were living reality. The most frequent comment made by guests and staff concerned the sheltered life our children were experiencing. I was asked if I was going to sit down with Kristy and Jeff before we moved and inform them that life wasn't the same on the "outside," and that even though you could trust people at Holden you couldn't always trust people in "real life" situations. I struggled with this. I finally decided that I would rather have Kristy and Jeff celebrate life and trust people than perhaps withdraw and live in unreasonable fear because of lack of trust in the broader society.

Living in a community also meant many faculty, guest, and staff wanted to help raise our children. We got a lot of advice, most of it appreciated. There were those who were concerned about the isolation and the fact that TV or even radio weren't available. Others had honest concerns about the lack of medical services. We even had someone concerned that Kristy's rosy cheeks might be caused by chemicals and acid in the tailings. A frequently mentioned concern was the quality of education available at Holden. My opinion was that the education was superior to what might have been experienced in a "normal" system. It's true that our children were at times the only students in their particular classes, but one-on-one education can't be beat. Learning social skills came from living in a caring community. Paraprofessionals in the school most frequently had PhDs. Their only experiences might have been teaching at the university level, but they were great to assist and encourage. The entire Holden Village community was the classroom, not just the hours officially considered "school."

Children in the Holden school were involved with all ages and varied experiences. One day they might be planting seeds in the greenhouse, the next they might be in the kitchen helping to cook or bake. If the school was planning a drama production, it was truly a community involvement with schoolchildren as well as adults sharing the stage. They had great opportunities for field trips, which involved a boat ride and overnight stays. On one field trip, the students went to Seattle, stayed in a hotel, and visited the King Tut display in the Seattle Center in 1978. Another field trip was to Pullman, Washington, to observe an eclipse because the mountain valley was frequently cloudy. Ironically, it turned out to be cloudy in Pullman with clear skies at Holden.

The one concern I had, especially for Kristy, was her lack of opportunity to interact with girls or boys her own age. Many of her friends were college-age staff. Many of her conversations were with adults rather than her peers. Once we left Holden, during the first parent-teacher conference after Kristy was enrolled as a student at Cascade School District, I asked her teacher if she was respectful toward her teacher and other adults. I explained that she grew up with more adult interaction than with children. Her teacher said that Kristy was a delight to have in class. She asked good questions and wasn't satisfied until she received an answer.

Holden Village was a good educational experience for both Kristy and Jeff. Kristy completed school through the seventh grade and Jeff through the third grade before we moved to Leavenworth. Ultimately, Kristy graduated from Pacific Lutheran University with a teaching degree and continued on to receive her master's degree in elementary school counseling from St. Martin's University in Olympia, Washington. Kristy now teaches full time in Puyallup, Washington. Jeff graduated as valedictorian from Cascade High School and received a bachelor's degree in food science form Washington State University. As a student, Jeff worked in the cheese division of the WSU Creamery. Before graduating, he was the student supervisor with certification to make cheese, especially Cougar Gold, the cheese with a worldwide reputation. He later decided to pursue commercial flying and is now a pilot with Horizon Air.

Holden Village was also a place to be exposed to life and death. Fortunately no humans died at Holden during those years, but there were traumatic experiences when animals suffered and died, creating an emotional experience for children as well as adults. One summer a deer climbed the steps on the east end of the hospital, apparently to eat some plants in the flower box. Something startled the deer and it leaped down about ten feet from the small porch, breaking its back legs in the fall. It pulled itself into the brush behind Lodge 3 and bleated with pain. People began to walk over to observe. Adults and children shed tears. I called the fish and game department via the forest service, but they said that this was nature and nature will take its course. The vespers service was about to start, and we asked that everyone go down to vespers. Our mechanic was a hunter and had a gun. I asked him to assist the deer and relieve the pain of a slow death. The deer was disposed of before vespers concluded. Many prayers were offered for the deer, and many conversations occurred between parents and especially younger children.

One spring, Kristy and Jeff along with their friends Matt and Erik Fish discovered a bobcat under the porch of Chalet 14. It appeared to have just recently died, and they knew not to disturb it until we made contact with the forest service and game department. I bagged the carcass and put in the freezer until it could be transported downlake for analysis.

A small number of families, primarily associated with faculty positions, lived in the community for two or three months for numerous summers. Our own family lived at Holden Village perhaps longer than any other family, including most if not all of the families involved with the mine. The children of some of the faculty families literally grew up within the Holden community. Carroll and Mary and their children—Marin, Johan, Elise, Paul, Mary Alete, and Andy—were in the Holden community for various lengths of time during the years Carroll served as director. The two families who were the longest participants were Rudy and Doris Edmunds with their children—Diane, Jan, and Linda—along with Beany and Gertrude Lundholm and their children, Peter, Mark and Martha. Al and Jean Swihart and their daughter Bonnie were also in the village community for many summers. These children were in their early years of education when they first participated in the Holden community, and some were in college before their regular summer Holden experience ended. Their lives at Holden involved two or more months each year, and it's my impression that the Holden experience had a significant impact on their lives. Other faculty families who experienced Holden as family in the community included Paul and Julie Heyne and their children, Margot, Eric, Brian, Michelle, and Sarah; and Rich and Liz Caemmerer and their children, David, Kathy, Mike, and Matthew.

Holden Village was a new venture within the church, and I was always sensitive to any criticism of my involvement on the management team. Criticisms were rare, but I did have a beard. Beards were associated with the hippie generation, and hippies at the time were suspect for everything. Carroll was a maverick in the church, understood criticism, and was more comfortable dealing with it. During the winter of 1967, he received a letter from a guest who thought it was inappropriate for the manager of Holden to have a beard. Sometime in the spring, Carroll shared this criticism with me via a letter. He didn't ask me to cut off my beard, but almost immediately I shaved, not wanting anyone to be upset with Holden. When I told Carroll what I had done, he more or less ordered me to grow the beard back, saying that no one would tell us how to run Holden Village. My beard has now been in place for forty-seven years. It became clear to me that Carroll understood the need to have good relationships with our guests and have some type of approval from the church but also knew what was important and what was trivial. The manager growing a beard was trivial.

Since Holden Village was a community with a strong spiritual emphasis, we began discussing the feasibility of having an official congregation at Holden. One of the reasons for considering this was the fact that it was impossible for Holden residents or long-term staff to participate in the life of a congregation, including sharing gifts with other communities and the work of the national church organization. A practical earthly reason was that organizational protocol dictated that we officially needed to notify the Lake Chelan Lutheran Church of the number of people taking communion. Lake Chelan was our official sponsoring congregation that authorized our communion. It looked strange in the records when Lake Chelan Lutheran Church, with a membership of seventy-five, had four hundred communicants on a Sunday in the summer. Keeping track of these statistics was always questionable in my mind, but it's what the church organization needs to determine progress.

Carroll and I worked with Dr. Clarence Solberg, bishop of the Pacific Northwest District, through the process of establishing an official congregation. Holden couldn't offer a normal community structure for a congregation. Only a handful of people actually lived at Holden over an extended period of time. Church attendance would vary from seventy in the winter to four hundred in the summer with perhaps fifteen official members. Dr. Solberg authorized a congregation, and we chose the name Fullness of God Lutheran Church. Fullness of God had Carroll as its pastor. It had no building to maintain or even any kind of a mortgage and therefore no expenses. One hundred percent of the contributions to Fullness of God would be contributed to others. Fullness of God Lutheran Church became official in 1972.

Initially the Holden Village congregation was considered more of a functional addition to the Holden ministry rather than a congregation that would have any significant input to the Holden Village program. Fullness of God might even provide some public relation benefits to Holden since now its pastor and a delegate could participate in district/synod meetings. After Carroll was officially called as pastor of the congregation, I was elected president. Over the years the pastors were called for one to three years at a time. Arnie Ohakes, Nancy Winder, and Jim Fish were some of the first pastors called. During the years Carroll was the pastor of Fullness of God congregation as well as the director of Holden, there was very little notice of the congregation within the community. Once the decision was made for Holden to hire a village pastor who would officially serve as the pastor of Fullness of God, the village pastor became an increasing presence within the community and program.

After several years of existence, Fullness of God congregation had the opportunity to help a congregation in Leavenworth, Washington, resurrect its ministry. Faith Lutheran in Leavenworth had been closed for approximately ten years, and the property was about to be sold. Newell and Nancy Arntson put an article in the *Leavenworth Echo*, a weekly newspaper, and suggested that people around Leavenworth who were interested in a Lutheran congregation should let them know. Nancy Arntson, as well as Nancy's parents, had been on the volunteer staff at Holden. Nancy's father was one of the individuals I transported downlake for medical treatment. As I remember, he was helping load a water heater onto the pickup, and it fell on his finger, crushing it.

Sufficient numbers of people in Leavenworth responded to reopening what had been Faith Lutheran. Newell contacted me about helping to provide weekly pastors, and we informed them that we would help in any way needed. During the summer, Holden had "surplus" clergy, including seminary students. It wasn't difficult to share these people, especially since the people of Faith Lutheran would supply housing for several days while the helpers were downlake. Arnie Ohakes was at the end of his two-year service as village pastor when he was called as the first pastor of Faith Lutheran after it was officially reopened. Holden Village gave Faith Lutheran retired hymnbooks, offering plates, and other materials critical to the life of any congregation.

The Leavenworth community already had Holden connections. John and Karen Rieke had been on the volunteer staff at Holden in 1971–1973 and moved to Leavenworth to start a toy shop with homemade wooden toys. Some of the original toys sold in The Wood Shop were actually made in the Holden woodshop before John and Karen moved to Leavenworth. John was the nephew of Vern Rieke, Holden board chairman. John was an ideal Holden staff person. He was actually an ideal person, no matter where he was or what he did. He graduated from Pacific Lutheran University in three years, went to seminary, and was an ordained Lutheran pastor. He then went on to law school and passed the bar in Minnesota. At Holden, John was the plumber.

John had grown up in a rather high-powered family. His father was director of the national Luther League in the American Lutheran Church and later president of Texas Lutheran College. His uncle Vern taught at the University of Washington law school and was at that time also Holden's board chairman. Another uncle of his, Bill, was a medical doctor, taught at the University of Iowa medical school, and then became president of Pacific Lutheran University.

My theory was that John really loved to work with his hands and be creative building things. Holden attracted numerous people who loved to express themselves with creative handiwork but who were encouraged by family or tradition to seek professions and live lives working in fields that weren't their first loves. John was certainly one of these people. He proved to himself and to his family that he could be a pastor or a lawyer, but then he was honest with himself and did work that he loved. He built three or four houses in Leavenworth, invested in several properties in downtown Leavenworth, and operated at least two businesses with his wife Karen. I joined a partnership for several years with John and several others in a fixed-net fishing permit in Bristol Bay, Alaska, which was even more remote than Holden Village. Holden at least had the sheriff's radio for emergency communications. Bristol Bay relied on National Public Radio to get messages to the remote fishing camps.

After John and Karen Rieke and their family left Holden and moved to Leavenworth, Washington an increasing number of Holden related people also made a similar move. Fritz and Gertrude Norstad moved to Leavenworth after they left the village in 1978. Karen Strom, long time registrar at Holden, moved to Leavenworth. Rich and Liz Caemmerer moved to Plain, fifteen miles north of Leavenworth, to start the Grunewald Guild. Bev and Merrill Cagle moved to Leavenworth several years after leaving Holden, and John and Mary Schramm and Bill and Carol Lehman also retired in Leavenworth. Dan Stata also moved to Leavenworth some years after completing his time at Holden as a conscientious objector. Maynard Johnson also took up residence in Leavenworth a few years after leaving Holden. Dawn (Smith) Kranz was one of the first potters at Holden and later took up residence in Leavenworth. Reed and Amy Carlson served on the volunteer staff and then relocated to Leavenworth. Reed was on the volunteer staff right after graduating from college. Reed helped to establish a credible photo lab at Holden Village and then relocate the lab to a more permanent location in the basement of Chalet 4.

Our family moved to Leavenworth in September 1983. We purchased our Leavenworth home in 1973. Arnie and Sharon Ohakes had been making plans to move to Leavenworth from Holden for Arnie to become the pastor of Faith Lutheran Church, but they couldn't find a place to rent. I told Karen Rieke if she could find a home on the Wenatchee River, we would purchase it and rent it to Arnie. Karen wasn't in real estate, but she knew everyone in Leavenworth and saw the For Sale sign on the property at 9766 East Leavenworth Road with 140 feet of riverfront. We made the purchase, and Arnie and Sharron rented it. Arnie and Sharron have just recently retired. It's my understanding they have moved back to Leavenworth, thus again increasing the number of former Holden residents living in the Leavenworth area. Both Leavenworth and Chelan became recipients of many former Holden staff. The mountains, the lake, and the close-knit communities attract those who enjoyed the Holden community experience.

For a period of time, Faith Lutheran in Leavenworth was about 50 percent former Holden residents. The Holden influence was noticeable, which caused some minor problems since the former Holden Village members were definitely more liberal than the local Lutherans and definitely more liberal than many of the people in Leavenworth. Faith Lutheran has continued to exist and thrive. It has developed in a unique way with strong emphasis on the proclamation, music, art, peace activism, environmental concerns, and declaring its affirmation as a "Reconciling in Christ" congregation, welcoming lesbian, gay, bisexual, and transgender people. For many years, Fullness of God Lutheran at Holden and Faith Lutheran in Leavenworth were the only two "Reconciling in Christ" congregations in the Northwest.

The most important factor concerning life at Holden Village was that a variety of people were always in the community, allowing relationships to develop and healing to occur. Holden Village was never without people hurting and suffering, but fortunately there were also people who had experienced hurt and suffering and could relate to and provide strength to those needing friends. Holden from the very beginning was a place of healing. I personally think Wes needed Holden. Wes needed a community where he could have value. What would have happened to Wes without Holden? His naïve quest for a community provided a community not only for him but also for many thousands over the years. I don't know where I would be without Holden. My entire life, at least from age twenty-four to the present, has involved Holden in some way.

I've already shared some stories of healing. One traumatic experience involved a couple from Eastern Washington. It was a unique occurrence of apparent demon possession. I can't document that demon possession was actually involved, but I'll share what I observed. The husband had a drinking problem. He was a small business owner. His wife arranged for him to join the volunteer staff. His wife may have had some difficulties that intensified her husband's drinking problem. The husband was much better after being in the village by himself. One weekend his wife came to visit, and the day after her arrival, she appeared to have a seizure. We didn't have a medical doctor in the village, and the nurse wasn't sure what to do since the wife's condition didn't seem to originate from a physical problem. I got Carroll, and he went to their room in the hotel.

Carroll was convinced that the woman was suffering from demon possession. He had counseled with her earlier in the day. He asked her husband and the nurse to leave the room but asked me to stay as a witness. He began quoting scripture and then commanded the demon to leave her body. Carroll repeated this procedure a second time, and the woman gradually calmed down. He speculated that the husband's alcohol problem was intensified by his wife, who appeared to fear her husband losing his dependence on her. I don't know if she was possessed by a demon. The word we received a year later indicated the couple was doing well.

A pastor contacted me about a young man from his congregation, Dale, who had the choice of going to the county jail or spending an extended time at Holden. Dale had assaulted another person and fortunately had no previous record. We welcomed him on staff. He had extensive experience with vehicles and mechanical equipment. Dale ended up living at Holden Village for a year and became the village mechanic. He was also the Sasquatch prankster who added enjoyment to the community.

Since Holden Village depended on volunteers to develop and grow as an exciting community it was most fortunate that relationships developed over the years benefited the rather rapid growth of the Holden Village reputation. One of the many gifts Carroll provided was the involvement of many of his friends, even some from Norway. One summer Carroll invited Wilhelm Andresen, who owned a well-loved bakery in Gjvoik, Norway, and had become friends with Carroll some years earlier. Wilhelm agreed to spend a period of time at Holden as long as we would provide the ingredients he required for his baking, especially his cakes. Carroll instructed me to make sure that we had five pounds of cardamom in the kitchen before Wilhelm arrived. I made a trip to Pacific Fruit and Produce in Wenatchee and requested five pounds of cardamom. They had never had an order of this quantity but did have a case of cardamom in two-ounce containers. I bought what they had in stock and put in a rush order for the balance. Wilhelm's cakes were out of this world, but it was the frosting that always drew attention. He rolled out the frosting and then laid it over the cake. Wilhelm was a delight. Even though language was a minor challenge, his smile really communicated and his cakes and other pastries won over the hearts of everyone in the village, especially those who had birthdays.

Communal meals with the same people, especially during the winter months, could result in a less than exciting experience. The Holden Village food service played an important part in providing occasions encouraging dress up or food style diversity. Occasionally the kitchen staff would put together one dinner with a 1950s theme or another night with a French restaurant motif. These special dinners provided the opportunity to look forward to a night out. We started having homecoming, including football and tailgating. Wes was a contributor to this make-believe and always had an appropriate costume for the occasion. Wes's ability to invent characters and willingness to be the target of laughter helped the community to celebrate life with less seriousness and personal concern for acceptance. All of us in the community had times of depression and times of concern for mental health and safety. Unfortunately some of these feelings were at times generated through the actions or attitudes of Carroll.

If Carroll felt threatened in terms of theology, employment, or anything related to family, he often cast a shadow over the community, more specifically the staff. Guests were generally less impacted since they were in the community for short periods of time, didn't understand, and were more easily able to dismiss Carroll's words or actions.

During these years Holden Village was never advertised or promoted as a place of healing although healing definitely occurred. It was essentially the volunteer staff structure that absorbed individuals who came to Holden for help or were sent by a pastor or a parent for a shot of community adrenalin. Individuals joining the volunteer staff because of social or mental challenges weren't always easy to deal with. Since they were on the volunteer staff, I was generally the first line of involvement. A guest once told me that he envied me. He wished he could have my job and live in such an ideal community. I informed him that he was the lucky one. I helped him understand that I dealt with problems 24-7. Normally in society you can go home at night, close your house door, and find relief from the outside world if you so desire. Because I was always on duty, there was never anyone to call in terms of medical help or law enforcement. I went to sleep each night hoping the alarm wouldn't go off or there wouldn't be a knock at the door.

I remember one night around eleven o'clock I was notified that the daughter of one of our faculty had fallen off the shoulders of someone carrying her from the Jacuzzi. She had hit her head and appeared to be unconscious. Fearing a concussion, the village nurse requested she be transported to a hospital as quickly as possible. Fortunately it was a clear night with no wind. I contacted Cascade Helicopter by radio, and they agreed to fly to Holden if we could provide a large circle of lights, giving them a lighted area to land. We took all of the vehicles we had, drove them to the upper mine level, and arranged them in a large circle with lights pointing inward. When we heard the helicopter arriving, we turned on all of the vehicle lights, and within a short time the young girl was on her way to the hospital. No serious injury occurred, and she was back in the village several days later.

Whenever I was out of the village for a meeting in Seattle or just for R and R, I would delight at hearing sirens, knowing that I wasn't responsible for dealing with that emergency.

We seldom had people arrive at Holden without prior application and acceptance, but it did occur. One interesting person was Scott Bacon. Scott was from New York and had been hiking in the North Cascades. He was not only hiking; he was hiking barefoot. At least he was barefoot when he entered the village. He had no knowledge of Holden but happened to walk in one morning just in time for coffee break. He couldn't figure out what was going on in this community. Scott was directed to me, and I explained what Holden Village was and its general mission.

He appeared to be in a daze and said he knew he had entered a mystical place. He explained that he had studied several years in New

York with one of the premier piano technicians but after receiving his certification, he wasn't sure what he wanted to do. He came west and was hiking in the mountains to seek direction in his life. Scott asked to be on staff, and we added him to the volunteer ranks. He was obviously a very interesting person. Holden thrived on interesting people. Scott, after leaving Holden, married one of the volunteers he had met. He became a massage therapist and had a highly respected business in Chelan before moving to the west side of the state.

Maynard Johnson and his friend Karen arrived at the village without any prior contact. He wanted to be on staff and was insistent as to his value to Holden. I think he had heard of Holden while living and working in Minnesota. John Schramm and I met with Maynard and Karen. Maynard laid out all of his abilities, which were extensive. He was a master printer, he had advanced training as an organist, he had a master's license to pilot river tugs on the Mississippi, he had a commercial pilot's license, and he also was experienced as a heavy equipment operator with equipment such as the D6 Caterpillar and the road grader. John and I looked at each other, not knowing if Maynard was a gift from God or if we were being overwhelmed with false claims. Maynard also informed us that he and Karen weren't married, but they would be living together. This was a potential difficulty. We decided to add Maynard and Karen to the volunteer staff. It did appear as if Maynard had all of these talents and was definitely an asset to Holden. It became obvious that part of Maynard's plan was to replace either John as director or myself as manager. He obviously felt that he was more qualified than either of us.

Maynard continued to pressure us to put him on salary, which we couldn't do. About this time, Holden was starting to operate the Lucerne Resort. It proved to be the ideal location for Maynard and Karen to live and work and even receive a stipend. After the summer at Lucerne, Maynard and Karen decided to attend Capital Seminary in Columbus, Ohio. They both graduated from the seminary and were ordained. They were married and later divorced. Maynard's last relocation was to Leavenworth, where he purchased five acres of property. He worked for

Marson and Marson Lumber as a delivery truck driver. He also built a home and worked until his recent death on installing a pipe organ in his home.

Among other activities, Maynard was involved with the Leavenworth Summer Theater. He was perhaps too talented, and it was my impression that he was either unwilling or hesitant to dedicate himself to just one of his many talents. He appeared to work at a job, often involving manual labor, and then overwhelm everyone when he excelled with one of his many other talents. I think his hesitation to settle on one of his talents resulted in a challenging life and at some times developed feelings of bitterness as he observed the recognition and stability of others around him. Again, Maynard was one of the unique gifts that dropped into Holden Village.

Community at Holden wasn't created through the specific efforts of Carroll and Mary, or Fritz and Gertrude, or John and Mary, or me, but rather community developed when the village was given the freedom to react to opportunities and needs without specific requirements and set regulations. A tightly controlled environment does not allow a vibrant community to develop. When it was obvious that someone needed a friend or needed someone to talk with, there was no community flowchart that funneled the person in need to a trained counselor or even the village pastor. Real community encourages everyone to be a friend and a healer. Community happened when it was allowed to develop without manipulation or being initiated by anyone with a specific title requiring participation or taking credit for any positive outcome. Community is created when all ages and levels of intellectual capabilities are allowed to interact in a natural way. Our three-year-old son, Jeff, was a healer to Omar, and sixty-eight-year-old Omar was one of the developers of the person Jeff became.

Community at Holden also allowed friendship to develop without the need for organized get-acquainted parties. Working or eating together, hiking together, or sitting at coffee break and arguing about the impact of a lecture all built community. When a person arrived at

Holden Village, the initial need for developing trust to get acquainted disappeared. Once one was in the village, friendship was almost immediate and conversation was natural. The advantage of being in an isolated setting without phones, without TV, and without radio was that more time was available to interact person to person. The village itself created the points of discussion through worship, lectures, and prayer time. Another element that helped create community was confinement in an isolated valley. Even though we were comfortable and had a lot of entertainment and intellectual stimulation, there was always an element of survival involved. Fire was a danger. Lack of communication added an element of uncertainty. The inability to summon help such as ambulance, fire department, or law enforcement also added uncertainty not experienced in most living situations.

We did experiment with possibilities for receiving a TV signal. I personally purchased an eleven-inch portable TV, and we carried it around the village and up to the mine area. It took several people to conduct the experiment. There was the TV, a battery pack, and then the large antenna that needed to be carried. We were able to pick up a signal from Spokane. It was apparently bouncing off the snow or glaciers on Bonanza Peak. The video, at times, was watchable. The day President Nixon announced his resignation we had a TV in the dining hall so people could witness this major event. We had the small TV in our chalet for several years, but the signal was barely watchable. The audio had a good signal, and we were able to listen to some of the significant news events when desired.

Those who had created community in Railroad Creek Valley prior to Holden Village becoming a retreat center also enhanced the Holden community. Those seeking out mineral claims created the early community. The mine operation created a very strong community over its twenty years. Families worked and lived together. Children were born and went to school. Deaths occurred that necessitated compassion and comfort. All of these factors increased the intensity of community. Someone once suggested that where community once existed it's easier for new community to be initiated. The mine community in many ways helped give birth to the community of Holden Village, the retreat center.

Huldreich Schmid and Karl Wyssen, the Swiss loggers, owned and operated the Wyssen Cable Crane system for selective logging in the Railroad Creek Valley. They were from Switzerland and moved to the United States to introduce the Wyssen Cable Crane to the West Coast. Their uncle Jakob Wyssen invented and was now manufacturing the cable crane in a factory located in beautiful Reichenbach, Switzerland, not far from Interlaken. The highline system was used in various parts of the world for construction projects as well as for logging.

For ten years the Swiss loggers worked in the valley from mid-May into October under a logging contract with the forest service. Their presence was an important part of the larger community in the Railroad Creek valley. The valley wasn't conducive to standard logging practices requiring road building. The Swiss loggers used an environmentally sensitive and effective system involving a highline attached at the top of the hill and at the bottom to a landing accessible to trucks. The highline cable lifted the logs, and gravity propelled them down the hill to the landing. A diesel engine at the top of the hill provided the lifting and braking capacity.

I was in Switzerland in 1969 and had the privilege of meeting Jakob Wyssen and staying with his family. When I visited the factory, it was unrecognizable as a factory. It looked more like a Swiss resort with beautiful landscaping around the Swiss architecture of the factory buildings. No rusted machinery sitting around and not a sign of discarded oil or other petroleum products. Jakob was a religious man and conducted weekly worship services in his factory. He would drive around in his Volkswagen bus and pick up people wanting to go to Saturday afternoon services. On the Sunday morning of my visit, he asked me to preach during the service he held each Sunday just for his family and any guests. That was the first and only time I preached in Europe, and it was a touching experience.

The Swiss loggers became an important part of the village. They offered to help in many ways, especially with removal of large trees that might be threatening our buildings. They also, on a couple of occasions, allowed Holden to use their D4 Caterpillar allowing us to open the last mile of road in the spring, enabling Holden to get ready for early summer activities. They volunteered their time to build the road from the upper mine level to the proposed site of the upper diversion dam. The road was created so we could transport materials to build the diversion dam and then also lay the fourteen-inch penstock pipe along the inner edge of the roadbed, which they then covered to hold it in place. Although they weren't on our volunteer staff, their willingness to work with Holden was invaluable to the work and daily life for the ten years they were logging in the valley.

Karl Wyssen was also a wood-carver and carved the alpenhorn that still hangs in the dining hall. Karl presented the alpenhorn to Holden as a thank-you gift. He wasn't very verbal, but his gift of the alpenhorn spoke eloquently about his feelings for what Holden Village meant to him. Karl moved to Leavenworth, and I visited with him each time I saw him walking past our home on the way to his workshop.

Many of the activities we enjoyed each year at Holden helped to bring everyone together in the community. The Fourth of July parade, the talent shows, or even the times when the community needed to draw together to deal with challenges were community building and broke down any barriers within the community. The annual "homecoming" game included cheerleaders and a homecoming dance. The flag football game was at the Holden ballpark, west of the village at the edge of the wilderness area.

The Railroad Creek valley is spectacular and provides some of the unique hiking and climbing opportunities in the North Cascade Mountains. With the three hundred to four hundred people at Holden Village in the summer and with the added hikers, climbers and hunters arriving to enjoy the remote areas, accidents were inevitable. Once or twice each year we dealt with a hiking or climbing accident and would have to institute a rescue. We gradually became more organized in our rescue efforts in terms of training our staff and adding some basic rescue equipment. We also updated our radio system to accommodate both the sheriff's frequency as well as the radio frequency used exclusively by Holden Village. Not all of the rescues involved Holden staff or guests. We provided rescue for a hunter who had shot himself in the leg and for several hikers who had eaten poison mushrooms in the meadow below Cloudy Pass. On one rescue of a Holden climber, we called in a helicopter. Steve May from Wenatchee was a mountain rescue paramedic and flew in with the helicopter. The injured staffer was on a slope without any location for the helicopter to land. Steve jumped out of the helicopter about eight feet above the ground so that he could stabilize the climber. The Holden crew then carried the climber to the upper mine level, where it was possible to load the patient into the helicopter for a trip to the hospital in Wenatchee.

The entire village community would be involved with a rescue, especially if it was somewhat visible from the valley floor. I had a telescope that was put on the lawn below the Jacuzzi, and people would gather around to observe the progress of carrying an injured person down the hillside.

Living in the community over an extended period of time was enjoyable, but it was also great to live in a chalet that offered some privacy. I found it challenging to eat meals with new guests each day. Perhaps my greatest talent was answering the same questions over and over as I talked to new people each day, responding in such a way that sounded as if it was the first time that a particular question had been asked. Living in the village for numerous years had the benefit of becoming acquainted with people who returned every year. I developed many deep friendships and although at times I would see these friends outside of the village, it was primarily a friendship based on being together at Holden.

At times, I joked with people that I really worked for the US Forest Service even though I was paid by Holden Village. Since the Forest Service was our landlord it was vital to develop a positive owner-tenant relationship. Part of my responsibilities was to serve as the Holden Village representative to all of the various governmental agencies. Bill Rines was the first Chelan District ranger I worked with. Holden was most fortunate to begin its history with Bill. He was definitely dedicated to his government work, but he seemed thrilled with being a district ranger, unlike some others I worked with who were only interested in being district rangers on their way up the management ladder. I knew Bill had the ultimate power over us, but I also knew we had the right to express our opinions and fight for our convictions. He always respected our convictions and ideas.

Holden had a love and concern for the environment. When Bill saw that we had many of the same goals, the relationship became very enjoyable. We definitely had disagreements, but overall, it was a friendship and partnership. The fact that there was forty miles of lake between Chelan and Lucerne helped develop a trust level, since it was impossible for the forest service to have someone watching over our every move. It would have been easy for us to get away with some inappropriate actions, and we probably stretched the limits a time or two. However, I knew any flagrant violations of our special use permit would destroy an important trust relationship.

After retiring as Holden manager in September of 1983, I remained on the payroll as a consultant for one more year. The forest service presented me with a letter of appreciation dated March 27, 1984. The following is from this letter:

> Please accept this letter as a token of our very great personal appreciation for all you have done to benefit the Wenatchee National Forest and the public during your 22 years as such an important part of the heart and spirit of Holden Village.
>
> Werner, as the person who has dealt with the Forest Service for Holden Village day in and day out, you have given special meaning to the terms, "cooperation" and "coordination." The excellent understanding you have developed of Forest Service resource objectives and management, coupled with your knowledge of the forest environment, has made your contribution uniquely valuable.

It is no accident that Holden Village is in such close harmony with its forest surrounding. Your personal concern for the environment has helped to mold not only the programs at the Village, but also the attitudes of the forest visitors and the Forest Service employees you have met. Your personal high standards for maintenance and operation of Village facilities have made them a national example of tasteful community construction and operation within a sensitive forest ecosystem.

Your willingness to tackle tough problems has helped lead to positive improvements in the difficult tailing pile situation. Your concern for the public well-being has been shown by your longtime support for search and rescue operations, active encouragement of fire prevention in the area, and assistance to the avalanche information system. The Holden Village bus system has been a great service to the general public. Somehow you have maintained your openness and willingness to cooperate with the Forest Service in spite of the frustrations of dealing with a bureaucracy.

This letter was signed by Donald Smith, forest supervisor; Richard Buscher, deputy supervisor, and Robert Hetzer, Chelan District ranger.

And here is a portion of the letter I received from Bill Rines, former Chelan District ranger on the occasion of Holden's twenty-fifth anniversary:

Werner was the ever present force and the congenial host whenever we were at the Village. Simultaneously though, he was also an advocate for the enhancement of the Village's future.

Whether the issue was road maintenance, resolution of differences of opinion regarding the taxi service being provided by the Lucerne Resort, installation of the new (at the time) hydro units, chlorination of the Village's water system, or planning for the construction of the new (at the time) dock at Lucerne,

Werner, Carroll and their associates were always active and productive participants in the dialogue.

Residents of the Village were always willing to help in times of
emergency. One such occasion was the time when Stan Mettler,
the Lyman Lake wilderness guard, was seriously hurt in a horse
accident. Medical professionals who were guests at the Village
at the time made him comfortable, and members of the Village
staff made the necessary arrangements for his helicopter transport to Chelan.

A willingness to help out was always noticeable with the people who stayed at the Village. Their close association with Henry
Schwecke and readiness to spend hundreds of hours laboring
in the construction of the new powerhouse and related pipeline
demonstrated their dedication to a cause.

Later, their cooperation with the Forest Service in the construction of the new Port of Holden dock at Lucerne proved to
me that the two outfits could work well together. (Werner's fears
to the contrary.)

Thanks again, and in the words of the immortal (he hopes)
Werner,

Peace and Joy
Bill Rines

As Holden Village and its program developed over the years into a
nationally and even internationally recognized retreat center, it also became a showplace for the forest service. It was recognized as a prime example of the rehabilitation and use of private facilities on forest service
property. We began receiving more high-ranking forest service personnel from the regional office in Portland. One fall, the Northwest Region
of the US Forest Service chose Holden Village as the site for its annual
management retreat.

Holden had another connection with the forest service. Rudy
Wendelin, the artist who was the creator of Smokey Bear, was on the

faculty at Holden. Rudy happened to belong to one of the Lutheran churches outside of Washington, DC, and volunteered to come on faculty. Then Chelan ranger, Bob Hetzer, and several others from the Chelan District ranger office brought the Smokey Bear costume to Holden and conducted an official welcome for Rudy. Rudy and his wife had made the first Smokey costume for the Macy's Thanksgiving Day Parade in New York in 1950.

While Rudy was in the village, he did many drawings and caricatures. Some of these were used in Holden promotional materials and have been on display in the museum. Rudy also donated six original paintings to help raise money for the tractor fund. The auction of his paintings to Holden guests raised over two thousand dollars.

Owning 240 acres of land including mineral rights surrounded by national forest land should be a positive attribute but it really didn't benefit Holden Village and in some ways was a negative. When the issue of solving the environmental problems caused by the abandoned mine and tailings were raised there was always an attempt to place some of the responsibilities back on Holden Village. All of the operational buildings with the exception of the garage and new museum were on forest service land, and therefore, the forest service has always been Holden's landlord. During the first years, the forest service had more of a tolerant, wait-and-see attitude. As Holden matured, the relationship became more of a partnership. I always knew the forest service had the power in the relationship, but as we proved in the efforts to have the new US Forest Service dock built, Holden can muster the political forces to add power to Holden's voice.

The fact that Holden existed because of a past mining operation continually impacted life within the community. Living next to eighty acres of mine tailings and owning 240 acres of land without well-documented property markers always created a bit of a mystery for our work and life. The primary mark that identified all of the property and mining claims was the Mineral Marker No. 1 (MM1). MM1 was noted on maps, but the location of the actual marker on the side of Copper Mountain hadn't been seen for many years. Beginning in perhaps 1970, Howard Gylling, Holden Village accountant and long time Village participant and his son James made finding MM1 their quest. At one point, the forest service brought Wimpy Phillips to Holden to join the search.

Wimpy was, perhaps, the longest employee of Holden Mine and was at the time living in Chelan. He was sure he could hike right to MM1, but when they began exploring, his memory and efforts failed. Howard and James would make at lest one attempt to find MM1 each time they were in the valley enjoying other hikes. They finally succeeded at finding MM1, or perhaps accidently stumbled across it, on July 4, 1978. Howard and James became the Indiana Jones team of Copper Mountain.

Holden Village had two major operational challenges. No road access existed to Holden Village necessitating a Lake Chelan passenger ferry or barge transporting people or freight. There was also a ten mile road trip between Lucerne, on Lake Chelan, and Holden Village requiring the operation of a fleet of buses and trucks. The second challenge was communications. During the twenty years I managed Holden Village no phone service of any kind was practical. Because of the remote location, deep within the Railroad Creek valley even radio signals were a challenge. Amateur Radio would be a possibility for emergencies and general communications but could not be used for any business activity. I received my license, personally purchased a radio/transmitter, and went on the air as WB7CVM. It was a personal hobby, but my motivation was communication for the welfare of the Holden Village community. An amateur radio operator is literally connected to the world or at least to whomever hears a call, which is dependent on time of year, sunspots, and even time of day. "Hams," or amateur radio operators, spend way too much money on equipment. In order to justify their expenditures, they are always looking for contacts, especially those that might involve emergencies originating in unique locations.

We were enjoying an exciting Halloween with the kids one year, trick or treating. Kristy was a princess and Jeff was a record. (That's correct, a record. Jeff loved 45-rpm records in his earliest years, so we put a sheet on him, painted on a black beard and hung 45s on him.) There was twelve inches of snow on the ground. Late that night, Sid Burns drove up from Lucerne. Sid was living in the forest service ranger's house and had injured his hand with an ax. Our nurse cleaned the wound but decided that since it appeared as if tendons had been cut, she couldn't stitch the wound. I tried, without success, calling the forest service on their radio. It was close to midnight. I got on the ham radio and made a call for anyone listening. I finally received a reply from a man in Sacramento, California. He had never heard of Lake Chelan or the Chelan County Sheriff's Department but was more then willing to call them on the landline. The sheriff's department contacted the forest service, and Sid was on his way to the Chelan hospital.

Another emergency occurred when Gertrude Lundholm became very sick. The village nurse did what she could but indicated she needed consultation with a doctor. I made a call on the ham radio. This was around noon, so there were lots of people on the open frequency. I connected with a lady from Shelton, Washington, who in turn connected me to a man in East Wenatchee, who in turn called Central Washington Hospital and made a phone patch with the emergency room doctor. Another radio operator was also on the phone, calling the Cascade Helicopter, which was immediately dispatched to Holden.

The ER doctor, from the information provided by the Holden nurse, figured the problem was most likely congestive heart failure, and time was of the essence. Gertrude was in the hospital in less than an hour from the time of the initial call on the ham radio. She was back in the village in less than a week. For my involvement in possibly saving Gertrude's life, I received a Certificate of Acknowledgment from the American Amateur Radio League, the national association of amateur radio operators. The certificate is in a museum box.

I also made calls for some guests, staff, and faculty when they received messages concerning some type of emergency. One summer, when Dr. Al Rogness and his wife, Nora, were on faculty, Nora received word that her mother was taken to the hospital. Nora asked if there was any way to call her brother, David Preus, president of the American Lutheran Church. I contacted a fellow radio operator in Seattle, established a phone patch and requested a collect call to the national headquarters office so Mrs. Rogness could speak with her brother and determine the seriousness of their mother's illness.

Emergencies didn't occur frequently, but when they occurred, communication was critical. One of these emergencies occurred when Ray Courtney was involved in a horse accident on the trail in the area around Hilgard Pass above Holden Village. Ray's son ran perhaps four or five miles down to the village and contacted me. I called the sheriff's department, and they dispatched a helicopter with medical personnel. Unfortunately Ray died as a result of his injuries prior to the helicopter's arrival.

We often dreamed of a phone that would allow us to make business calls. One winter our Snow Trac broke down and we needed a part. We only had one operational Snow Trac at the time. If we ordered the part by mail it would take two to four days. I broke the rules and used the ham radio to order the part, and we had it on the next boat. I rationalized that it was an emergency. Occasionally, the Holden board would discuss potential negative impacts of phone communications at the village. These discussions were hypothetical during my years; an option for other communications didn't exist. This discussion is somewhat similar to the discussion of turning the lights off at ten o'clock each night to maintain a tradition. Part of the value of a retreat is being isolated from outside forces. Gradually the isolation is being diminished for Holden as technology advances. Everyone knew enhanced communications at Holden would change the experience, but no one could really outline the impacts or document that those impacts would be negative.

In the mid 1970s a group associated with the National Weather Service started the Northwest Avalanche Forecasting Program. They heard that I had a ham radio and asked if I would call in daily weather and snowfall statistics in winter. They didn't have any reporting stations located in the remote mountains. I continued calling in data for several years.

One radio call and phone patch that wasn't an emergency but did involve the ham radio was a call I arranged for Leo Bustad. The day after Leo arrived in the village to serve on the faculty, he received a written message via the boat indicating he must get to a phone as quickly as possible. Leo was dean of the School of Veterinary Medicine at Washington State University. He was negotiating a multimillion-dollar grant with a government agency. Leo asked if there was any way to place a call with the ham radio. He didn't want to leave Holden and spend a night in a motel. I arranged for a phone patch through a fellow amateur operator in Seattle. Leo was on the radio for forty-five minutes, successfully negotiating what Leo told me was a forty-five-million-dollar grant.

The building at WSU that now bears his name as Bustad Hall was listed as a ten-million-dollar project, so the rest of the grant must have been for other aspects of the veterinary school. They didn't mention Holden Village or the ham radio on the building plaque.

I actually received a citation from a volunteer monitor for arranging this call. The volunteer monitor decided it was a commercial call and therefore not appropriate over a ham radio. I was later told that it was perfectly OK; WSU was a state university with nonprofit status. I guess it was the $45 million that made it sound like a commercial negotiation.

Leo was definitely multitalented. He had a double doctorate, one in veterinary medicine and a PhD in physiology from the University of Washington School of Medicine. He was also an avid birder, and it was his routine to head out early each morning with binoculars around his neck. In fact, the binoculars were around his neck all day long, even when eating or lecturing. This routine was followed no matter if he was at Holden, at our home in Leavenworth, or even in Washington, DC. Leo was a scholar but also knew how to work the political scene. When Holden was beginning to plan for a new hydroelectric system on Railroad Creek, Leo urged me to travel back to Washington, DC, with him and meet a few people who might be helpful.

Leo was a close personal friend of Tom Foley, Washington state representative, and at the time of our visit, the Democratic majority whip, later to become speaker of the House. Leo and I headed to his office, and Leo narrated helpful instructions each step of the way. Leo was always a teacher, no matter what he was doing or where he was. Prior to reaching Tom Foley's office, he instructed me that it was most important to become acquainted with the person who occupied the desk at the entrance to any politician's office. He suggested bringing a small gift and learning about his or her family, and especially their children. He said that it made no difference that this person may be the lowest-paid office personnel; the person at the front desk controlled the office traffic.

There was no problem with Leo. He was well known in this office, and we walked right in. The Foleys had a much-loved dog, and Mrs. Foley happened to be at her husband's office with the dog when we arrived. Leo did a quick exam of the dog and declared him in top health. It was a courtesy examination. Leo emphasized that you needed to stay in contact with helpful politicians and keep them informed of what was happening that might require their future assistance. He talked about WSU and the School of Veterinary Medicine, and Leo also introduced me. We talked about Holden and the need for an expanded hydro system. The fact that Representative Foley was a ranking member in the House made it more convenient if problems with a project developed.

Leo was also a member of the Cosmos Club in Washington, DC, and arranged for me to be his guest for three nights. I had never heard of the Cosmos Club. I later discovered that the club was, at the time, a men-only club. In 1988, it opened membership to women. I learned that the Cosmos Club had a rather distinguished list of members, including three presidents, two vice presidents, twelve Supreme Court justices, thirty-two Nobel Prize winners, and fifty-six Pulitzer Prize winners.

I don't know if WSU was paying for Leo's membership, but I was grateful for this unique experience. I did have an opportunity to look through the membership registry. There were definitely recognizable names, such as three of the Kennedys, Alexander Graham Bell, Rudyard Kipling, Theodore Roosevelt, and Carl Sagan. There was no plaque above the bed in the very small room assigned to me, so I assumed that no actual members had used this particular room. Membership was by invitation only. I'm sorry that I didn't talk with Leo about the background of his membership. He must have paid for my three nights' stay, since there was no charge when I checked out.

Isolation and solitude is a matter of perspective. Holden Village was very remote without the normal options for communications but with up to four hundred people in the village, solitude for those living there was sometimes lacking. It was ironic that guests from all over the United States would come to Holden to enjoy the solitude of the community, but the staff would go on overnight hikes to Lyman Lake or beyond to find solitude from Holden. The routine of the Holden day or even the week could at times become troublesome. Set routines can eliminate the need to plan the day's activities. At least in the winter, I felt a definite routine also reduced the motivation to work most efficiently. We all work more efficiently with deadlines. The winter boat and mail schedule made mail-departure mornings the most efficient for accomplishing work. I guess in a retreat setting, efficiency wasn't the highest priority.

Looking back on the experience, I'd say it's very possible that a strict routine might have been critical for life in an isolated community. Knowing exactly what was going to happen at specific times during the day eliminated the feeling of isolation or uncertainty. Now that I'm retired, I find that I need to generate a routine so I can look forward to specific actions at specific times. I always have an egg omelet on Sunday mornings and popcorn with real butter Sunday afternoons. I listen to specific news programs at specific times each day and dislike weekends and even extended holidays because it ruins my routine.

I don't know if this is a result of living at Holden for twenty years or if I have just learned that for mental health, routine can be a gift. At Holden, mealtimes were always the same. Mail needed to be in by a certain time. The bus left and arrived at the same time each day. The boat schedule dictated the daily schedule. The days the boat didn't run in the winter were like minivacations—no arrivals and no departures and no deadline for the mail.

We were always looking for opportunities to grow our own food or prepare meals without using pre cooked items. When the kitchen started to bake bread, we purchased a small electric flour grinder. We also arranged gifts of wheat from several farmers around Waterville, not far from Lake Chelan. This allowed Holden to grind its own flour and bake its own bread at minimal cost. We did notice one negative effect of the early homemade bread. The heavy bread was difficult on the human digestive system, and lack of complete digestion apparently resulted in a problem with flatulence. I trust the recipe and the skill of the bakers in the twenty-first century solved this community dilemma.

Fruits and vegetables were grown in Eastern Washington and not too far from Lake Chelan. One year we received five hundred pounds of carrots. We didn't have sufficient winter refrigeration for that volume of carrots, so we dug them into the ground under the front porch of Koinonia. Unfortunately, in January we not only had heavy snow but also several days of hard rain. The artificial root cellar filled with water, and the carrots soon began to rot.

We contacted friends in the orchard business, indicating we could send volunteers to glean the fruit trees. Several friends designated two or three trees for Holden, which amounted to several hundred pounds of cherries, apricots, or peaches. We brought some of the fruit to the village, and the kitchen added it to the meals.

Since the winter community was growing, we also wanted to utilize this gift of the fruit during the winter. We discovered a small custom cannery outside of East Wenatchee, where we could have the fruit preserved in No. 10 cans. I would take four or five volunteers downlake in my boat to spend the day canning fruit for the winter. The cannery eventually closed, eliminating this option. All of these experiences helped to create community not only at Holden but also in the larger North Central Washington area.

Holden Village was surrounded by nature. Deer, bear, ground squirrels and humming birds were all part of daily life at certain times of the year. Observing wild animals provided fun and enjoyment for those living at Holden Village but family pets also became a part of Holden from the beginning. During the years Ruben Thomson was caretaker, his little black dog, named Bugger, was an important part of the village. Bugger was always Ruben's responsibility, and it was evident that Bugger knew who his best friend was, following Ruben wherever he needed to be.

Karen Buege, one of our first secretaries, thought we needed a companion during our first winter and suggested a cat. I wasn't all that excited about cat ownership, but there were more than adequate mice around for cat entertainment and food. I jokingly told Karen we would love to have a cat if she could find a black cat with four white paws. Guess what? We became parents of a beautiful little kitten, from 1966 to around 1978. Jeremiah was the name of our new family member. I guess we must have been studying the Old Testament at the time. It was amazing that she lived so long. She was definitely an outside cat. With the coyotes, bobcats, cougars, and other animals always looking for a meal, a cat had a challenging existence. Jeremiah entertained our small winter community and died a natural death at perhaps age twelve. Perhaps she had an agreement with the other animals in the forest to live and let live. Animals do communicate, and life in the wilderness is one big community of survival.

Terry Sateren had a beautiful white Samoyed dog when he was in the village the first winter of operation. The Samoyed, named Lucrece, and was also a gift from Karen Buege.

In 1971 our family added a St. Bernard puppy, Bernie, to our household. Bernie grew to be a big, big dog. That is the nature of a St. Bernard. We even found a whiskey barrel that Bernie wore around his neck for the many photographs. She was definitely big and admittedly not well trained but was well loved by most of the community. As a pup, she had the habit of eating small pebbles, which eventually caused her some problems with bowel movements. Hortie Christman was our unofficial pet doctor (as well as plumber—as well as bus driver, as well as barber, as well as civil engineer), and he came up with a plan to encourage Bernie's digestive system to flush out the pebbles.

One time Bernie made contact with a porcupine. Leo Bustad happened to be in the village and assisted us with the extraction of many quills. After Bernie made a second contact with a porcupine, Leo concluded that Bernie had "an IQ of zero." Leo was one of my favorites, and I considered him to be a brilliant person and a close friend. I thought Leo was a bit harsh with his analysis of Bernie's intelligence, even though he was the dean of the School of Veterinary Medicine.

I am sure that Bernie had an IQ above zero. She definitely had a high score for compassion and community involvement. Bernie unofficially participated in one of the village baptisms. It might have been the baptism of Jean Swihart. It was a river baptism at the river sauna. Carroll stood in Railroad Creek, with his white robe staying white, until Bernie elected to cool off in the river a short distance upstream. Bernie inadvertently stirred up the yellow deposits on the bottom of the stream, which made the baptism and Carroll's robe more colorful. After about four years, we found a new home for Bernie. Trips to the vet were very inconvenient.

As more staff families were staying for up to two years, a few of them brought pets. As more pets became part of the community, some people felt they weren't appropriate, partially because they impacted the natural environment, especially with the deer. The community finally made a rule that dogs weren't allowed. The deciding factor was a concern by Sig Schroeder, director of the tape ministry. Sig spent several winters in the village and was very upset about the dogs dropping their "left-behinds" in the narrow paths in the snow.

As hikers traveled through Railroad Creek valley we had the opportunity to meet some very interesting people. Because of the remote location it wasn't a trip that hikers and climbers planned for only one or two days. The Railroad Creek Valley and the mountains that towered over the valley were definitely a destination adventure requiring multiple days, even for basic hikes.

One afternoon in early August, Willi Unsoeld and his wife Jolene walked into the village. They had just completed a climb of Bonanza

Peak. Several years earlier, Willi, together with his climbing partner, Tom Hornbine, had been the first to climb Mount Everest via the more difficult West Ridge. Willi had been the director of the Peace Corps in Katmandu, Nepal. I was more of a reader about mountain climbing than an accomplished climber, so I knew the history of Willi Unsoeld and was thrilled he was in the village. He was now employed with Outward Bound, an organization working with youth growing up in inner cities to learn wilderness survival skills and the advantage of working together rather than relaying on the power of the individual. Willi was doing reconnaissance of the area between Stehekin and Holden with hopes to include this area in the Outward Bound itinerary.

We invited Willi and Jolene to stay in the village for a couple of days, which they graciously did. Willi gave a living room talk in Chalet 14, our home at that time. In 1969 Willi was killed in an avalanche on Mount Rainier. Jolene later became one of Washington State's US representatives and was one of the early voices in Congress for the environment.

Willi and Jolene had climbed Bonanza Peak as recreation, since it wasn't intended to be part of the Outward Bound itinerary. Bonanza Peak, at 9,511 feet elevation, is the highest nonvolcanic peak in Washington State. The original name of the peak was North Star, but when the US Geological Society provided its first topographic map it mistakenly swapped the names of North Star and Bonanza. This mistake caused some confusion in some early surveys of the area. I had the privilege of climbing Bonanza prior to the climb by Willi and Jolene, which is about the only claim to fame I have in the mountaineering history.

Outward Bound did receive a permit from the forest service to conduct a month-long trip into the wilderness area for the physical, mental, and spiritual growth of young boys from the inner city. The first trip they conducted in the area was during a period of almost continuous rain. The leaders came into the village to pick up supplies they had stockpiled there, but they were so discouraged by the weather that they were ready to cancel the remainder of the trip. They asked if they could use the river sauna and also take the boys to the snack bar to lift their spirits. This was normally against all rules for Outward Bound, but under the circumstances they elected to break the rules. It saved the trip for them, and they were grateful.

I asked them if they would be willing to have a session for the community in Koinonia. It was amazing to hear the stories of these boys. One boy admitted that he wasn't afraid of the streets in the gang areas of Chicago, but he was petrified of being in the wilderness at night when only the stars provided light and the coyotes were singing. Others related how the total experience, including Holden, had been a spiritual experience for them. Several years later the forest service withdrew the permits for these trips.

Larry Penberthy was another unique visitor who traveled through Holden several times during his research into the use of citizen band radios for mountain rescue. Larry was known as the "Ralph Nader" of climbing equipment. He was a thorn in the flesh for Recreation Equipment Incorporated (REI) since he claimed some of the climbing equipment they were selling wasn't safe. He started a company called Mountain Safety Research to manufacture climbing and high-altitude gear that was safe. REI later purchased his company.

Larry contacted me upon his arrival at Holden and asked if I would work with him on his radio tests. It was Labor Day and the weather was marginal, but Larry and his climbing group were planning on climbing Bonanza Peak. I monitored his base station, and he was scheduled to call every fifteen minutes. The radios worked for the first test, and after that no signal. CB radios are more or less dependent on line-of-sight communications, which is problematic in the mountains. There was some speculation that mineralization in the mountains around Holden also made CB communications difficult. We'd had the same experience the year prior to these tests. We had hoped that CB radios would work for communications with the snow vehicles between Holden and Lucerne.

In the Holden community, Larry Penberthy was best known for his excellent photographs of Holden, the mine, and especially excellent photographs of the underground mine. His book of photographs is still available in the Holden store. I contacted Larry when we were opening the new Holden museum building, and he graciously gave us permission to use his underground photographs in the museum. Larry ran for the US Senate on two occasions without success.

Rudy Edmund was, for me, the most significant faculty member. Because of his geological as well as his business experience, he wasn't only a lecturer on valley geology and the mining operation, but he was also a business consultant. I trusted his wisdom and honesty because of his knowledge of Holden and its challenges.

Rudy was a hero for many people, including me. I valued Rudy's advice and wanted to get his counsel when I received the job offer from Holden. Rudy was involved with Holden for at least thirty-five years. He died in 1997 after a very complete life. Rudy had power, not because he demanded power or provided a powerful stature or had a powerful voice, but he had the best kind of power, given to him by those around him who respected him for his compassion, intelligence, and insight. He also valued others. I think everyone, including myself, felt special when in his presence. I think I would be accurate to say that Rudy was consulted on more issues by more board members, faculty members, and staff than any other person from 1962 until he died in 1997.

I have so many memories of Rudy. He was a perfect match with Holden Village, its program, its relationship with people, and the work required. He was an intellectual with a common touch. His humility made it easy for everyone of every age to relate to him. Rudy didn't try to impress anyone, but people were lined up to be his acquaintance or friend. His knowledge of geology allowed people to understand the mine, which was the reason for the existence of Holden Village as a retreat.

On several occasions I joined Rudy and an engineer who worked for Howe Sound in touring a small portion underground in Holden Mine. I respected the danger of any abandoned mine, but trusting Rudy and the mine engineer who had specific knowledge of this mine, I couldn't wait to go underground.

It was surreal to see where hundreds of men had worked. We visited the hoist room that contained all of the machinery to hoist men and minerals out of the depths of the mine. The ceiling of the room was strengthened with steel and concrete to avoid potential damage to the expensive equipment. We went past the portal leading to Copper Basin. It had been sealed because of insufficient copper ore. We took turns climbing a wooden ladder attached to a shaft that appeared to go straight up to multiple levels above.

The most amazing experience was going into the main stope, where all of the ore was extracted. It had been partially filled with tailings, so the ceiling was only about four hundred feet above us. It appeared to be four hundred feet wide and, according to old maps, around eight hundred feet long. Our battery lamps didn't penetrate the length of the stope and its darkness.

Cavities had been blasted out alongside the main haulage tunnel, forming underground rooms for work space, where there were still maps on the tables when we visited. The cavity that served as the lunchroom still had lunch pails, magazines, and several flip-top boxes of cigarettes waiting for someone to return. It had been at least twelve years since any mine operation had taken place, but we got the feeling that it might have been only a few days since workers had occupied the space.

I have always had an environmental concern about the mining process, but I must admit that underground mines always intrigued me. It seems rather magical to have valuable ore hidden in such small quantities but still retrievable. Copper extraction helped the Allies win World War II. My uncle, Martin Janssen, was a medical doctor who flew to various parts of the war in airplanes that relied on copper, zinc, silver, and perhaps even a little gold—all metals extracted from some mine, perhaps Holden Mine. Uncle Martin returned safely to continue his medical career. We can be upset at the environmental damage of any and all mines, but we also must admit that we all rely on copper in our daily lives, and we love that Holden Village came alive as a result of a bit of environmental death within the Railroad Creek Valley.

The mine was a marvelous teaching tool for Rudy. At one point, the Holden board gave us permission to hire a consultant and investigate the possibility of reopening a small portion of the main mine shaft for instructional tours inside the mountain. A requirement by the Bureau of Mines to have the mine shaft inspected for safety each day tours were offered made it financially impractical to seriously consider this project.

Rudy wasn't only a teacher but an important community member. One summer we had a cloudburst, and the heavy rains diverted Copper Creek, our source of drinking water, around the intake supplying water to the seventy five-thousand gallon tank. Rudy immediately suggested that he take a small crew to the diversion dam to see if they could move sufficient rocks to reestablish water flowing into the pipe. Rudy and the volunteers, some of the summer volunteer staff but also guests who wanted to help, worked four or five hours, successfully reestablishing the flow of water into the diversion intake and allowing water to flow into the tank and down to the village.

Rudy was dedicated to saving the mine documents but he also looked forward to hikes, especially a hike involving fishing. Rudy, his daughter Diane, and I planned a trip to Dole Lake around 1964. At that time I don't think anyone had been to Dole Lake since the mine closed. The word in the valley was that a Department of Fish and Game–chartered airplane taking trout fry to Hart or Lyman Lake had weathered out. The fish wouldn't have lasted for a return trip to Chelan, so they were dumped at Dole Lake. The rumor was that there were large trout, but they were difficult to catch.

We followed deer trails up the draw and finally made it to the lake. We saw evidence of three lakes, each at a different level, one below the other. Our trip was in mid-July. The lower lake was visible with the outlet of the second lake visible, but the third lake was completely covered by snow. Rudy always caught fish, although I think he worked harder at Dole to catch fish that day than he had at any other lakes in the area. The trout were eighteen to twenty-two inches and great tasting. Rudy had a spiritual connection with trout. The trout knew that Rudy was their friend, and he valued them as special creatures of God. It's my theory that the trout wanted to be caught by Rudy because he understood their being such beautiful creatures. I apparently didn't have that connection and certainly didn't have the same success at catching trout.

I had no other explanation for Rudy's success catching fish. I'm sure that his ability as a fly fisherman, his knowledge of the right fly, his sense for the right time of day, and his keen ability to understand where the trout might be all contributed to his success. It was his theory and his advice that unless you had your fly in the water, you didn't catch fish. I guess my interest in having a conversation along the shore with Rudy didn't count as important in terms of impressing the fish. The next morning we got up to continue fishing, but the lower of the three lakes had a thin layer of ice on the surface that slowed our pursuit. I was always more interested in being with Rudy for our conversations than for the actual fishing.

Domke Lake was almost a spiritual home for Rudy. Domke was three miles by trail from Lucerne, not a difficult hike, but sufficient work to enjoy the thought of a cold beer with Gordon Stuart upon arrival at his cabin. It was always a privilege to be on one of Rudy's trips to Domke. In the early years, Rudy would fish Hart Lake or Holden Lake on occasion, but from the mid-1970s on, Domke was about the only lake that Rudy would fish. If the schedule allowed, it was a weekly trip. Most of the Domke trips involved camping along the lake, renting a boat, and rowing a set pattern that he had established for the most productive fishing. The pattern would depend to a certain degree on the time of day and wind conditions.

For thirty years, at least once each summer, Rudy, Leo Bustad, Fritz Norstad, and I would be together at Domke Lake. Depending on the year, my son Jeff would join us along with one of Rudy's grandsons. Rudy may have gone alone to Domke on a few occasions, but usually he invited someone to share the experience.

The meals at Domke were always the same. When you fished with Rudy, you didn't take back-up meals, because there was always plenty of trout. Rudy was the master chef. No one ever attempted to fry the trout when Rudy was present, and I don't think he would have ever shared this responsibility. I never knew if Rudy did most of the cooking because of his desire to serve others, or if he didn't trust anyone to cook his trout and potentially desecrate what he had so lovingly caught. No matter if it was over a camp stove in the campground or on the wood stove in the cabin, the process was always the same. The other constant was the fruit soup. As soon as we arrived at the camp, a variety of dried fruit was put into a kettle of water to soak. Then, in the evening after the fish were fried, the fruit soup was put on the fire to heat. The next morning the soup was the first thing we ate, either cold or warm, depending on the fire situation.

When we stayed in the cabin, it was traditional for Rudy to bring a bottle of Harvey's Bristol Cream to share in the evening. Even though we had the Bristol Cream and sometimes a six-pack of beer, drinking was never a significant part of any trip. It did, however, add enjoyment to the evening conversations. On many trips we ended up leaving surplus beer with Gordon rather than carrying it back. Gordon never drank beer. He kept whatever beer we gave him in his root cellar for his guests while he sipped expensive scotch, which he always appreciated receiving as a gift.

Leo was always the camp organizer. I quietly waited for instructions and then was delighted to be part of the process. I generally was trusted helping with dishes. On one Domke trip, Leo brought a cooler full of clams. He had been visiting friends on Puget Sound, and they insisted that they dig clams for him to take along to Domke. It was difficult to add clams to the menu when there was plenty of trout. We ended up with fried clams as well as clam chowder for breakfast along with the abundant supply of fresh trout. We considered adding one day to the trip to finish the clams.

On one of the trips that involved just Rudy, Leo, and me, we were together in one rowboat—it was a bit tight. I was sitting in the bow of the boat, Rudy in the middle, fishing and manning the ores, and Leo in back. Leo was working his fly, and I could hear it whip past my head. It made me nervous, but I was hesitant to show my anxiety. All of a sudden, I had this sharp pain in the lobe of my ear and found Leo's fly attached to it. We rowed back to shore, and Leo was going to do the extraction. After all he was a veterinarian. The problem was, he had a slight hand tremor. Rudy recognized the problem and took over the operation. Rudy knew the procedure well, and he had a steady hand. Soon we were back on the lake, fishing into the evening.

During the summer of 1993, I joined Rudy, Leo, Fritz, on a chartered float plane trip out of Chelan to fly to Domke Lake to celebrate the thirty-year anniversary of our Domke fishing trips together. This was our final trip as a group. Fritz Norstad died in 1995, Rudy in 1997, and Leo in 1998. It was the end of a special friendship with these fellow life travelers.

There are certain people who should remain on earth and not be taken from us. Besides Rudy, Fritz, and Leo, there were Hortie Christman and Al Swihart. I thought God should have allowed them to continue their work here on earth forever. God has sufficient good people in heaven. My life, as well as the lives of many others, could have benefited from these saints remaining on earth to continue their work and assist others in celebrating life.

Since Holden Village had no road access and limited communications and was fifty miles form the nearest store, ordering supplies was a challenge. The US Postal Service was our only means of communication. It was necessary to plan ahead, making accommodations for the time lag in ordering and receiving items. Fortunately we had sufficient storage capacity. Dry goods and food could be ordered in sufficient quantities to eliminate too many embarrassments. The Lake Chelan Boat Company barge ran once each week for approximately six months each year If an item missed the barge, its arrival waited another week. Perishables came on the passenger boat, which arrived each day from mid-April to mid-November. If ice cream, and especially the popular flavors, ran out before the next shipment, that was the most noticeable shortage and created the greatest number of complaints. If we ran out of fresh milk, we used our supply of powdered milk.

Shipping gasoline and diesel fuel was a major inconvenience. For many years Holden didn't have a crane to unload full fuel tanks. During the months the barge ran, we transported two five-hundred-gallon tanks of diesel fuel each week and one two-hundred-gallon tank of gasoline. We were always planning ahead during the summer to stockpile sufficient gas and diesel so we had an adequate supply of fuel for the winter. When the barge stopped running in the fall, there was no option to get fuel to the village until early May, when the barge was running and the roads free of snow.

Holden initially only had one two-ton flatbed truck. We unloaded the fuel tanks onto the truck as the barge was going uplake, transported them to the village, emptied the fuel into storage tanks, and then transported the empty tanks back to Lucerne and loaded them onto the barge as it was going downlake. Until another truck was available, the other supplies from the barge were loaded onto the truck on the downlake trip after the fuel tanks were on the barge. The barge brought freight every Thursday when on the summer schedule and it generally involved one full day of work for two or thee staff members. Once the ordering of supplies and shipping schedules became familiar, ordering was routine. There was always the unexpected, which most often occurred with maintenance items. The cooks were very creative with menus if they ran out of supplies.

In August 1964, the first phase of the hydroelectric system became operational for the first time and from then on provided reliable power. The work during that summer was primarily on the technical end, so the number of volunteers needed for that project was minimal. Henry Schwecke was our hired engineer. The diesel-electric units were designated as backup but were still used as the hydro was shut down for adjustments. The completion of the first phase, utilizing the lower diversion dam, provided twice as much electric power as each diesel generator unit.

Prior to Christmas 1964, I drove to Minneapolis to operate the Holden Minneapolis office while Carroll was in Europe for three months. I lived at Luther Seminary, in a dorm room, while taking care of Holden responsibilities. Living at the seminary provided an opportunity to enjoy attending some classes and be exposed to exciting teachers. Holden Village shared an office in Minneapolis with Merton Strommen, director of Lutheran Youth Research. Mert was a frequent faculty participant at Holden. Spending one winter in Minneapolis was sufficient for me. January never got above zero degrees.

On the drive back to Chelan in April, I visited a Holden supporter in Minot, North Dakota. He owned a car dealership but also happened to be selling a twenty-one foot inboard-outboard boat with trailer. I ended up buying the boat and towed it back to Chelan. This was the first of three boats I owned while working for Holden. One boat sank in Refrigerator Harbor during a windstorm. The boats I owned were personal, and I paid for fuel, insurance, and maintenance. Holden did reimburse me for business use. The boat was seldom used for pleasure.

Without options for communications at Holden and the necessity of obtaining parts for critical repairs, it was most convenient for me to use my boat rather than make overnight trips to Wenatchee. I could leave Holden at 6:00 a.m., be in Wenatchee by 9:00 a.m., spend a full day, and be back at Holden before dark. These trips involved long days and also personally loading and unloading lots of freight, including everything from toilet paper to sacks of cement. On occasion I even picked up Chivas Regal whiskey for a faculty member. I also made some emergency medical runs when the injuries weren't time critical.

One morning I arrived at the Twenty-Five Mile Creek dock, the dock located at the beginning of the road and where we kept our car and on my way to the parking lot, I noticed a pile of metal with a scattering of glass that was completely wet. The cars in front and behind were in perfect shape. I went to the ranger station and asked if they knew what had happened. They explained that a helicopter had been dipping water out of the lake to deal with a fire up the Twenty-Five Mile Creek Valley and dropped its water bucket, with six hundred gallons of water (five thousand pounds), on the car. He thought it was probably someone at Holden who owned the car. He gave me the license-plate number and told me that he had salvaged the radio out of the debris, since it looked in good shape. When I returned to Holden, I found the owners, who happened to be from Spokane. This was their first trip in their newly purchased, used VW Rabbit. I told them that the ranger had salvaged the radio, and they began to laugh. The radio was the only part of the car that didn't work. Later that year, they documented their experience and sent it to the VW magazine . The article was titled, "Roy Rogers Shoots Rabbit." It so happed that the name of the helicopter pilot was actually Roy Rogers. I recently found the printed article in my files and gave it to the Holden museum.

I was also the transporter of cash. We had a safe in the village, but we had no way to deal with the accumulation of cash that needed to be deposited once or twice a month during the summer. One trip to the bank was with my briefcase and perhaps eight thousand dollars in the case.

I was wearing dark sunglasses. I set my briefcase on the teller's counter and opened it. Following the deposit, the manager came out, and in a very kind manner, let me know that they almost activated the silent alarm, thinking it might be a robbery. He advised me not to wear dark glasses and suggested I bring the cash in a bank sack rather than in the briefcase. The bank manager also advised me to keep the cash deposits under ten thousand dollars. Regulations required banks to report deposits over ten thousand dollars. I assume this regulation was instituted to catch drug dealers. Another trip involved leaving the sack with cash in the vehicle parked at Refrigerator Harbor. I didn't realize my mistake until I was in Wenatchee. I quickly completed my business, and when I got back to Refrigerator Harbor, the cash was safe.

The use of the personal boat was a late-spring, summer, and early-fall activity. I did keep track of each trip, and by the time I retired in 1983, I had logged over fifteen hundred hours on the lake in our personal boat. I had a love-hate relationship with Lake Chelan. It could be a magical trip, or it could be a trip that only Satan could arrange. Chelan is a dangerous lake because of the unpredictable winds. Waves could build to three feet or more, which is uncomfortable and dangerous in a small boat. I never had any form of communication. If trouble occurred, no immediate help was available.

There were numerous trips when I wondered if I would safely make it to shore. Only one trip involved mechanical problems. The Holden chef and I had attended a restaurant show in Seattle. Our chef had picked up some samples of items that we considered using at Holden. We had a small aluminum tray of stuffed chicken breasts and also a small tray of petit steaks. We made it to Little Goat Creek, which was just over halfway to Lucerne. The vertical shaft in the lower drive unit broke, and there was no way to make repairs. At that time I didn't have a small outboard motor for emergencies. We paddled to Little Goat Creek, tied the boat to avoid damage, and waited for a rescue. We had no communication. It was a Saturday in early April, so the commercial boat wasn't running that day. We saw Ernie Gibson in the floatplane fly uplake. We went up on the rocks and started a fire, gathering items that would make lots of smoke. When we heard Ernie coming downlake, we piled items on the fire to produce as much smoke as possible, but Ernie didn't see us. We prepared to stay the night and knew it would be below freezing.

We found a sheltered site along the shore and built a fire for heat and cooking. We enjoyed stuffed chicken breasts and petit steaks for dinner and breakfast. We kept the fire going all night and kept turning around so that only one side of our bodies froze. We knew the commercial boat would be running on Sunday. Prior to the commercial boat reaching Little Goat Creek, a private boat saw us and towed us to Refrigeration Harbor. Following that experience, I mounted a seven-and-a-half horse-power outboard motor on the boat as backup, something I should have done years earlier.

Anyone who frequented Lake Chelan during the 1960s into the 1980s recognized the sound of Ernie Gibson and his Cessna 180, which was the entire fleet of Chelan Airways. Ernie flew charter flights. No schedule, but basically flights were available seven days a week, weather permitting, as long as daylight existed. The weather conditions at the south end of Lake Chelan and at Stehekin were reliable for takeoffs and landings. The winds and waves around Lucerne were problematic, but those who knew the lake and wanted to fly to Lucerne would charter flights in the morning. If Lucerne was too rough to land, they would remain on the flight until Stehekin and then take the passenger boat back to Lucerne on the downlake run.

Ernie was a man of few words. Until one became acquainted with him it was easy to feel as if paying him to fly uplake was an inconvenience for him. He always clarified at least one safety requirement, but generally only to first-time passengers. Conversation was minimal. He generally wore rubber waders. He would turn off the engine and then hop on the pontoon. As the plane was approaching the shore, he would step into the shallow water and pull the pontoons to the shore or dock and tie up. Often when there was minimal freight, he wouldn't even tie up but turn the plane around and head right out.

At times during the flight, I thought Ernie was asleep, but he was just relaxed. The plane seemed to have a honing device that always followed the same route over Manson and then as straight as possible to Lucerne or Stehekin. Ernie flew a few people downlake for medical reasons, but most of the flights were to eliminate the four-hour boat ride or to fly to Domke Lake for a fishing trip.

Ernie started flying Lake Chelan around 1945. At various times he would have a partner in the business, but the years I knew him he was generally alone. He would make many trips into Domke Lake with fishing parties. Until the National Park Service took over the Stehekin Valley, he would also fly into Trapper Lake. I was scheduled to fly into Trapper Lake one summer to do a little fishing but then got word from Ernie that he had just been notified that Trapper Lake was off limits to float planes. I understand that Ernie also made a few flights into Lucerne during the mining days delivering liquor to some thirsty miners. Ernie was one of the great people who brought business as well as transportation to residents of this remote area. Ernie was one of the "characters" who made Lake Chelan special. Everyone claimed to be a friend of Ernie's, but Ernie's facial expressions seldom changed, whether in the presence of a longtime customer or meeting someone for the first time.

Boat travel on Lake Chelan was a way of life for anyone living uplake of Twenty-Five Mile Creek. During the early years of Holden's existence, George Pennell owned the Lake Chelan Boat Company. For me, initially, the Lake Chelan Boat Company was greatly appreciated as a necessary and unique service.

Travel on Lake Chelan was always interesting because of weather conditions, lake level and wildlife along the shore. Lake Chelan averages a mile wide so both sides of the canyon are very visible. The lake can be lowered in the winter months to a minimum elevation of 1,079 feet, which makes it twenty-one feet lower than the full summer level. The Chelan County PUD operates a hydroelectric generation facility at Chelan Falls. The winter lake variations are dependent on the precipitation in the mountains that feed water into the lake. The PUD keeps track of snow depth, snow density, and lake levels and adjusts the lake level to eliminate problems with the spring runoff as well as to meet the requirements of their license to operate the power plant at Chelan Falls.

Before the new Lucerne dock was built with a floating section to accommodate the various lake levels, people and freight were unloaded on the rocks as the lake level decreased. That inconvenient and somewhat dangerous process continued until 1972, when the new dock was available. In the winter, under certain conditions, the rocks were icy, which made getting to the vehicles extremely difficult, especially when carrying crates of milk or eggs. It was great when Holden guests arrived so at least more people were available to help carry the freight, mail, and other items to the vehicles. One winter we were making plans for a new tile floor in the kitchen. The schedule for this work was made during the early winter but not in time to order the tile before the barge stopped running. The tile arrived in March, and we carried several thousand pounds of tile up the rocks before loading them on vehicles.

I always considered George Pennell to be very kind and helpful, especially as Holden was beginning an adventure with no experience in a remote operation dependent on lake travel for passengers as well as freight. George died in 1972 just as he was in the process of having *Lady of the Lake II* constructed. Paul Bryant and then Jack Raines were the subsequent owners of the boat company. Jack Raines was a more difficult person to work with. It appeared as if in owning a monopoly, he made the rules for his personal benefit, not taking into consideration his service being an important lifeline for those living uplake.

Listening to opinions of those he supposedly served wasn't high on his list of priorities. It didn't appear as if Jack understood how dependent those living up Lake Chelan were on the commercial boat service. Since his operation was the only option for passengers, he didn't value the concept of service as compared to maximizing profit. The Lake Chelan Boat Company was the only game in town. It was and continues to be a state-sponsored monopoly, protected by the Washington State Utility and Transportation Commission. Their rationale for this monopoly protection is that the boat company has the mail contract and is obligated to provide service year-round. Any competing boat service could merely operate during peak tourist travel, skim off profits, and potentially jeopardize the Lake Chelan Boat Company's survival.

Wes Prieb even got involved with the boat transportation issue. While living in Seattle he became acquainted with several people who were designing a small hydrofoil, designed for recreation as well as commuter use. The company was called Hydro-Marine. Wes contacted them and told them about Lake Chelan and Holden Village. They expressed an interest in testing their design on Lake Chelan. Wes contacted me, and we were invited to do a demonstration run on Lake Washington. Several weeks later they arranged to haul their vessel over to Lake Chelan. I met them at Twenty-Five Mile Creek with my boat and was going to follow them uplake. Shortly after leaving Twenty-Five Mile, they had a malfunction and I towed them back to the dock. We never heard from them again.

During 1971 and 1972, a small group of us living in the village began discussing the possibility of starting another passenger boat service on Lake Chelan. This was going to be independent of the Holden operation but would be available to serve Holden and its guests. We requested a certificate of operation from the Utility and Transportation Commission, and a hearing was scheduled in Chelan. We were a bit naïve and figured it was a routine hearing. I found out that the Lake Chelan Boat Company had a high-powered attorney to oppose our application. I hadn't retained an attorney to represent this new commercial venture, but it so happened that John Rieke, Holden volunteer who also happened to be part of the new venture and also an attorney, was downlake. We pressed John into service as our legal representative. He did an excellent job representing the new application for service, but we were notified a few weeks later that the application had been denied.

In 1974, Holden Village purchased a forty-foot boat, designed as a houseboat but without out any of the houseboat amenities. Bench seats were installed along the sides of the interior. The plan was that Holden could add convenience for some of the guests, provide unpaid passage for staff and faculty, and also transport a portion of our considerable freight. Purchase of the boat was made possible through a generous gift from Stephanie Larson, daughter of the owner of Larson Chevrolet in Minneapolis. The Holden Boat was christened *Happy Exchange.* John O'Neil and Merrill Cagle were initially the operators.

When we purchased the *Happy Exchange,* we knew we wouldn't be able to charge passengers. The decision was made to proceed since we at least could take staff and faculty, freight, and guests whom we hoped would be grateful for the passage and would increase their gifts to Holden on a yearly basis. Holden operated the *Happy Exchange* for a number of years and then sold it to The Cove Resort and Marina on the south shore of Lake Chelan in 1979. The *Happy Exchange* added convenience to the Holden operation, but it was decided that the overall cost didn't justify the convenience. The Lake Chelan Boat Company wasn't always the best friend but did provide dependable transportation.

Cliff and Jim Courtney, businessmen from Stehekin and sons of Ray Courtney, attempted twice to obtain a permit to operate an additional passenger service on Lake Chelan, but their applications have been denied both times. When they filed a suit against the state Utilities and Transportation Commission, they were able to gain assistance from the legal department of the Institute for Justice, which claims to be the nation's only libertarian, civil liberties, pubic interest, pro bono law firm. Their application was denied primarily because they couldn't prove to the state that the Lake Chelan Boat Company wasn't providing adequate safe service.

George Will, conservative columnist with the *Washington Post* even wrote an opinion piece on December 16, 2011, condemning the state for protecting a monopoly on Lake Chelan. I did whatever I could to support Cliff and Jim. I have admired the Courtney family since first meeting Ray and Esther in 1964. I always value conversations with Cliff and consider him a great friend.

Managing Holden Village, especially as one person without any administrative assistance, was a unique job with new challenges almost each day. The community spirit and well being was by far the most important. During my years of working in the Holden Village community, I attempted to patiently work with those who tried to manipulate what life within Holden Village was all about. I considered it my ministry to help them celebrate the daily mystery. It was my observation that the community was one big committee and didn't need to meet and come to a consensus before discovering the next exciting adventure. The input and advice from the community might have been subtle, but it allowed each day to be new and exciting. The community expressed itself through conversations at coffee break or letters received from people with lives transformed. The community participated by being observant, with adjustments made as it became evident what was important and what allowed lives to experience the new along with the traditional.

To describe living within the Holden Village community is complicated. Life at Holden was like a smorgasbord: so much to choose from, and the opportunities just kept coming. Life in the village definitely had a routine, but each day was new with the frequent arrival and departure of guests as well as almost daily adventures that weren't planned. It's difficult to outline what was the most important or the most interesting or what had the greatest value. The experience was unique for each person because each person was able to choose and participate based on his or her hopes, dreams, or desire to explore the new and different. I was most fortunate to experience twenty years with a great variety of people and experiences.

Worship at Holden for me was more than matins or vespers or noon prayers. Worship was also observing the change, the healing, the joy, and the sorrow in the lives of everyone involved. The program couldn't be separated from the work or from the variety of guests or from even working with the forest service. In the end, the worship, the program and the operation of the village were all a single effort. I didn't have a favorite season, only favorite experiences. Most days, our remoteness and the potential dangers involved were forgotten no matter if it was winter or summer, day or night.

Even the fear and anxiety of dealing with facility problems or human challenges was part of the program and part of the worship. Perhaps the greatest joy during those first twenty years was being able to operate without committees, which have a tendency to slow innovation and eliminate miracles. None of the directors I worked with liked formal office or management meetings, so life was good. To manage Holden was to make sure the facility and the operation functioned in a manner so as to not interfere with the personal adventure of any individual. It was critical to do whatever was necessary to eliminate the meaningless and encourage that which might lead to a new breakthrough. Operating with a management team of 'two' allowed decision making to be very efficient.

CHAPTER 10

Holden Village Board
of Directors

BEING EMPLOYED AS HOLDEN VILLAGE business manager was the first opportunity I had to work with a not-for-profit organization and interact
with a board of directors. The board officially hired me as manager, but
it's my understanding that it was at Carroll's request. Carroll was officially my boss, but because of his hesitation in terms of working with those
who controlled his employment future, I generally prepared and also
presented many of the reports offered at the board meetings. Carroll
always dealt with all of the reports and information in terms of program
and faculty. Initially, the board had two people to deal with in terms of
all aspects of the village operation. Carroll had overall responsibility
but specifically for the program and worship. I had responsibility for
everything else.

Initially, membership on the board was established to include men
who were involved with the beginning of Holden, especially if financial
gifts were involved or if their participation would open doors to the various national Lutheran Church bodies. For the first twelve years, there
were no women on the board. In 1978 Ellen Gamrath became the first
woman to chair the Holden board. Ellen served as a director for several
years prior to being elected chair. Ellen remains the only woman elected
as Holden board chair, but at least other women have been selected
to serve as directors. Ellen and her family have been involved in the

Holden Village community for many years and made valuable contributions to the life and ministry of Holden in many significant ways.

The youth directors of the three national Lutheran bodies were initially given board positions. Holden Village was originally envisioned as a youth or young-adult-oriented program. Therefore the youth departments would need to be represented. The other aspect of the youth departments' involvement was financial. If Holden were to receive any direct funding, it needed to come through an established department with a budgeted line item. None of the Lutheran groups had a department of young adults or a department of family integration. The board automatically included one member from the Lutheran Bible Institute in recognition of LBI initially accepting the gift and having ownership until the not-for-profit corporation was established. LBI also retained 50 percent of the mineral rights of the mining claims and 50 percent of any value derived from the mine if production were ever to be resumed. Eventually, the LBI position was revised to be advisory and nonvoting, then finally eliminated all together.

In addition to the national youth directors, many of the board members were from the Northwest. Holden had started as a Washington State activity initially providing most of the technically experienced volunteers needed to help bring the facilities into operational condition. The assumption was that the Northwest churches would be the source of the greatest number of registrations, at least initially. It was deemed important to assign board positions to a few Northwest pastors.

From the very beginning, Holden Village was envisioned to be a project of the three major Lutheran groups. In the Northwest, all of the Lutherans seemed to have a good working and worshiping relationship. A specific effort was made to involve pastors from the Lutheran Church–Missouri Synod who were known to have worked with other Lutherans on other projects or activities in the Northwest.

The board also included a number of professional men who could help fund the early years and influence others who might provide financial support. Many of the initial board members stayed involved with Holden for many years, and wonderful friendships were developed through their participation. Term limits weren't strictly adhered to initially. Some members were asked to remain on the board when many challenges and uncertainties existed. When the national youth offices dropped their financial support and the program moved away from a youth or young adult approach, the board removed the requirement for representatives from those offices.

The board initially met once a year. The executive committee, with members living in the Seattle area, was authorized to act on behalf of the entire board between board meetings if the need arose. In between board meetings we had very little contact with the board. Since the US Postal Service was our only communication at Holden, the board or the executive committee seldom communicated with us unless either Carroll or I contacted them. Many of the board members in those early years were active in the church both regionally and nationally, so they maintained social contact with each other even if it wasn't directly dealing with Holden Village business.

One of my favorite Holden board members was Dr. Erik "Bill" Pihl. Bill was an orthodontist from Mount Vernon, Washington. He became involved with Holden from the very beginning and was a contributor of time, money, and labor as well as landscaping materials. Many of the early board members as well as supporters were people recommended by the various Northwest bishops. I think Bill was really a gentleman farmer who became an orthodontist so he could afford the tractors and other farm implements he loved.

Bill came to the village each spring for at least a week to work with the landscaping. Many of the trees in the village that are now fifty years old were planted by Bill or volunteers he directed. In the early winter of 1964, Bill and his wife, Louise, called me and indicated that they would donate money to purchase a small snowmobile so Ruben, the first Holden Village caretaker, would have some transportation. I researched possibilities of snowmobiles that were commercially available.

It's difficult to imagine, but in 1964 there were only two dealer-
ships in Seattle that carried any kind of a small snowmobile. The one
was Polaris, and the other was the Canadian logging equipment company called Bombardier. (Bombardier is still in existence but is now
heavy into aviation. In fact our son, Jeff, flies the Q400 Bombardier for
Horizon Air.) We purchased the single track Bombardier. It would hold
two riders, and if the snow conditions were OK, would pull a sled. The
total cost was less than $1,000.00. Bill, Louise, and I hauled it over to
Chelan and loaded it on the passenger boat. We had rented a toboggan
from REI to pull behind the Bombardier to help haul a little luggage
and freight. We made it to Holden in reasonable time, and Ruben was
delighted to see some transportation other than snowshoes and skis. It
was a delightful weekend. Bill was on the board of directors for Holden
for at least twelve years.

Bill was very generous in many ways and introduced many people to
the village over the years. He and Louise opened their home in Mount

Vernon to me numerous times in the first few years of Holden, and I have fond memories of our conversations, eating fresh shrimp from La Conner and enjoying a few beers. The Pihls were great friends, and I visited them many times as I was trying to learn how to work with Carroll and the complexities of being the Holden Village manager. We discussed Holden and the challenges of beginning this unique operation. I may not have lasted through those first three years without the kindness of Bill and Louise. Bill was a member of the Lutheran Church in America and was a valuable national contact with that branch of the church.

As a result of the job history Carroll experienced as a maverick in the church and his fear of those who controlled his employment, he didn't relate to the board between its meetings and would frequently ask me to communicate with the board on his behalf. Board members during those years were very supportive of the village and its needs. The greatest value of board members might have been to introduce others to Holden and encourage pastors and churches to become involved. All board members were financial contributors, but none were major contributors. I have heard that Vern Rieke took a second mortgage on his home to help finance Holden in the beginning. Vern and his wife Jane were invaluable to Holden in many ways, but to my knowledge, their taking a second mortgage on their home wasn't factual. It's possible that this occurred without my knowledge, but I was maintaining the financial records for Holden Village and would have been aware of any major gifts—even if the gift occurred prior to 1963.

Until perhaps 1980, board members were more active in the village through visits with families rather than participation as members of the faculty. Through this involvement, the members had a thorough knowledge of life and work within the village through direct observation. During my twenty years, the board was never involved in "running" the village. In fact, it was my experience that the board spent very little time or effort on the operational aspects. It's true that perhaps half of the early board members came to the village and volunteered their time in landscaping, general cleanup, or maintenance projects, but this was because of their love for Holden, not because of their board involvement. Board members were more program oriented and spent more time discussing and listening to reports concerning the program.

The board never established a program for sustainability or fundraising. Carroll did the fundraising based on his extensive contacts with acquaintances around the country as well as generous relatives and past members of congregations Carroll had served. He was frequently invited to preach and address groups, which also provided fundraising opportunities. The quality and impact the program was definitely the force behind fundraising.

During one board meeting, a member and business owner suggested that the board set up a committee to establish a mechanism to solicit wills and insurance policies put in the name of Holden to assure future financing. Carroll literally jumped out of his seat and notified the board that as long as he was the director, Holden would never be financed with what he called "dead money." At least while Carroll was director, the issue remained off the table for further consideration.

Budgets were always presented conservatively based on the previous year's actual income and expenses with only minor increases for the next year. Although we applied for several grants, we received no grants or major gifts during the first twenty-two years. We made contacts with specific people if we had projects to fund such as the Jacuzzi therapy pool or passenger snow vehicles.

The major fundraising event was the annual year-end letter sent to the entire mailing list. Holden Village stayed alive and gradually grew through small gifts received from many enthusiastic supporters. The first major fundraising attempt involving a project was money needed to replace the maintenance garage destroyed by fire. We sent out a letter, and within four weeks, received over $20,000. For Carroll and many board members, the success of this fundraising confirmed the idea that Holden Village didn't need fire insurance because it had an excellent mailing list.

One of the board members, also a successful businessman in Minneapolis, took note of the generosity of those on our mailing list. He stressed that Holden had a gold mine in terms of potential fundraising and suggested hiring a professional fundraising team to mine the potential funds available. Carroll refused to consider involving a professional fundraiser. This was another sign that the Holden board could approve what Carroll suggested, but the board didn't dictate to Carroll what the village might do to sustain itself in the long-term or what approach should be taken in terms of the program. Carroll was definitely interested in sustaining the Holden Village program, but only if it was based on the generosity of people who supported the village because of the positive impact Holden was having on their lives and not because a professional fundraiser got paid to extract money from those who loved Holden Village.

During the years Carroll was director, the board basically met to receive reports from the director and manager and verify that Holden was paying its bills as well as not getting into trouble with the forest service or other government agencies. The board was especially important in terms of raising the prestige of Holden and its program and as quickly as possible making Holden Village into a national and even international retreat. The function or purpose of any not-for-profit board is to pick management leaders and then trust management to effectively run the operation.

As long as the board wanted to retain Carroll Hinderlie as director, it appeared to pull back from some of its responsibilities in order to keep Carroll happy. Carroll had definite convictions as to how Holden should be run and financed. It was evident that he wasn't about to allow the board to establish any fundraising programs that didn't match his convictions. Holden Village initially had no operational history, and it was evident that the remote location and limited history made it a potential challenge to hire a good director. I would suggest that the board members greatly admired Carroll for his many positive attributes but were perhaps too tolerant of some of his eccentricities and emotional challenges. It's sometimes difficult to define that fine line between allowing creativity and implementing oversight to eliminate potential problems.

The board did eventually begin meeting in the winter in Seattle and then in the summer or fall in the village. As often happens with new, nonprofit boards, the director—in this case Carroll—basically chose board members who were friends and who he thought would understand his personality as well as his program preferences. This process gradually changed, but even with the board loaded with specifically chosen members, Carroll was paranoid about board meetings. I always assumed his concern was the fear of being criticized by the board or potentially not having his employment continued as director. He didn't deal well with criticism.

Prior to the board meeting in 1965, Carroll was especially nervous for some reason. Four days before the board arrived, he informed me that we were going to Seattle to relax. He also informed our secretary, Karen Buege, that she was coming with us. Carroll's cousin had given Holden a sixteen-foot aluminum boat with an outboard motor. Carroll insisted on taking this boat from Lucerne to Twenty-Five Mile Creek. We made it downlake and arrived in Seattle about eight o'clock that night.

Carroll loved Peter Sellers; he informed Karen and me that we were going to enjoy a series of Peter Sellers movies at three separate theaters. The first one ended at ten o'clock that night, the next one at one o'clock the next morning, and the third at three in the morning. We went to a steak house for a very late dinner—or early breakfast—and then took Karen to the YWCA. Carroll and I went to the YMCA. We enjoyed three or four hours of sleep and then headed back to Lake Chelan and a return ride uplake in the sixteen-foot boat. This was another time when perhaps a "flock" of guardian angels watched over us and allowed us to survive. The board meeting a couple days later was a delight, and we were thanked for the great job we were doing. I interpreted that to mean that the village was still operating, and we even had a small amount of money in our bank account.

The Holden board during the first thirteen years was generally an effective governance organization, but it's my opinion that the board had some failings. It faced a major challenge, giving birth to an entirely new community and program without funding to assure success. Direct communication wasn't even available for the board to maintain minimal verbal contact with either Carroll or me. People returning from Holden were generally delighted with their experience, which most frequently didn't involve insights into operation or community challenges. Perhaps out of necessity, the board allowed Carroll and me to operate with the bare minimum of direction and monitoring.

With the limited funds, it was a miracle for Holden Village to continue from year to year. I got the impression that the board was so grateful that the program was meaningful and the facilities were usable, they didn't pay a lot of attention to potential problems. The board probably heard a hundred positive comments to any one negative. With a dynamic and controversial personality such as Carroll, the board was bound to hear some complaints.

It was fortunate that Holden Village attracted a person with the stature of Vern Rieke. Vern wasn't only respected by the Lutherans throughout the Northwest but also nationally and internationally. He was considered to be one of the leaders throughout the Northwest in terms of social issues. He was the Holden board chairman from day one of the nonprofit corporation being established. Vern was a brilliant person and was also a respected theologian. I must admit that I was always somewhat nervous when I was in his presence, especially if it was just the two of us. Vern was a very loving and compassionate person, but he was so brilliant and logical that it was intimidating for me to carry on a conversation with him, especially a conversation in which I was trying to lead to a logical conclusion. I was thrilled that Vern was the one who called me to offer me the position of business manager of Holden Village. I was twenty-four years old and had no training in terms of the responsibilities that the position would require.

Vern remained chairman of the Holden Village Board of Directors until 1978. It was a pleasure to be in meetings with him, since he never allowed them to get out of hand or too far off the track. He rarely offered an opinion during a meeting and was an excellent listener. He had an uncanny ability to wait until just the right moment and then inform everyone that all of the points had been made and it was time to vote on the issue. I think everyone always felt they had ample opportunity to contribute, and everyone felt their comments were valued.

Vern had power in any meeting because Vern was Vern, and it was difficult for anyone to counter his final conclusion. On the other hand, I think everyone felt that his conclusions had portions of their own comments, so how could Vern ever be wrong? To me, he always appeared to be thinking and analyzing a conversation and could sort out all of the points and accurately summarize what was being said. He wasn't afraid of dealing with tough questions or sensitive situations, and he was also one of the people who would keep Holden on the straight and narrow. His power and his leadership resulted from the respect and stature he held. I experienced several times when the board members' conversation was headed in one direction, and in Vern's wisdom it was the wrong direction. He would listen patiently, and then he would share what he considered to be a summary of the issues. When a motion was offered, it was basically Vern's suggestion, and there was a unanimous vote.

Vern was dedicated to working through the governmental and legal system to bring about social action changes, especially in terms of family law. I remember his leading sessions in Koinonia during the years he was working with the state legislature to change the divorce law to a "no fault" system. Prior to his work on this issue, the divorce courts were dedicated to destroying one or the other spouse in the process of divorce.

I always appreciated the fact that Vern was available to me if I needed counsel or guidance on some aspect of Holden. There were times when I had some concerns, and especially if they related to Carroll, it was difficult to know how to approach the situation. Vern always had time for me on the phone, in his office at the university or in his home.

Vern had the respect of many people and many segments of society. His association with Holden helped the village in the early years gain some credibility in the Northwest. Vern was the chairman of the board of Cashmere Valley Bank and therefore was well know and respected in the business community of North Central Washington. I was told, although it was never confirmed, that Vern was encouraged by an influential group to run for governor of Washington State. Vern elected not to enter elected office.

All of this respect within the government and within the church helped when we needed consideration with the many issues involved in establishing a credible operation. His association with the University of Washington Law School and the state of Washington helped Holden as it dealt with the forest service, Chelan County, and the state of Washington. His reputation definitely made a difference as Holden began to build respect as a creditable organization. As far as I know, Vern never pulled any strings with any government agency or within the church organization on behalf of Holden, but I do know that he didn't allow any agency to take advantage of the very inexperienced team that was establishing the Holden operation. One of Vern's important directions for the board and for Carroll was that he felt strongly that

1. Holden should maintain a connection with the church, and
2. Holden should remain separate from the church organization.

I originally wrote many of these comments concerning Vern upon hearing of his death. Vern's death in 2003 marked another passing of a significant person who kept this world from losing its balance and laying the ground work for Holden Village to be established on a sound foundation.

I always enjoyed working with the Holden board. I felt intimidated at times but generally felt supported and appreciated. Perhaps I was fortunate to be on the management team with Carroll Hinderlie. This partnership may have encouraged the board to show greater appreciation for my ability, my enjoyment—in general—of working with Carroll, and providing some emotional stability to the overall operation.

CHAPTER 11

The Dark Side of Holden

I HAVE STRUGGLED FOR THE past thirty-seven years, dealing with the memory of what I call the dark side of Holden. I love Holden, and it has been an integral part of my life for the past fifty years. However, for me, a bit of the luster of Holden's image was tarnished because I knew sexual misconduct occurred during its history. No community or ministry can achieve its maximum potential unless it's honest about its accomplishments as well as its faults and humbly enters into confession and seeks absolution.

These comments are made to share a part of Holden history that still needs healing. The lack of any public acknowledgment regarding these events was perhaps tied to where the church and society were at the time they occurred. It's not clear why healing was never offered for those who were hurt. Since Holden Village was in its infancy, it's likely there was concern over hurting the positive reputation Holden enjoyed in the church and society. Acknowledging that one of Holden's heroes had a flaw was apparently a major problem for the board.

The tragedy is that those who suffered abuse were never helped. The people who experienced this sexual misconduct were unfortunately forgotten, and they have had to assume that Holden didn't see the need to address their mental and spiritual damage.

Carroll Hinderlie was very much a part of the organized church community, but he was also a free spirit. Organizational policies often irritated him because they generally had little to do with the gospel of living in the freedom of grace. Carroll had a loving and compassionate side. It was easy to accept his flirtatious nature as a part of his innocent and at times playful personality. His free spirit delighted many, but in all likelihood his free spirit and the power of his position as pastor and Holden Village director created a dangerous combination in a remote community where he reached hero status.

Rumors began circulating indicating Carroll was acting inappropriately with some women in the sauna. It was virtually impossible to confirm these accounts, and I have no knowledge as to when these problems actually began. I made inquiries and was told staff women were aware of this problem. Apparently the rationalization for not coming forward was their fear of Carroll. He was the director, and he controlled communication within the village. He could be an emotional person when he was challenged. I understood those who expressed this fear of him. I was told that staff women circulated a warning to other women in the community, suggesting it was best to stay out of the sauna when Carroll was present.

Carroll loved the sauna and actually developed a "sauna culture" in the village, with announcements concerning the healing qualities of the sauna and its important function in creating community. He even scheduled Bible studies and discussions of current subjects of interest in the sauna. He created a perception that the sauna provided healing for body as well as the soul.

This sauna culture at Holden may have been even more dangerous because the 1960s and 1970s were periods when young adults were interested in rebelling against a prudish society as it related to drugs, sex, and nudity. All of these conditions intensified the dangers of a person in authority misusing his position of leadership and power within the community. The church, especially through the power of a pastor as leader has, at times, been a potential danger point because the church too often defines what is acceptable and at times when wrong can be overlooked. Holden was isolated geographically, and perhaps the assumption was that what happened at Holden stayed at Holden.

After this problem of sexual misconduct became apparent in the summer of 1976, I tried to work with a close friend of the Hinderlie family to investigate and deal with this situation, but that effort wasn't successful in addressing what was obviously a serious problem.

A young couple on sabbatical from Valparaiso University contacted me and reported that Carroll had been very inappropriate with the wife in the sauna. A newly arrived staff woman reported that she and Carroll had been alone in the Jacuzzi late at night and Carroll had engaged in inappropriate touching. She elected to leave the village. An adult counselor with a youth group from First Lutheran Church in West Seattle told me that one of the high school girls in the group had been in the sauna with Carroll and that Carroll had engaged in inappropriate touching. The counselor demanded action to deal with this problem.

In late summer of 1976 I received letters from a couple in Minnesota who were frequent Holden faculty members. They knew Carroll well and recognized the positive impact of the Holden program. The wife wrote a detailed letter concerning what she indicated was a serious problem involving Carroll. She also mentioned she had a conversation with a pastor and counselor in Minneapolis who shared he had previous knowledge of Carroll's problem. They also contacted Bishop Clarence Solberg (now deceased) of the North Pacific District concerning Carroll's inappropriate actions at Holden. They indicated individual letters had been sent to each of the Holden board members in 1976 but received no response. A retired pastor who was on the volunteer staff shared with me, during the summer of 1976, he spent more time counseling and helping staff women deal with Carroll's actions than he did in terms of his regularly assigned job.

I sent a letter to Vern Rieke and asked that we meet as soon as possible. At that time, no other means of communication was available other than US mail via the boat. I indicated that I had a concern regarding Carroll that needed immediate attention. Vern was chairman of the board of Cashmere Valley Bank and indicated he would be in Cashmere (eight miles west of Wenatchee) for a meeting. He suggested meeting in

Cashmere. I met with him and we talked for a couple of hours concerning this serious problem.

It was my impression from this conversation that some of the other Holden board members had strong suspicions of Carroll's problem. No one will ever know why this issue involving sexual misconduct hadn't been dealt with earlier. The concerns surrounding Carroll were now in the hands of the Holden board. Vern later notified me that the board's executive committee would meet in October to discuss this misconduct involving Carroll. A special meeting of the entire Holden board was subsequently scheduled for January 1977.

Our family had been granted a three-month sabbatical, and our time away from Holden was scheduled to begin November 1,1976, returning to Holden early February, 1977. We spent this time at our home in Leavenworth. Vern Rieke asked me to attend the January 1977 board meeting, which was held at Glendale Lutheran Church in Burien, South Seattle. Carroll wrote to me prior to that meeting, asking to meet and come up with a plan to deal with the board. He apparently knew the nature of the board meeting. I elected not to meet with Carroll prior to the board meeting since it was now a Holden board issue.

I had no advance indication if my job with Holden was in jeopardy, but following the meeting my job status didn't change. It was my understanding that the decision was made that Carroll would be granted a three-year period with full pay plus travel expenses to write a book but not return to Holden and not have any direct contact with any aspect of the Holden operation. It was my impression that no one on the board ever expected Carroll to actually write a book, and he didn't.

The Holden board apparently decided that this was the best way to protect Holden's reputation and minimize the hurt to the Hinderlie family. I wasn't aware of any attempt by the Holden board to work with Carroll to arrange counseling or therapy. To my knowledge, Carroll returned to Holden only once following his removal as director. The Holden board invited Carroll to visit during the summer of the twentieth anniversary celebration of the Holden Village ministry.

Carroll's removal created an unsettling time within the Holden community. Vern came to the village in early February 1977 to visit with the Holden community about Carroll being removed as director. Vern announced that Ron Vignec would be the acting director until an interim director was available. Ron was completing an internship with the Fullness of God congregation and was highly respected for his compassion and people skills. It's interesting that Carroll had, in a very real way, helped Ron discover a new life ten years earlier by bringing him to Holden. Now Ron was helping to rescue the Holden community and perhaps its future operation.

Our family returned to Holden in mid-February and immediately experienced an extremely uncomfortable situation within the Holden community. I was thankful that Ron was acting director, and I felt comfortable working with him. I'm forever grateful that Ron was helpful and supportive as I continued my work.

The arrival of Jim and Kay Fish with sons Eric and Matt was most fortunate for our family. Jim and Kay had been on the volunteer staff ten years earlier when Jim was finishing his theological training at Wartburg Seminary. Jim was an excellent preacher, counselor, administrator with a brilliant mind and healing humor. Kay was equally talented in administrative and planning abilities. They were taking a family sabbatical and happened to return to Holden during this rather traumatic period in its history. For me, and probably for my entire family, the fact that Ron Vignec was the acting director and Jim and Kay, long time friends, were now in the community were blessings. This allowed me to mentally and physically survive the next months prior to the arrival of Fritz and Gertrude Norstad as the interim directors.

My daily activities and responsibilities continued managing the operation. The three months prior to the arrival of Fritz and Gertrude were, without a doubt, the most difficult and stressful time I have ever experienced. I was isolated in a remote community. I felt as if my pastor, the pastor of Fullness of God congregation, eliminated me as a person within the community. Rather than helping the community heal or acknowledging that others had been mentally and spiritually hurt, some in the community adopted an attitude of loyalty to Carroll and denial of any misconduct. Unfortunately this attitude continues to this day for a segment of those who were aware of this sexual misconduct.

As fellow sinners we all have flaws, and we all need guidance and forgiveness. The need to identify someone to blame appeared to be a high priority for a group within the Holden community who couldn't accept the removal of Carroll as director. This exposed another aspect of the dark side of Holden Village and illustrated how much elements of life within the Holden Village community mirrored the shortcomings within society. Holden Village is a unique healing community, but it has always been far from perfect. Remoteness doesn't eliminate the sinful nature associated with the human spirit.

I never knew if some within the community who were very angry over Carroll's removal really understood the reason the Holden board felt it necessary to take this action. When Vern came to the village to talk with the community, it is my understanding he didn't go into detail as to the specific reason for the change in directors. Fortunately, Ron was an excellent acting director with the ability to relate to all within the community and literally keep Holden Village from disintegrating.

When it was obvious that Carroll couldn't continue, the Holden board was presented with the serious challenge of finding a new director. Knowing how difficult it would be for a director to step into this position, the board made a brilliant choice urging Fritz and Gertrude Norstad to rescue Holden Village. Fritz and Gertrude had been life-long friends with the entire Hinderlie family and were essentially considered part of the family. Fritz and Carroll had been classmates at St. Olaf and Luther Seminary. I had known Fritz for the previous thirteen years, and we had developed a great friendship and respect for each other.

Fritz and Gertrude agreed to serve as interim directors until John and Mary Schramm arrived in 1978. Fritz and Gertrude were the first directors to actually live in the village full-time. Since the Norstads were close friends of the Hinderlie family, the healing process began immediately upon their arrival. Fritz and Gertrude allowed the Hinderlie family a gracious way to make a transition away from Holden. With the reputation that Fritz enjoyed in the church and in society, his leadership allowed Holden to maintain its integrity, reputation, and respect.

Gertrude was the quintessential hostess to all in the village and was a healing force for everyone, no matter which side of the issue one might maintain. She was a special favorite with the children in the village because she knew how to feed the lollipop tree. During the winter and spring, Gertrude would tie treats to the branches of a small tree in front of Chalet 4, and the children would harvest the goodies. Our children, Kristy and Jeff, were seven and four years of age respectively at this time. The children of the village may not have known the details of what had occurred with Carroll's departure, but they definitely felt the tension within the community. Fortunately, Gertrude allowed the children to be children and not suffer from the attitudes and actions displayed by some of the adults during those months.

Fritz was a great communicator, not only preaching the gospel but also in sharing healing words with many individuals. His unique human spirit allowed attitudes to be healed. Fritz was highly respected by everyone, and many of Carroll's friends were also dear friends of Fritz and Gertrude. Fritz had been involved in a new healing program at Lutheran General Hospital in Chicago and also had a PhD in physiological counseling. Fritz was, in my mind, the best of the best. Fritz and Gertrude left Holden when John and Mary Schramm arrived and they moved to their new home in Leavenworth. After I retired from Holden, I was fortunate to enjoy a continued close friendship with Fritz and Gertrude during their remaining years in Leavenworth.

This episode was a very sad period in the life of Holden Village and during the community's development as a significant influence in the church and society. It's sad, but for whatever reason, Holden Village and at least some of its leaders protected Carroll and the Holden image without dealing with the hurt experienced by numerous women and others who had knowledge of Carroll's misconduct. When a lie exists in an organization, the organization cannot rise to the level of excellence that would be possible if the truth and the resulting healing could be a part of its ongoing growth.

It was unfortunate that when Elmer Witt became director in 1984, he was also involved in a questionable personal relationship situation. The Holden board was again faced with a dilemma and the need to replace another director.

The Holden board, or at least some of its leaders, having the authority and opportunity to deal with and initiate healing for all involved, chose the approach of burying the information concerning sexual misconduct by two of its directors. Carroll Hinderlie was a Holden saint and hero, but like so many other saints in the church, this Holden saint had a serious flaw that was ignored by too many for many years.

In 2013, while writing these memoirs, the Holden board of directors publicly shared a statement with the village constituency concerning sexual misconduct involving directors during the 1970s and 1980s. The names of the directors weren't shared, but the statement did indicate both directors were deceased. The full statement was this:

> Faithful to Holden Village's vision of God's love making new the church and world through the cross of Christ, we recognize that we are all both saints and sinners. During the 50th anniversary celebrations of Holden Village, we heard of many fond memories and significant positive life-changing events. Regretfully, it came to our attention that pain and suffering were also a part of our history. Specifically, the Board of Directors learned of sexual misconduct by two former executive directors, now deceased, that impacted female staff and guests decades ago. We acknowledge and lament the pain and suffering these actions may have caused. It is our mission and ministry to respond to this pain, offering hope in God's

reconciling love and seeking healing for those harmed. We are dedicated to preventing such occurrences in the future. Strictly administered policies and procedures are in place to deal with any harassment, sexual or otherwise, that occurs within the village community.

I applaud the board for at least publicly acknowledging the extended silence concerning this tragedy of sexual misconduct and also admitting that no action was initiated by previous Holden Board of Directors to address the spiritual and mental pain of those suffering directly or indirectly.

I fault the 2013 Holden board for remaining silent as to the identity of the directors involved. If the silence of the board was necessary to garner majority approval regarding this public statement, so be it. Their silence fails to completely deal with this tragedy, but the public statement was an initial positive step in the healing process.

The current Holden board has demonstrated how difficult it is to live the message Holden Village proclaims with a community "Amen" at the end of each day. This struggle has happened within a spiritual community that believes God helps each of us deal with our sinful nature through honesty and healing while allowing us to celebrate the freedom to explore daily challenges in our journey through life and our struggle with faith. Being open to help those hurting and also facilitating healing doesn't come easily, even for the directors of the Holden community.

CHAPTER 12

Valley of Innovation

In 1970 I spent several days in the Seattle Public Library investigating articles written about Holden Mine. (These were the pre-Google days.) I was surprised how many articles were written involving the mine and amazed that so many of these articles indicated the innovations for which Holden Mine was credited. One year a national mining magazine had articles about the Howe Sound mine at Holden in eleven out of its twelve issues. The mine was responsible for innovating operational techniques that became standard for the industry. Some of these innovations involved the methods for hard rock mining, while other innovations involved the health and safety of the underground activities.

As I became acquainted with residents of the Railroad Creek Valley, I also learned that the Holden miners weren't the first innovative people in the valley. Anyone who lives in a remote area and without easy access to transportation or communication needs to be innovative. Oscar was perhaps the earliest innovator in the Railroad Creek Valley, at least beginning around 1918. Gordon was an innovative person who naturally knew how to partnership with nature for survival and enjoyment of life.

Over the years, an increasing number of Holden miners returned, giving us an opportunity to learn directly from them about working in the mine as well as living in the larger community. It was always interesting and emotionally touching to see how much those who worked in the Howe Sound operation loved the work, the beauty of the valley, and the strong community ties. I never heard much about labor problems or even criticism of the Howe Sound Company, although I knew that there had been labor problems and strikes.

The fact that there was already a real community in Railroad Creek Valley may have increased the innovation and ingenuity of the workers. Being dependent on each other and sharing individual talents quickly creates community, reducing or minimizing internal competition. Talent that can't be hired is available free as abilities are shared. It's my guess that being isolated increased the opportunity to work together no matter what levels of management or labor jobs they occupied. It's also possible that because of the community that existed, there was greater willingness among the miners to solve problems for mutual benefit rather than live with constant labor conflicts.

One summer, William Barquist and his wife returned to Holden for a visit. Mr. Barquist was the exploration engineer hired by Howe Sound around 1928 to determine if the volume and concentration of the ore was sufficient to justify the investment needed for full production of the mine. Mr. Barquist and his wife had lived in the Honeymoon Heights the first housing area for the exploration team. By the time they left in the mid-1930s, he had submitted the reports indicating Howe Sound would make 10 percent on its investment with an operation lasting twenty years. These were the minimum conditions set by Howe Sound to begin a production mine. Mr. Barquist had followed the Holden Mine operation and its closing and then learned about Holden being given to an organization for a camp or retreat center. After visiting with us, he was convinced that God wasn't only involved with the current activities but also with the mine operation that allowed Holden Village to now exist.

When the Holden Village retreat came into existence, a new community took up where the mine community left off, even though the emphases of the two communities was totally different. In 1961 and 1962, all who were working to open the village for a religious endeavor were volunteering their time and abilities. No one was receiving a stipend or receiving any payment for services. This was the ultimate in community but unrealistic for future operation. Starting in 1963, the village began paying its first full-time director and manager. During the first ten years, the volunteers outnumbered paid employees by a factor of up to fifty to one. This ratio was probably not realistic for the larger, more complex operation of the future, but perhaps initially was important to generate the relationships needed to create a unique community atmosphere.

The community was critical to drawing an increasing number of guests from literally around the world. Organization and management activities were really a minor factor initially. The community felt that everyone in residence at any one time was totally involved and supportive of each other. Separation among guests, faculty, staff, management, and even government representatives was minimal and not generally apparent.

The remote location without transportation to medical facilities or to the source of repair parts increased the motivation for innovation during the mining operation. Knowing that the Holden Mine hospital had limited options very likely helped everyone to think in terms of safety and how blasting rock underground could be done in a way to create the least amount danger to everyone. Howe Sound was better funded than Holden Village, the retreat center, and could warehouse and store items to assure an efficient and productive operation.

Holden Village was started on a shoestring budget, but the junk pile that the mine left as its final legacy gifted a supply of items that provided plumbing parts, building and construction items as well as an unending supply of "stuff" for art projects. The mineral rights to the patented claims never really benefited Holden Village, but the junk pile left by the mine was a real gift. Terry Sateren began art welding, and Dan Erlander found a photographic paradise in and around the mine mill structure and the accompanying junk pile. Very few people in this time in history in the United States have had the joy and excitement of walking through a junkyard and discovering treasurers. The junkyard I remember outside of DeWitt, Nebraska, was a constant source of treasures similar to the treasures left by Howe Sound. It remains a fact that what is junk to one person or operation becomes treasure to another person or operation.

The Holden Village Science and Technology Committee was instituted to add some innovative power to Holden not only for operational necessities but more importantly, to keep the innovative atmosphere alive that had been in the valley over the years. The Science and Technology Committee supported the innovation already occurring in the Holden community. Some innovative ideas came from guests, more ideas from staff, and a few from my interest in various projects.

The first compost system was actually started around 1973. Brooks Andersen, a campus pastor, and his family from Duluth, Minnesota, came to Holden on sabbatical. As soon as they arrived, Brooks and his wife asked me if Holden could start a compost system. I wasn't into composting at the time and thought it a little strange. I finally told them that they could start a system on their own and operate it as a personal project, but the village wouldn't be getting involved with composting. They immediately set up several fifty-gallon barrels behind Chalet 2, where they were living, and started Holden's first compost system. They were very dedicated to this cause and collected horse manure from some forest service horses in the area, adding the manure to the kitchen scraps. They were ahead of their time, even ahead of Holden Village. Brooks and his family were the pioneers of the green movement at Holden. Within a few years, Holden jumped on board to expand their pioneering efforts.

I enthusiastically endorsed composting several years later when Russ Wold and his wife arrived on staff in the 1970s. I had gradually been learning and gaining knowledge and convictions in all things dealing with the environment. I was evolving into my "green" phase of life, which has intensified ever since. Russ was a professional horticulturist and had retired from one of the large pineapple plantations in Hawaii. He indicated that he had developed a simple compost system that was adaptable to large volumes, requiring minimal daily attention. He labeled it the "sliding air tube compost system." A year later he won a national award from Rodale, Inc., publishers of *Organic Gardening* as the organic gardener of the year in the United States.

Russ built Holden's system and it continued to operate for forty years. The only alteration we made to Russ' initial design was adding an electric fence to discourage bears. Some years later I was working for Harriet Bullitt, developing the Sleeping Lady Mountain Retreat in Leavenworth, and attended a conference in Washington, DC, featuring green living and biofuels. In the vendor displays I saw a large poster with a picture of Russ Wold. He had sold the manufacturing rights to the Sliding Air Tube Composting System, and it was now being commercially manufactured.

Herman Propp, one of our great innovators and craftsman, arrived in the village and seemed to have a talent for attracting some of the mature single women in the community. He had a flirtatious smile and was a great teller of stories. To my knowledge most of his stories were true. As I became acquainted with Herman, I found out that he had lived in Waverly, Iowa. I had attended Wartburg College, also in Waverly, but of course had never met Herman, who owned a local Buick dealership.

When he retired he signed up to go to New Guinea to work as a volunteer in the mission field. While in New Guinea he built a water wheel for an irrigation project. I had always been intrigued with water wheels, their beauty, their mesmerizing musical sounds, and of course, their ability to do work. Herman must have been close to eighty but still very active, and I asked him if he would be interested in building a water wheel at Holden. He didn't hesitate. I think his first interest was a justifiable excuse to spend extended time living in the Holden community.

It took at least two summers to finish the project, but Holden finally had an eight-foot water wheel. We even installed a small generator so it actually produced a small amount of electrical power with one light bulb to prove it was functional. Since diverting water from the creek would have required permits, we used the water being discharged from the hydroelectric plant. We didn't need permits if we utilized the water before it reached Railroad Creek. We constructed a wooden flume with lumber from our sawmill. The water wheel didn't do much other than provide another educational model along with the visual and audible music resulting from the mechanics of the wheel, while the water gave up its power to another form of energy. Herman was a great person and another shaper of the Holden community.

Another valuable volunteer with an innovative mind was John Nyquest. John had worked for and retired from the Great Northern Railway, which allowed him to ride the train without cost from Minneapolis to Wenatchee. John was a member of the volunteer staff for several summers. Some of these people, such as John, Omar Cline, Hortie Christman, Herman Propp, and Al Swihart, were unofficially my executive management team, although that isn't how they were identified. It was impossible to give these people a title since they did so many jobs and always responded to any new opportunity I presented to them. They spent multiple years at Holden because they had talents that were extremely valuable to the operation, but even more importantly, they added life and joy to the community. Since none of them were paid, they felt free to be honest with me if they made observations that needed attention. Holden enriched their lives, and I'm sure they felt they received as much or more than they gave to Holden.

John had worked as a surveyor and maker of maps for the railroad. He was a detail person, frequently frustrated because the maps that we had of Holden Village and the mine weren't accurate in terms of measurement and location in relation to other structures. I encouraged him to relax and enjoy life and not worry about a few inches or one or two degrees. John was always interested in a new project. Much of the time he was working on maps or plot drawings involving a project where more detail was needed in order to be submitted to the forest service. As Holden would add a small structure such as the greenhouse, John would add it to the map so its existence, as well as its location, was accurately documented.

John and Omar were responsible for the vast majority of the brick pathways around the central part of the village. The bricks were salvaged from the chimneys of several of the mine buildings, including the assay house and warehouse and engineers' office. Salvaging and using brick for the walkways wouldn't have been economical if we were paying for the installation costs, but with volunteers it was possible to be inefficient and use many existing materials. The brick paths were a great addition, but they also absorbed moisture, which, when freezing temperatures arrived, made for slippery walkways.

I always had ideas to pursue, but I was never the one to pursue them. We were trying to think of ways to win the battle with the tailings from the mine. I read an article about a company in one of the Caribbean countries with a process for making building blocks out of tailings. I discussed this with John, and he was excited at the possibility of experimenting with our tailings. As he had time, outside of some other projects, he made several molds and began experimenting, combining the tailings with lime and cement. He was successful in making several sample blocks that probably could have been used for some construction projects. We didn't expand this project into a production volume, but we did provide another point of interest and education for the community. At least one or two of the tailings blocks were originally on display in the museum. John was another example of a retired individual who provided a valuable service to Holden and in turn benefited from being part of the Holden family.

Hugh Davis was a miracle find for Holden. Actually we didn't find him; he and his wife, Melba, accidently found Holden. They had no tie to the Lutheran Church but were taking a day-trip to Stehekin one fall. Hugh, a retired Boeing engineer, had a conversation with a fellow boat passenger who was traveling to Holden who mentioned the hydroelectric plant Holden had built. Hugh was the "father" of the propulsion system for Boeing's commercial hydrofoil and an expert with turbines. After he graduated, he first worked for the Leffel Turbine company engineering turbines for hydro projects. His specialty was "water cavitations effects." He was a brilliant engineer and, in his university training, had had the opportunity to attend lectures by Albert Einstein.

Hugh was excited and intrigued with the Holden hydro generator project. Melba agreed to change their plans, and they got off of the boat at Lucerne rather than continuing on to Stehekin. I gave Hugh a tour of the hydro generator and had a great conversation with him. We immediately bonded. Hugh not only agreed to be a volunteer consultant for us on the hydro installation, but he almost begged me to allow him to be involved and test our units and calculate efficiencies. Hugh loved numbers and lengthy calculations and solving challenges. I guess that's why he was a brilliant engineer. I personally was more interested in the philosophical or societal aspects of engineering. That's probably why I retired early in my engineering career.

Hugh was brilliant but also humble. He realized immediately that technically we didn't know much about improving the efficiency of our hydro system, yet he approached any suggestion he had as a partner rather than someone with superior knowledge. In the next years, Hugh and Melba made numerous trips to Holden, and Hugh spent much time working to help us increase the efficiency of the hydro turbines. He also worked with us as we investigated several new options for additional hydro production. This included a pump storage system and a low-head system on Railroad Creek.

Hugh was another example of the many non-Lutherans who became involved with Holden. He also fit into the category of a person who had spent all of his life in exciting projects and traveling around the world, in demand for his technical knowledge. In retirement he needed—and in Holden found—a project that could keep him active and excited, looking forward to each day.

Hugh had a real interest in the Seattle Supersonics, the professional basketball team. We gathered in our chalet to listen to the game on TV when they won the national championship. We couldn't really watch it because of the poor reception.

Now that I have personally joined the "mature" category of society, I understand how important it is to feel as if I still have some value. At twenty-four years of age, when I started to work with the retired volunteers, I had a great relationship with them. I recognized their involvement as a valuable asset to the Holden operation, but I didn't understand how much the involvement on the volunteer staff meant to them in their lives. The retired staff members weren't only accepted but perhaps even elevated in status to a point they never experienced in their home communities or occupations.

We were interested in reviewing as many alternate energy options as possible for the Holden operations as well as program or educational possibilities. I found an article and plans in the *Whole Earth* catalog for solar hot-water panels. We were interested in anything that would help reduce fuel-oil consumption. Fuel was costly, especially when adding the cost of transportation up the lake and then trucking to the village. It was also exciting to make use of the sun to heat water for the laundry, a rather new concept in the early 1970s. Our maverick crew got busy after we discussed some options and reviewed the challenges. Before long we had eight low-cost, solar hot-water panels ready to install on the roof of the hospital building.

The primary expense was the copper pipe and the differential temperature valves controlling the circulating pumps. The village laundry was in the basement of the former hospital, and it already had a two-hundred-gallon tank that could be used for circulating and storing hot water. We added a circulation pump and electric temperature sensors that regulated the flow of water as the sun did its work. After a little trial and error, the laundry, serving up to four hundred daily guests and staff, was being supplied by solar hot water from mid-May through September. The main disadvantage of the system was the necessity of removing the panels before the snow arrived so that the four-to-six feet of accumulated snow wouldn't tear them off the roof each spring. The homemade solar panels weren't the most efficient, but we weren't after the highest efficiency as much as reducing costs and providing educational examples. We were able to make solar panels at a minimum cost with our volunteer labor and by using parts from our stockpile of materials from other projects.

We also experimented with heat recovery systems that would preheat the cold water going into the kitchen boiler. The water for the dishwasher was required to be 140 degrees and then boosted to 180 degrees by an electric booster. Normally the hot water went directly into the sewer lines after use. We ran the hot water coming out of the dishwasher through a homemade heat exchanger, which resulted in heating the forty-to-fifty-degree incoming cold water up to about ninety-to-a-hundred degrees without the consumption of more fuel. Consequently, it took less oil to heat the water going through the boiler, saving oil and money. The heat exchanger was built at the village and installed by our plumber. Some years later it was decommissioned, since it didn't meet the manufacturing requirement set by the health department.

We took a look at vermicomposting, which is the process of converting organic material into very rich soil using red wiggler or garbage worms. I found a government research paper that indicated even large metropolitan systems were experimenting with this approach. It wasn't practical for Holden since the worms worked most efficiently at around seventy degrees. Not a good system for perhaps nine months of the Holden operation. I have personally made use of vermicomposting at our home for the past thirty years, even transporting "red wigglers" to Tucson, where we now live.

With the cost of shipping food, we were always discussing options we might have to produce some food in the village. The first project we considered was raising fryers. They were seasonal. Chicks would be easy to ship in around mid-May, and we would harvest them in September or early October. We even had an area in the old mill structure that had three very high concrete walls. It would take only a good fence on one side to keep the coyotes, weasels, and other hungry predators from living off our fryers. I can't really remember why we decided not to proceed with this concept, but we knew we couldn't outsmart the predators.

We knew that gardening was a lost cause except for small volumes of salad material and perhaps some other cool-weather crops. We did have a demonstration garden, but production for the community was

minimal in terms of volume. Rabbits, ground squirrels, and other crit-
ters benefited more from the garden than we did.

Growing pigs was one possible option for food production. Leo
Bustad was known as the "pig man." One of his research projects at
Hanford was developing a miniature pig that could be used to experiment with radiation and its effects on skin. Leo informed us that physi-
ologically, pigs and humans had a lot in common. He tried his best to
improve the reputation of pigs. He had clip-on ties with pigs on them.
He wore hats with pigs on them. He even presented a few vespers featuring lessons from pigs. He did help people understand that the concept
of pigs being a dirty animal wasn't true. He convinced us that if you keep
a pigpen clean, the pigs would be clean. It was the humans' fault that
pigs got dirty. Pigs can consume lots of garbage. Holden produced a lot
of garbage. The experts told us that the only way our garbage could be
safely fed to pigs that are then used for human consumption was to boil
the garbage before feeding it to pigs. We elected not to pursue this.

The one option that did seem to have merit was trout production.
Trout grew naturally in the stream, so the climate was favorable. I contacted the state fish and game department to see if we could get some
trout fry (baby trout). The department had a hatchery at Chelan Falls.
To our amazement, they offered to ship us thirty-five hundred Spokane
strain of rainbow trout as long as we were using them for an educational
project and not for commercial use. We didn't have the funds to construct a pond for the trout, but we did have the river sauna plunge. The
water flowing into the plunge was coming directly out of Copper Creek.
After the water ran through the hydro turbine it ran into the plunge
and then into Railroad Creek. Sauna lovers could no longer use the
plunge, but we assured them that the creek was just as refreshing.

In early June, the hatchery shipped us the trout fry in a large vat
that was equipped with an aeration system, with oxygen percolating in
the tank for the duration of the trip. Our first choice was to find natural food for their feed but discovered that was virtually impossible. We
ended up having to purchase pellets that were also used by the hatchery.

About this time, Meredith Olson arrived on the volunteer staff. She had just received her master's degree in aquaculture from the University of Puerto Rico. Meredith was the perfect fit as director of the aquaculture project. She was in charge of feeding and record keeping, including recording water temperature and calculating conversion of food into protein in the fish. Meredith also was an excellent teacher, spending a lot of time explaining the scientific aspects of raising fish to the many people who visited the project.

The project was very exciting and attracted a lot of people to observe the progress and watch the frenzy of the fish when food pellets were distributed on the surface of the water. We didn't give up trying some natural feed. We purchased a small device that was suspended directly above the plunge. It had a light to attract the bugs and then a fan that blew them down on the water surface. It worked but didn't come close to supplying sufficient feed for the fish. Growth of the trout was very promising. In late September we had our first fish fry in the dining hall. The next harvest was over Christmas vacation that year. We invited everyone in the village to grab a pole from the Hike Haus and catch a trout for dinner. The young people loved it, and even some of the adults who had never caught fish found it a memorable experience. Standing on top of four feet of snow with over three thousand trout waiting to be caught in the plunge below wasn't really a challenge, but it was either one person catching sixty trout with a net or thirty people each catching two trout while having the time of their lives.

The trout continued to do well until April and early May of the next year. We went to the plunge one morning and found all of the fish floating on the surface. We had no idea what had happened. An animal hadn't killed them. I froze six of the deceased fish and wrote a letter to Leo, who was a friend of Dr. Lauren Donaldson at the University of Washington. Dr. Donaldson was a world-recognized teacher and scientist in the area of aquaculture and in fact had, through the technique of selective breeding, developed a new strain of trout called the Donaldson trout. (Dr. Donaldson later came to the village with Leo on an informational trip when we were investigating the development of Lucerne with a possible aquaculture project in Lake Chelan.)

Leo instructed us to send the frozen fish to the University. An analysis determined the trout were poisoned by copper and zinc. That made sense. The sauna plunge wasn't well built, had cracks in the bottom, and was sitting on tailings. As the snow was melting in the spring, the water table increased until it was pushing tailings through the cracks in the concrete and infiltrating the water. Tailings, of course, had zinc, copper, and probably a few other items that weren't fish friendly. It was a great project, but we made the decision not to invest the money into constructing a pond that could guarantee contamination-free water.

The tailings covered approximately eighty acres with Tailings Pile No. 2, the largest over sixteen-hundred feet long. We were always looking for some positive use for the tailings surface or the tailings material. Small, single-engine airplanes had landed on the tailings several times, so we knew that was feasible.

Once, three Piper tail draggers flew up the valley and circled the tailings a couple of times, and then all three planes landed. They had no identification markings on them. Rumors got started that they could be flying illegal cargo in or out of Canada. The small community was interested in some excitement. One of the planes experienced some minor damage when landing and our mechanic helped make the repairs. The pilots never came down to the village, and the mechanic was the only one to talk with them. We assumed that he had been sworn to secrecy. It was important for the community to have some excitement to break the routine and also to generate some new points of conversation.

Since Tailings Pile No. 2 made a reasonable runway at our elevation of thirty-two hundred feet, I decided to check on the possibility of a flight service from Boeing Field in Seattle, flying charters between Seattle and the Holden tailings. The charter service I contacted was familiar with Holden and the tailings, and they thought it was worth considering. It turned out that if a full plane of six passengers flew each direction, per person costs would be competitive with the road and boat trip, especially when considering overnight lodging. The winds in the valley weren't predictable and neither was the forest service. We didn't pursue the project. It appeared that the permitting process would be endless, plus uncertain weather conditions and the need to maintain the surface of the tailings would add too many complications.

From 1972 to 1973, the US was experiencing a fuel shortage, and there was interest in the possibility of using dirigibles (blimps) for at least freight and possibly passengers. An article I read indicated that the federal government was looking for a route to test the use of dirigibles, but it must be a route not currently subsidized by the government for commercial passenger transportation. I thought I had the perfect route. A dirigible could be based at Pangborn Airfield in East Wenatchee, fly up the Columbia, pick up passengers at the Chelan airport, then fly up-lake to Holden and on to Stehekin. I imagined that when the dirigible was approaching for a landing, a group of volunteer staff would run up to the tailings and help with the landing and unloading procedures. I imagined the announcement over the public address system: "The blimp is coming. The blimp is coming."

I didn't know that much about dirigibles or blimps, so during a trip to Wenatchee I put in a call to Goodyear Aerospace in Akron, Ohio. It took a while to get to the right person, since they thought I wanted to advertise on the side of the blimp. I was finally put through to the person in charge of the aerospace division, who seemed thrilled to talk with someone about the use of dirigibles for something other than advertising. The important factor was that he assured me they could maneuver in a space that was adequate for any single engine plane to maneuver.

I read in one of the national magazines that Senator Barry Goldwater, Senator from Arizona, was interested in this concept, so I wrote to him about my idea. I received a nice letter back from him with a copy of a speech that he had just given to a group involved with transportation and aeronautics. Senator Goldwater was encouraging, but we didn't pursue this project. I guess we were just too far ahead of the time. I gave Senator Goldwater's letter to the museum.

During the mine operation the tailings were flushed out to the settling area as slurry. Over time, the tailing dried to a fine powder and the dust blowing off the tailings on windy days was always a concern. Most frequently, the wind and airflow were downvalley, so the village itself didn't experience the major portion of the tailings dust. We began doing experiments on mixing compost in small sections of the tailings and planting pine seedlings and some grasses to see what might grow. The forest service also sponsored a project through one of the government agencies. They completed a more scientific study of various grass seed and various combinations of nutrients. Some of these combinations worked rather well, but there were too many variables. We cooperated with the forest service by helping set up a sprinkler system and doing some of the weekly monitoring and record keeping.

Through our contacts with Leo and his colleague Al Halverson at Washington State University, we worked with one of the graduate students to investigate the actual volume of tailings being deposited down the valley and also determine the distance down the valley and the spread across the valley. We set out buckets of a given size at various distances and then at the end of the season determined the volume of the tailings at the various locations. The results of these tests may still be in a box in the museum storage or in some report at WSU.

The sewage system, transportation of fuel, and dust generated from the tailings were all major challenges that were constantly on our minds. At the same time I did the Holden Mine research in the Seattle library, I also made an effort to find plants that might grow in soils with wide pH ranges. The tailings were high on the acid side. I discovered that Jerusalem artichokes not only were tolerant of a wide range of pH levels but also had very few enemies in terms of disease or pests. The exciting discovery was that they were also a great source for producing ethanol alcohol, which could be used as vehicle fuel. This was like Christmas: a solution for tailings dust, disposal of sewage effluent, and production of fuel onsite!

We were having serious problem with the sewage drainage field. Dr. Eleanor Schwecke, Chelan-Douglas County health director and wife of Henry Schwecke who engineered our hydro plant, had threatened to close the village unless we could come up with at least a temporary fix to the drain field problem. The mine had used the tailings as a big evaporation pond for its sewage system. I figured if it worked for them, it should work for us. I met with a civil engineer in Wenatchee to draw up plans for using the tailings and sizing the pumps and pipes. I submitted the plans to the forest service and to Dr. Schwecke, and they were accepted.

Washington State University was just completing a research project using Jerusalem artichokes as a substitute for sugar beets for the production of sugar. WSU offered us eight hundred pounds of artichoke tubers free of charge if we would pick them up at their research station in Prosser, Washington. We took them to Holden and planted all eight hundred pounds of tuber in a section of the tailings, irrigating them with effluent we pumped from the septic system. Later that summer we had Jerusalem artichokes growing eight feet high, but we discovered that if we didn't continuously sprinkle the plants with the effluent, the deer would graze and eliminate part of the crop. The stalks were high in sugar content; it was like the deer had discovered a candy store. The trick was to keep sprinkling effluent on the plants. The article I read in the Seattle library hadn't mentioned deer as a threat to raising Jerusalem artichokes.

Since we were experimenting with Jerusalem artichokes, we decided to also plant tomatoes in the same area to check their growth possibilities. They grew well, but we didn't plan to eat them because of the chemicals in the tailings and the use of sewage effluent for irrigation. That summer we had a guest who was director the Weyerhaeuser Corporation laboratories. I asked him about the danger of the tomatoes being grown on the tailings in terms of human consumption. He offered to take some of the ripe tomatoes back to the lab and unofficially test them. Several weeks later I received an unofficial report indicating that there was no reason that they couldn't be consumed because of pathogens or tailings chemicals, but of course we weren't about to add them to our salad bar.

Artichoke tubers are excellent for salads and have the crunch and moisture of chestnuts. The tubers are high in starch, in addition to the high sugar content of the stalks. Ethanol alcohol could be made from either the tuber or stalk. We were interested in using the stalks, leaving the tubers in the tailings for next year's crop. Dan Lofgren, an enthusiastic young man from St. Paul, Minnesota, who appreciated his experience at Holden, was interested in this project and offered to give us $2,000 to purchase a twenty-five-gallon electric still. Making ethanol from a crop that was being grown to solve the sewage system problem, decreasing the dust problem, plus producing low cost fuel for the vehicles used around the village was an interesting prospect.

After the successful tests on Tailings Pile No. 1 with the artichokes, we put together an initial plan to use Tailings Pile No. 2 to establish two or three effluent evaporation ponds and sufficient acreage to plant Jerusalem artichokes. The majority of the forty acres of Tailings Pile No. 2 would be irrigated with effluent to eliminate a portion of the dust problem and also produce a source for biofuel for at least the vehicles used in and around the village.

The Science and Technology Committee reviewed and refined the plan. Then we turned it over to an engineering firm, Haner, Ross and Sporseen from Portland. One of the company's engineers had been a frequent visitor to the village and had also worked with us on the Railroad Creek hydro project. After the engineers confirmed that it was a viable project, we turned it over to the forest service and the country health department. Approval came just as I was retiring from Holden in 1983, and the new management team elected to begin anew, considering a more traditional sewage system. The still was purchased but never used, and the plans for the Jerusalem artichoke project were assigned to the Holden museum. The tailings sewage project could have saved Holden considerable money compared to what was subsequently spent, but it would have required more monitoring and labor.

Not all of the projects we initiated dealt directly with the operation of Holden Village. Most projects were discussed with the Science and Technology Committee or were ideas directly from the committee. Some projects just sounded interesting and would also provide an opportunity for educating the Holden staff and guests. Leo loved animals, and he loved people. He was always thinking of ways for people and animals to interact. He helped write and lobbied for a congressional bill that allowed pets to be taken into government-supported retirement and nursing homes. It's my understanding that Leo was present when the president signed the act into law. Leo was convinced of the healing properties of pets in their interactions with humans.

He also had an idea that involved the use of pigeons and retirement homes. Pigeons make great pets and are fascinating to observe. Why not send messages between retirement homes via pigeons? Leo suggested that Holden experiment with pigeons to see how complicated it was for the average person to raise them. He, of course, had friends who raised pigeons and supplied us with three-day-old chicks. The first question was whether pigeons needed to be hatched on the site for them to return or whether introducing chicks to a new location would work. Our initial pigeon coop was the Chalet 1 garage.

Once we proved our competence, our volunteers built a more sophisticated pigeon coop. It was an A-frame just to the north of Lodge 2 and the greenhouse. After several hatches, we built up our stock to about twenty-five pigeons. Each morning around coffee-break time, we would release them for exercise. It was a delight to see them go through their exercise flights. Pigeons are easy to train as long as they know where and when food will be served. We started transporting the adults down the road, increasing the distance each week to make sure they could find home. We found out the pigeons were smarter than we were.

Eventually we took them to Lucerne for multiple practice runs. Then I started taking a small group of them down to Twenty-Five Mile Creek in my boat. I would record the release time. Pigeons always head out and initially make three circles over the launching point and then head home. From Twenty-Five Mile they didn't fly uplake but rather headed to the north and west, taking the most direct route even though they had never made the trip from Twenty-Five Mile to Holden. When I arrived back in the village later that day I inquired if the pigeons had returned. It turned out that they were back in the village within approximately thirty minutes of my releasing them.

We continued training them through the summer and fall. Unfortunately, during Christmas, a weasel got into the coop and killed all of the pigeons. That was the end of the project. We had done all we could to seal and secure the coop, but the weasel was smarter than we were. To my knowledge, Leo never did try the pigeon message-carrying concept in any retirement home. Over the years I have heard and read different stories about the reason Holden had pigeons. Most of the stories were inaccurate. Now you know the real story.

Howe Sound did an excellent job of constructing the company town with craftsman quality. Howe Sound also located the town site at a location in the valley that minimized the danger of destructive avalanches. For years, mine locations were notorious for being built in mountainous areas without consideration to avalanche danger.

It's not likely that there were building codes in 1935 in Chelan County that would have specified snow loads for buildings. One factor that helped was that much of the lumber used for building construction was cut and milled in the valley. The lumber was full dimension, so a two-by-six was actually two by six and not milled down to one and a half by five and a half. The buildings were constructed in 1935 and 1936, thus seventy-five years old when the village celebrated its fiftieth anniversary in 2012. The Village Center is the only building that was built with steel girders.

The domestic water system was also well built. The seventy-five-thousand-gallon storage tank was a metal tank with a wood covering and sawdust insulation on the sides. Much of the eight-inch waterline bringing water form the diversion dam to the storage tank was cedar wood stave pipe. Wood stave pipe lasts forever. If they spring leaks, they're easy to repair by tapping in cedar wedge. As soon as a cedar wedge absorbs moisture and expands, it seals the pipe perfectly.

The original village builders had also installed fire hydrants in the supply line in the mine area as well as in the village. Gravity pressure provided eighty-four pounds per square inch (psi) of pressure in the village. Water pressure in most metropolitan areas is forty psi out of the hydrant and then increased by fire truck pumpers. The eighty-four psi out of the Holden hydrants was somewhat dangerous when using the two-and-a-half-inch fire hose. It definitely takes more than one person to hold and control the hose.

The vehicle bridge used during the mine days was built from wood and was gradually deteriorating. We knew from the beginning that it would need to be replaced. At the same time the Lutheran Bible Institute received Holden Village, Howe Sound contracted a salvage crew to remove the mill and other buildings from the mine. The crew, from North Central Washington, didn't understand the complexities of this salvage job. They ended up taking the easiest items to remove and sell and then declared bankruptcy with the mess left for someone else to deal with. The Holden board actually gave them one extra year to do salvage work. Gil Berg had his eyes on two thirty-six-inch steel I beams that would work for the bridge replacement. The agreement was that the salvage crew would be allowed to come back for one more year if they would take the I beams down to the vehicle bridge and give them to Holden. Word has it that the only money the salvage crew made was by shipping out some barrels of concentrate that they recovered from several of the tanks they removed. The concentrate resulted from the milling process after removing much of the rock that didn't contain copper, gold, silver or zinc.

Holden didn't replace the vehicle bridge until the mid-1970s, with Hortie Christman engineering the plans for getting the thirty-six-inch I beams across the creek with basically no equipment.

During the years of the mine operation, the footbridge across Railroad Creek was covered. Pictures were still available, so we knew the original appearance. However, the roof over the original bridge had fallen off or was removed before 1961, when I first visited Holden. The original bridge continued to deteriorate. The original eight-inch waterline that supplied water to Winston Camp and the Holden Company town was attached to the bottom of the bridge and insulated with sawdust and wood chips available from the sawmill. In the early winters following 1961, there was minimal use of the village and therefore minimum water flowed in the pipe. The pipe froze several times, and there was increased concern that the bridge was deteriorating to the point that it would jeopardize the main waterline if the bridge were to collapse.

The first step to assure domestic water and fire protection in the village was to relocate the waterline. We decided to bury the line under Railroad Creek bed, just upstream from the footbridge. Fortunately we accomplished this work before the law changed and endless permits were required for any work done in or around the creek. The stretch of Railroad Creek that ran through the mine-disturbed area was more or less void of fish. Over the years the minerals and chemicals from the mine and blowing tailings had killed the potential aquatic nourishment for fish. Although the water didn't kill the fish, they didn't linger in the creek or spawn in the area along the tailings. The bottom of the stream had been coated with residue from the mine and mill.

Because of the potential problem with the water pipe being damaged by rocks or erosion, we used two sections of surplus fourteen-inch hydro penstock pipe as a sleeve for the waterline to cross the creek. We buried the sleeve two feet under the creek bed, which was as deep as we could go with the equipment available to us. We completed the work in late fall when the water flow was at a minimum. We pulled a six-inch pipe through the fourteen-inch sleeve and attached it to the eight-inch waterline on either side of the creek. The actual waterline was well protected by the fourteen-inch steel pipe. We relocated the pipe in the mid-1970s, and it was still in use in 2013.

This was another project involving volunteer experts in the field. Ralph Peterson provided the technical direction for all of the projects that involved water and sewage flow in pipes. He was a salesperson and technical consultant for Pacific Pipe and Supply Company in Seattle. He was a member of the Development Committee and put in countless hours and many trips to Holden to assist in its development, always on a volunteer basis. He had many friends and associates in the business; when we needed additional information or technical assistance, Ralph could always contact a technical associate for free advice.

With the pipeline secured under the creek bed, the integrity of the bridge was still a concern, but any further deterioration of the bridge wouldn't jeopardize the only source of water for fire protection and domestic use.

In order to replace the footbridge, we needed an engineering drawing to submit to the forest service. Ralph suggested his friend Les Erickson, city engineer for Edmonds, Washington. Les's professional license would help with getting approval from the forest service. He volunteered his time to design the covered bridge and do the needed engineering to determine the size of logs necessary for the structure. He studied the historical pictures of the original covered bridge so the new bridge would have a similar appearance. Work on the footbridge occurred during 1979 and 1980.

We made an attempt to obtain all of the materials for the footbridge from the forest in Railroad Creek Valley. As the plans became available, Ernie Zoerb, our Lutheran pastor and military chaplain turned logger and sawmill operator, began looking for appropriate logs to be used as the main stringers for the bridge. The lumber was also rough cut onsite. Even the cedar shakes for the roof were hand split from cedar blocks cut nearby. With the exception of the nails and metal hangers, the entire bridge was valley grown. Construction was the combined effort of the designer, Les; the logger/chaplain, Ernie; and the barber/logger/self-taught engineer Hortie Christman. No equipment was available to lift the log stringers in place, and it was again up to Hortie to engineer a system with the limited equipment we had available.

Within a year after the bridge was completed, word circulated about its construction. The Oregon Covered Bridge Society contacted me, expressing an interest in visiting Holden to document the bridge with pictures and a story. I made sure they understood that the Holden covered bridge wasn't the original, but that wasn't of concern. They indicated that there were limited numbers of covered bridges in Washington and Oregon, and they made an effort to document all covered bridges in existence in the Northwest. We were told that people traveled around the country to view and take photos of existing covered bridges. An article appeared in their association newsletter. I was aware of a few people who visited the village specifically to see the covered bridge, but to my knowledge it never involved a large number. The Holden Village covered bridge is on the Internet with excellent photographs; Google "Washington Covered Bridges List."

During the period of 1963 through 1983, the only major building we added to the Holden Village footprint was the mine and geology museum. Another project was the addition to Koinonia to enhance the options for the winter community, as well as new options for meeting rooms during the summer. However, the total building was still Lodge 5 or Koinonia. We also replaced the original garage following the fire that destroyed the original.

The Holden museum had been in the planning stage since Rudy Edmund first arrived in 1962. Rudy was a patient person. We initiated various options for the museum's location, but each time the space was taken by a function that was determined to be a higher priority. In the mid-1970s, we began in earnest to design and eventually construct a facility that would be exclusively a Holden mine and geology museum. The plan was to place the building on the foundation of the original mine assay lab. This was on Holden Village property, located on the edge of the processing mill building. It would have a view of the processing mill and tailings to the east and Bonanza Mountain to the west. It turned out to be an excellent museum location and layout. The assay foundation was a reasonable size.

Rudy was involved in all of the planning, and he specifically designed the interior. Dan Dierks, former volunteer staff member and now a licensed architect, agreed to do the plans pro bono. Even though using the existing floor and foundation of the assay lab put some limitations on the design, we felt that utilizing the space would add to the historical value of the museum. The museum project cost less than $40,000. Rudy finally had a museum, and it was a very popular point of interest.

After about thirty-five years of service, the Portal Museum was torn down in 2013 as a result of the mine remediation work, but money was appropriated through remediation funding toward eventually constructing a new and probably much larger and much more expensive museum facility within closer proximity to the Holden townsite. The mine and tailings remediation process was started in 2012 to clean up the environmental damage resulting form the original mine operation. This work is to be completed in 2015.

The fact that the electric power provided by the Chelan Public Utility District had been deactivated after the mine closed posed a serious problem for the future operation at Holden Village. There was no way that the use of diesel generators would be acceptable in the long term. Hydro electric power would be an ideal option for low cost power with minimal environmental impact. Copper Creek was immediately south of the village and an ideal stream for hydro utilization. Howe Sound Company and the mining operation had had a great demand for electrical power for its extensive operation. Prior to the mine opening in 1939, Howe Sound explored several alternatives for power production but finally contracted with Washington Water Power, a utility company out of Spokane, to provide power to the mine. This would necessitate running high voltage lines up Lake Chelan and into the Railroad Creek valley to the mine site. The lines were located on the north shore from Manson up to the area across from Domke Lake, then crossed Lake Chelan and into the Railroad Creek valley. The power line itself was a major construction project and was also a major expense for maintenance by the power company. Some of the sections of the power line were over bedrock, and they drilled holes into the rock. Poles were cemented in, with some of them sticking out of the rock horizontally, over the lake shore. This was done in the late 1930s with the mine opening in 1937. The Chelan County Public Utility District purchased the Chelan Falls hydro plant and associated power lines from Washington Water Power in 1955. What was formerly Washington Water Power is now known as Avista Energy.

The Howe Sound Company seriously considered a hydroelectric plant, utilizing Domke Lake for a reservoir. As a result of the decreased water flows into Domke Lake in the winter months, it was proposed to build a flume from the twenty-two-hundred-foot level of Railroad Creek into Domke Lake to supplement the available water for operating a hydro plant. They mapped the bottom of Domke Lake by using weighted lines to get an accurate idea of the volume of water in the lake. The hydro plant itself would have been located somewhere around the level of Lake Chelan, near Domke Falls.

According to records recovered from the mine operation, the fish and game department denied the permit request because of concerns over fish production in Domke Lake. Several natural streams feeding Domke from the Emerald Park area were used for natural spawning of trout. There was an official, natural fish hatchery at Domke Lake for some years. The trout fry were then transported to various high lakes in the Cascades. Many of the high lakes in the Cascades were originally planted with fish from Domke Lake.

Following the closing of the mine, the transformers and switching gear were removed from the distribution system that provided power to the mine operation, concentrating mill, Winston Camp, and the Holden town site. Since the power lines were basically intact when Holden Village began its operation, we made contact with the Chelan County PUD to investigate the feasibility of reactivating the power lines into Holden. Since the electrical use by Holden Village would be rather minimal, the PUD indicated that all costs to activate the system would be charged to Holden. I'm sure that a major factor involved was the uncertainty over the long-term future of the Holden Village operation. The Chelan PUD couldn't justify the high costs of reactivating the power lines without some guarantee of a long-term power purchase.

It would have cost an estimated $100,000 to reactivate the lines and transformers. The major problem wasn't really the reactivation costs but the fact that Holden would be responsible for maintaining the lines, which over the years would have exceeded the activation costs. Electricity would have been metered at Chelan, and Holden would be paying for the line loss for the fifty-five miles to the village.

It was fortunate that the PUD didn't make it easy to supply power commercially to Holden. It would have been a significant financial hardship for Holden to initially activate the system. More significantly, the annual cost of purchasing electrical power would have been a major expense.

Yet Holden needed electricity to operate, even on a minimal basis. Refrigeration of food was the basic requirement. Adequate lighting for the safety of guests was another critical consideration.

Gil Berg assigned the electric power challenge to the Development Council, tasked with helping to determine the most efficient approach toward accomplishing necessary improvements at Holden. The council was open to anyone interested. I was interested and joined in 1962. The council determined that the diesel-electric units would be an interim power source. The only practical way to supply electrical power in the long run was to use hydroelectric equipment. Lou and Jerry were generous people. They purchased the hydroelectric equipment and then donated the units to Holden.

The challenge of the hydro project was to find someone who had experience with hydroelectric installations and operation and who would be willing to install these units under rather primitive conditions with little equipment. Holden Village learned quickly that if they had a need and if they kept mentioning the need to the many people passing though the village and even along Lake Chelan, most frequently someone showed up who would respond to the need.

The hydroelectric project was a great symbol for Holden in terms of the accomplishments feasible with volunteers along with the generosity of many people. Carroll had made a presentation to a large congregation in Toledo, Ohio, and without any of the members ever having visited Holden, the congregation contributed $4,000 to help the hydro project get started. I think Umhau Wolf was the pastor of the church in Toledo, and he later took several congregational groups to Holden. A portion of the money for the hydro project was provided through designated gifts, but we built the hydro without any financing. It always turned out that adequate money was available to continue. No financial grants or bank loans were available to Holden at that time. The first phase of the hydro project was completed for $39,000.

The idea of the hydro came out of the Development Council, and it certainly worked out well for Holden and Henry Schwecke. Word traveled around the Wenatchee Valley that Holden Village was planning to put in a hydroelectric plant. Operators of the *Lady of the Lake* were a part of the important verbal communication system along the lake. Passengers in conversations with the boat crew or even overhearing conversations by the boat crews would share the information—in a positive way. It's possible that Henry first heard about the Holden hydro project from the boat crew. He was more or less retired, or at least available, and was interested in a project involving a hydroelectric installation.

Henry had worked with Seattle City Light for many years at the Cedar Falls hydro installation. His wife, Eleanor, was a medical doctor and, at the time, director of the Chelan-Douglas Health District. They had a home in Wenatchee, but even more amazing, they had 160 acres of land almost directly across Lake Chelan from Lucerne at Fish Creek. Henry's parents had homesteaded this property. Henry and Eleanor were using it as a getaway, gradually improving the property and facility for retirement. Henry and Eleanor had had a twenty-year courtship before getting married. During their dating years, Henry would drive down to Stanford Medical School on weekends from Seattle for dates. They finally married and moved to Wenatchee. Henry was also working on a project to install a hydro plant at their cabin at Fish Creek. He was interested in trading some labor to help him with his project in exchange for some of his involvement at Holden. Henry let the Development Committee know of his qualifications, his interest, and his availability. Holden found its man, and Henry found his project.

We agreed to send some of our volunteers over to Fish Creek in exchange for some of his time on our project. Henry also wanted to prove to the PUD that he was qualified to install a hydroelectric plant. About the same time Holden's hydro project was initiated, the Chelan PUD had decided to install a hydro plant in Stehekin to reduce the cost of supplying electrical power to the Stehekin community. Henry had submitted a proposal to the PUD to install the Stehekin plant, but he wasn't given serious consideration. He was an individual, not a corporation with a history, and he had no business license.

Henry was a mild mannered person whose facial expression turned from the one he wore 98 percent of the time to a bright smile when things really went well. He loved to tinker and design and invent. He was a quiet doer and didn't spend much time in conversation. The Stehekin project was completed in early 1963. They made a big deal of dedicating it, with invited dignitaries for the "throwing of the switch." The system didn't work when the switch was activated, and I think that Henry had one of his great smiles when he heard the news. Henry was definitely not vindictive, but I think engineering and constructing a hydro plant at Holden gave him a positive way of showing PUD officials they'd made a mistake by dismissing his capabilities. Holden Village benefited from the PUD's mistake.

Henry was the ideal person for the Holden project. He had the ability to deal with the electrical as well as mechanical challenges of the old system. I don't think we checked to see if he was a licensed electrician, but it really didn't matter to us at the time. We trusted Henry to know what he could do and also when it was time to call in additional help. He had a machine shop in the basement of his Wenatchee home and was able to machine missing parts, especially for the old mechanical governors that controlled the speed of the undershot Pelton wheels. In order to have sixty-cycle power, it was necessary to maintain the speed of the generator accurately.

The hydro project was almost a one-man show, with Henry calling in volunteers to help when more manual labor was needed. Many volunteers were utilized for pouring the concrete for the two units' substantial foundations. Henry purchased a boat to make transportation on Lake Chelan more convenient. The only hired help we needed during the project was having Dinsmore (Dinty) Bigger from Moore Point do the welding on the penstock as it connected to the Y at the hydro. In the earlier day, Dinty was also the welder for the Lucerne hydro project as well as one of the original welders for Holden Mine.

The summer of 1963 saw the completion of concrete work for the foundation and slab for the building. A significant amount of concrete was needed to provide the structure for mounting the turbines and generators. Initially the turbines would be powered from the original diversion dam used by the mine for its domestic water, water to run the mill, and fire protection. This would only power the turbines to supply less than half of the total potential of the designed output. We didn't have sufficient money or manpower to build a new diversion dam and pipeline at the same time the turbines and generators were being installed. A new diversion dam and two thousand feet of pipeline would be phase two of the project.

The construction project was primitive. We mixed all of the concrete with a small half-sack mixer, and we transported the concrete to the forms by several wheelbarrows. We screened and washed by hand the sand and gravel. We hauled the gravel to the site from wherever we could find it, including an old pit along Railroad Creek, west of the vehicle bridge. Excavation for the foundation revealed that the site was located over the sawdust piles from the original sawmill used by the mine. The location needed to be moved slightly.

Time wasn't a major factor, and by the end of summer the concrete work was complete. The turbines and generators were shipped uplake by barge and brought to the village on the flatbed truck. Lou and Jerry Sheffles knew that Holden didn't have equipment to provide the lifting capacity needed, so they purchased and donated a four-wheel military surplus vehicle known as the "bomb truck." It had a manual hoist on the back and a motor-driven hoist on the front. They also installed an A-frame for the front so the winch could be used to lift heavy loads. (I was delighted to see that the "bomb truck" had been reactivated and was still running when I visited Holden in 2012.) We placed the equipment on the concrete base and constructed the building to weatherize the equipment prior to winter 1963.

Before I officially accepted the manager's job, I participated in a weekend Holden Village work party in connection with construction of the hydroelectric plant. I recall that it felt strange to be working with the volunteers, knowing that there was a chance that I might be the manager directing the crews in the near future. The work involved manually covering the penstock in the area between the upper mine level and the powerhouse. One of the men close to the upper mine level, without realizing the consequences, tossed a rock down the hill, accidently hitting one of the other workers. It was an innocent mistake and to my knowledge the only accident and injury involved with the entire hydro project. The hydro project involved many hundreds of hours of volunteer labor over a four-year period. The young man sustaining only minor injuries was from Montana and had just returned from New Guinea, where he had been a pilot with the Missionary Pilot's Association.

In the winter of 1964, Henry machined many of the needed parts. As soon as the snow melted in the spring, he and his volunteers began to put the final touches on the equipment, and the extensive electrical work required connecting the system with the distribution lines. It took multiple tests of the system to verify the integrity of the equipment. We installed the safety relays and other electrical devices so protection was available if the voltage exceeded or dropped below the safe level. This also provided safety in case the water was cut off or reduced. This protection was necessary because low voltage could damage or destroy some electrical equipment being used in the village.

We also needed to connect the fourteen-inch pipe to the wood stave pipe bringing water from the lower diversion dam to the seventy-five-thousand-gallon storage tank. The first electricity was produced in August 1964. The system worked perfectly right from the beginning. Henry could take pride in his accomplishment, also enjoying the thought of his success in contrast to the PUD episode in Stehekin. Even with the water coming from the lower diversion dam, the units produced more electricity than had been available from the diesel units. The hydro plant was relatively easy to operate—also a major advantage. It wasn't necessary to hire a trained technician, and the process worked well to train volunteers over the years.

Plans began immediately to extend the fourteen-inch pipeline another two thousand feet to provide 639 feet of vertical head, allowing for the maximum output of the turbines and generators. This project would involve construction of a small diversion dam and collection box that would also serve as a settling box to settle out some of the sand, rocks, and other debris that would come down Copper Creek. Henry Schwecke continued to provide technical assistance and designed the settling box. He also determined the location of the diversion dam. The decision on the dam location was partly finalized by finding an area that could also be used as a staging area for mixing concrete.

Sophisticated equipment wasn't available to determine elevations, and we used a military altimeter from a World War II bomber as a good substitute. I kept the altimeter in my office and used it to monitor atmospheric pressure variations moving through the valley. The design of the diversion dam settling box allowed us to assemble it at the site. Transporting an assembled box would be impractical with the equipment we had available. We mixed concrete above the forms, employing gravity to fill them. We hauled sand and gravel up the hill in the back of the Jeep. Black flies were so numerous at the diversion dam site that, during part of the construction, we set up lights using a portable generator so crews could work at night while the flies were sleeping.

We needed a road from the upper mine level by the water tank to the site of the new diversion dam. The road needed to be at a grade that would allow a Jeep and the "bomb truck" to make numerous trips for materials and crews. We were fortunate to have the Swiss loggers in the valley during those years. They had the equipment and expertise to build roads in mountains as well as safely cut trees that needed to be removed. The plan was to lay the fourteen-inch pipe on the inside edge of the road against the bank. When finished, the Swiss loggers would use their equipment to cover the pipe with three-to-four feet of dirt pulled from the side of the mountain.

Each section of fourteen-inch pipe was forty feet long and weighed a thousand pounds. We strapped the pipe to the side of the "bomb truck" and hauled it up the mountain one section at a time. The pipe was connected with "dresser couplings," which used rubber gaskets and metal flanges to hold the pipes together. When the 639-foot head was available, the total pressure at the nozzle was 268 pounds per square inch. This produced close to 40,000 pounds of pressure, so the pipe needed to be well anchored—especially at the bottom. At the time of the dedication, someone pointed out that the 40,000 pounds of thrust was approximately the same as the thrust of the rocket that propelled the first American satellite into space. This second phase of the project was completed in 1966. Before the end of August of that year, the new diversion dam and the full length of the pipeline were being utilized.

Hundreds of volunteers worked on the Holden hydro project from 1963 to 1966. It was literally a miracle that the project was completed. It was a miracle that the Sheffles family located the equipment. It was a miracle that Henry was available and was so generous to provide his expertise and labor at a very reasonable cost. It was a miracle that the Swiss loggers were logging in the valley and were willing to help construct the road for the new diversion dam. It was a miracle that in 1963 the state and federal government had very little regulation on the construction of hydroelectric systems. It was also fortunate that Copper Creek didn't contain any fish. Initially the hydro plant was licensed for ten years by the state of Washington through the department of ecology. When the license was renewed, the state fisheries department wanted to impose restrictions on the system and install mitigation for fish. I didn't think they had ever been to Holden or seen Copper Creek. I invited them up for an inspection. After they hiked partway up to Copper Basin and observed the creek, they agreed that Copper Creek wasn't a stream that needed protection for fish.

The hydro installation wasn't only functional but also a point of interest for many visitors. It attracted some people who came specifically because of the hydro plant. Hugh also did extensive work on the Lucerne hydro plant and especially the unique mechanical governor that controlled that system. And he investigated and did extensive calculations on other options for hydro power when we were considering expanding the output. One option involved developing a system on Tenmile Creek. Ten Mile Basin, with its southern exposure, produced a greater volume of water earlier in the season.

The best option involved a dam at about Sixmile, four miles east of the village with a pipeline carrying water to an area around Sevenmile. Once we did initial calculations on this option and completed a preliminary survey of the site, we turned the concept over to the engineering firm in Portland—Haner, Ross and Sporseen—to develop the plans. This plan had the greatest potential, and we had sufficient engineering work completed to know that it was feasible.

When the forest service changed the wilderness boundary in about 1983, the boundary lines were adjusted to allow for construction of a dam and powerhouse. We submitted a proposal to the forest service as well as to Federal Energy Regulatory Commission (FERC) to begin the long process of permits. One of the requirements was the newly instituted archeological survey of any area on federal land that would be excavated or disturbed. A teacher and a group of students from Central Washington University did the archeological survey and found minimal or no significant indication of any Native American activity in that section of Railroad Creek.

As soon as the application was submitted to the FERC for approval, the project was noted in the federal registry. A group of attorneys, primarily in the Seattle area, had formed the Washington Water Watch. They filed a lawsuit objecting to this project. It was obvious that we didn't have the financial capabilities to work through the legal considerations. The Holden board was also hesitant to consider funding a project that could cost $750,000, and the project was dropped.

The mine remediation work that began in 2012 needs power for a water purification plant and, at the time of this writing, is considering building the hydro plant we engineered. Project engineers have copies of the plans from Haner, Ross and Sporseen. I trust that if this plant is built, it will have sufficient output to share with Holden. That would greatly improve the efficiency of the village's winter operation.

Electrical power was critical for the operation of the village but a dock at Lucerne was vital to transport people to and form Holden Village. The story of the Lucerne Dock—its removal and replacement— is an important part of the Holden history. As a tenant of the forest service, Holden has had great relations with this government agency. This episode also indicated that Holden had power, when needed, to promote its own welfare.

During the mining operation, Howe Sound maintained a dock at Lucerne to unload the processed ore from the mine onto the barges along with freight and passengers. During the exploration years, a tram was built up the hillside up lake of the present dock. It moved the freight up to what we call the top of the switchbacks. The grade used by the tram is still visible because of the difference in the tree and vegetation growth.

The road into Holden from Lucerne was originally the grade developed for the Chelan Railway Company. The railway would begin at what is now Refrigerator Harbor and would make one very long switchback to allow the proper grade to the top of what are now the switchbacks.

The grade was developed, but as far as I understood, no railroad tracks were ever laid. Howe Sound Company purchased the Chelan Railway Company and took control over the grade, which then became the road into Holden. The switchbacks were then developed, making vehicle access possible from Lucerne to Holden.

The dock, with movable crane, was built to service the needs of the mine operation. A dock house was also built at a site just south of the present dock and east across the road from the present A-frame. The dock house was the home of the person responsible for the dock and operation of the crane. The Fields lived in the dock house during most of the mine years. Mrs. Field was the teacher at the Holden School for many years.

After the mine closed, Howe Sound Company sold the dock house to the Swiss loggers. The dock and crane were a part of Howe Sound Company's gift of Holden Village. The dock wasn't in great shape, and the moveable platform to allow access at the varying lake levels was no longer usable. It did provide access for Holden guests at the high water periods.

When the Swiss logging operation began, the Chelan Box Company worked out a deal with the village to purchase the dock and crane for $2,500. They agreed to deed it back to Holden when they were done using it. Hullrich Schmidt and Carl Wyssen, the Swiss loggers, verbally indicated that when their logging operation was complete they would also give the dock house to Holden. Nothing was in writing.

The logging operation was nearing a conclusion during the summer of 1969. It was our understanding that the Swiss loggers would return in the summer of 1970 for at least a short period of time. It was expensive to bring all of the equipment uplake, but they knew they wouldn't be able to finish the sale in 1969.

I was away from the village for several months starting in September 1969. When I returned, the dock, crane, and dock house were all gone. The crane had been removed, and the dock and dock house had been burned. I never heard an official explanation, but the loggers told us that the forest service gave them no choice but to remove the dock house and dock.

Trying to piece things together, I believe that it appeared there was a mutually beneficial arrangement between the loggers and the forest service. It would have been expensive for the loggers to return the next summer. If they didn't finish the timber sale, the loggers would have to pay the government a penalty. The forest service wanted the dock house and the dock removed to cleanup Lucerne now that the mine was closed. My assumption was that the forest service agreed to release the loggers from a contract-related penalty in exchange for the loggers burning the dock house and the dock.

No matter what the real facts were, the dock was gone. For Holden, the impact wouldn't be great until the next summer. This gave us some time to decide what options existed. I contacted the district ranger and was told that the dock would definitely be replaced, but it wasn't likely any construction money would be available for several years. They had developed no plans and budgeted no money for the next couple of years.

After Christmas 1969, Dr. Quintine Kittner brought thirty-five youth from the Lutheran Church in Port Angeles, Washington. Because of scheduling, Dr. Kittner chartered a boat for transportation to Lucerne. He was very upset that there was no dock for them to use at Lucerne, and they unloaded on the floating dock at Refrigerator Harbor. Dr. Kittner wondered why we weren't putting pressure on the forest service for a new dock. We explained that we were somewhat hesitant to cause too much trouble since we depended on the forest service for our special use permit. He asked if it was OK for him to make some inquiries, and we encouraged him to do whatever he could.

It turned out that Dr. Kittner had a partner in his medical practice who was one of the campaign chairmen for Washington State Senator Warren Magnuson. Needless to say, when Dr. Kittner contacted Senator Magnuson's office, he received an immediate response. Senator Magnuson indicated that he would be in contact with the forest service.

This contact by Dr. Kittner put the process in motion, but it would take almost two years before a new dock would be constructed. The district ranger contacted me and indicated that activity in the higher echelons of government was beginning. Nonetheless, they felt that since the construction budget had been cut 70 percent by the Nixon administration, no money would be available for a lower priority project such as the Lucerne dock.

Our main concern was unloading people from the boat during the coming summer. I contacted the Cove Marina downlake about the possibility of our leasing one or two of the old Howe Sound barges that were moored there. We considered the possibility of towing them uplake and anchoring them to the shore. We would add a walking ramp to each barge to allow people to get to the shoreline at the various levels of the lake. This concept didn't work. The only other possibility was using the old crib dock in front of Oscar Getty's cabin, with all of the busses driving over to that section of Lucerne to load passengers and freight. I think Oscar actually enjoyed all of the activity, and he graciously allowed Holden to use his dock and access road. We used Oscar's dock for two summers.

Not much happened the summer of 1970. A few letters went back and forth as we tried to build up some interest in appropriating funding for the project. The district ranger and the Wenatchee National Forest supervisor basically told us that there wasn't much they could do, but if money became available they would certainly be grateful.

Dr. Kittner suggested that we get people from our mailing list to write letters to their individual congressmen. Since it might appear to the federal government that this was a small local project, I thought it might be effective if we went through our mailing lists and picked out all the guests with professional letterheads who might have more clout with their congressmen. This turned out to be very effective. We sent out several hundred letters to "significant" Holden Village friends involving as many states as possible. In the end, guests from over forty states participated.

The Forest Service Chelan District office was so supportive that two of their secretaries unofficially helped type some of these letters on office time in the rangers office. I'm sure that this wasn't officially authorized, but the Chelan District ranger felt it was a worthwhile cause. I honestly think that the Wenatchee National Forest discovered that it had been a mistake to remove the dock without any immediate assurance of replacement.

The letters used a little emotional appeal on the basis of this remote community in the North Cascades with the only access being the Lake Chelan Boat Company and a dock being essential to our survival. The letters went out January and February of 1971. When senators and representatives began receiving these letters, they applied pressure to the forest service to get a dock built as quickly as possible. A notebook with copies of most of this correspondence is in to the Holden Museum.

One Saturday morning in March of that year, we were having breakfast in Koinonia when we heard a small airplane circling above. We ran outside and recognized the floatplane from Chelan Airways circling lower and lower. We knew it was Ernie Gibson, owner/pilot of Chelan Airways, but this had never happened before. We were all concerned. Finally on one of the low passes, we noticed Ernie dropped a container from the plane. We saw it land, and fortunately we were able to find it in the snow because of bright colored plastic materials tied to it for identification. We retrieved the container and signaled to Ernie that we had the message. He turned and disappeared down the valley.

The container had a note from the forest service requesting my presence at Lucerne at eleven that morning to consult about the location for a new dock. They indicated that time was of the essence. I took the snow vehicle to Lucerne and spent several hours with the district ranger and several of the forest service engineers, along with a representative of the Lake Chelan Boat Company, to discuss the plans.

Official word came from Washington, DC, that money was available for the dock, but the process needed to begin quickly. Work needed to be completed before the lake began filling from the spring runoff. The runoff would increase rapidly in April and really increase in May and June. By July 1, the lake would be back to its full level of eleven-hundred feet. The lake hadn't gone down as far during this particular winter, so the window of opportunity to put in a bulkhead on the shore was even shorter than normal.

I made arrangements to travel to Chelan the next week. Holden had offered to provide much of the construction labor under forest service supervision. Oscar was so impressed with what was going on that he offered to pay $2,000 cash to help the process get started. He wouldn't give it directly to the forest service but would give it to Holden Village. Government regulations concerning material specifications and an open bidding process meant there was no way bids could be processed and sent out and materials acquired before the lake exceeded the required level.

I suggested that Holden Village purchase the materials needed for the initial work since we weren't under any bidding regulations and could basically call the supplier and order the material the same day. The forest service wouldn't let me make any of the phone calls to vendors from the forest service office. I went to the KOZI radio building to make the calls and within a very short time arranged for the materials. Holden Village contributed approximately $3,000 to cover the balance of the initial cost beyond the gift from Oscar.

The rest of the materials weren't as time sensitive. In fact, the pilings that would be driven into the lake bottom couldn't be driven until the lake was up to the eleven-hundred-foot level. Once the bulkhead was built and backfilled, the rest of the work waited for several weeks.

We not only had volunteer labors from our "maverick" crew, but we also had Franz Strandberg. Franz was one of our retired volunteer staff who had spent his life managing construction projects. He agreed to be construction manager. The dock construction continued all summer and into the fall before it was basically completed and ready for use. Even though it's considered a forest service dock, it was an honest community effort, including many volunteers from Holden, the Lake Chelan Boat Company, the forest service and, of course, Oscar with his cash gift. Oscar insisted that we not tell the forest service about his contribution.

The dock house, though it was burned at the same time as the original dock, was not replaced. We did get permission from the forest service to construct a small A-frame building just to the west of the original dock house to serve as a waiting and emergency winter shelter for people coming and going through Lucerne. The A-frame would replace the old bus with the wood stove.

Brad Brisbine had been a part of the Lucerne project development when he was a student at Washington State University. Following graduation he returned to Wenatchee and joined the architectural firm of MJ Neal Associates. Brad had also visited Holden Village on hiking trips and was familiar with Holden and its mission. I contacted him, and he agreed to design the A-frame for the winter waiting shelter.

The concept of a Lucerne development took on a more formal aspect after Holden Village was given the Lucerne Resort. The resort was located on forest service property and was under a special use permit. The resort changed hands frequently after the mine closed. The main source of business was selling gas for boats and beer for boaters. The necessity of gas sales was almost a safety issue. In high winds and rough water, boats would consume more fuel than normal. They might not be able to make it to Stehekin, the next available fuel source.

Mike Griffin had purchased the resort because he had an association with Holden and loved the area. He felt that it would be a wonderful business for his family to operate, and he could work closely with Holden for mutual benefit. After a short time, it became apparent to him that the ownership title was so messed up over the years that he would never be able to get clear title. The only way to solve the problem was to give it to Holden Village.

Holden actually operated the resort for several years. During that time we discussed options as to what might be appropriate and what would be compatible with the existing Holden operation. Since the land and operational approval was under a special use permit from the forest service, it was also necessary to have approval as to the type of operation that was acceptable. The forest service definitely required that the operation provide "public service." Most of the property uplake wasn't suitable for campground development or any commercial endeavor, so the parcels that could be developed and were under control of the forest service were required to provide some public activity.

Those who had lived along the lake for many years claimed that the only resort that was financially successful up Lake Chelan was the Moore Point Resort, located at Fish Creek. It had burned down in the late 1950s and was never rebuilt. There had been other resorts or rentals along the lake as well as in Stehekin. I guess one of the other successful ventures that occurred during the mining days was the brothel that was located just a short distance uplake from Lucerne during the mining days.

Reportedly, there was a trail that went from Lucerne to the brothel. A portion of the foundation of the house was built out over the lake, so rowboats or motorboats could deliver the men from Lucerne. I was told that most men took the boats to get there and walked back. Many men who worked at Holden were single, and in the beginning of the operation, the company didn't allow women or families to live at Holden. When they discovered the difficulty of maintaining good workers with a men-only situation, they changed the rules, invited families, and developed a section for family housing. Perhaps this brought about the demise of the brothel along Lake Chelan.

Through the Science and Technology Committee, we had contacts in the architecture department at Washington State University. They had wanted a project for their students to use as a design exercise. I met with the students and outlined an idea that I was proposing for the development of Lucerne. We developed a plan for Lucerne that would provide some cabin-type of housing for the public, educational opportunities, a restaurant that would feature trout raised in pens in Lake Chelan, and at least some vegetables that would be grown in greenhouses. The hydro plant would provide needed electricity. Most of the buildings would be wood heated. Plans were also made to have the Holden Mine museum at Lucerne. We felt that this would be a selling point for the forest service, and it would provide the public more access to the information and displays. The Lucerne plan was developed prior to the time that plans were made to have the museum at the mine level.

We utilized various staff members as part of the planning team and put together a rather professional proposal that was presented to the forest service. The proposal received enthusiastic support from the district ranger in Chelan and also the supervisor's office in Wenatchee. Before any final approval could be issued, it was sent to the regional office in Portland for final review and approval. The total investment and development was sufficiently big that the decision would be made beyond the Wenatchee National Forest supervisor's office.

The proposal was finally denied, and perhaps it was best that it was. It would have taken a lot of effort and finances, and it might have been difficult for Holden to operate two efforts and make them successful. It was an interesting process and probably involved some politics that could have negatively affected the decision. The regional supervisor of the forest service in Portland was an active Lutheran layman. We thought that might be a positive break for Holden, but it probably turned out to be one reason that it was denied. I could never verify some of this information, but I was led to believe that the regional supervisor, because of his Lutheran association, was extra cautious with the decision. We were told that he favored the proposal, but several people working with him were skeptical about Holden's ability to carry out a plan of this complexity.

Two of the men came to the village to talk with us and get acquainted with the existing operation before making a final decision. They were negative from the beginning and verbally indicated that they thought it inappropriate for the Lutheran Church to have the existing operation and then expand the activities to Lucerne. I always felt they were against religious activity on forest service property and had some concerns that we were a cult that might be developing negative influences. With their negative and biased attitudes, and with the extra caution that the regional director was taking, there was no chance that this proposal would be accepted. Perhaps it was the hand of God saving us from a mistake. It was, however, a very good proposal.

Over the next two years, we gradually dismantled and cleaned up the old Lucerne Resort as required by the forest service. Holden Village retained the lease of a small portion of land at the hydro plant for parking vehicles and equipment. Part of the reason for retaining this land was an attempt to maintain the old hydro plant, which would be more expensive to remove, and also retain the water rights for the hydro plant, which had potential future value. We even considered the possibility of producing power at Lucerne and building power lines back to Holden— perhaps not financially feasible but nevertheless a possibility to consider.

It is difficult to schedule innovations. A community living with the free spirit of conversation stimulating the thought process was the perfect breeding ground for many ideas for the craftspeople to pursue and implement. I'm still convinced that the lack of committees requiring a formal permission process allowed many exciting projects at Holden Village to move forward with at least some of these projects materializing. Life is exciting when people are encouraged to dream and live in a location where materials are available from the forest and a junkyard.

CHAPTER 13

Life after Holden

RETIRING FROM MY POSITION AS manager of Holden Village initially seemed easy and even invigorating. I think I was tired. Some of the negative experiences and what I saw as obvious changes at Holden were starting to impact me. It appeared to me that the program was making a fundamental shift. The responsibilities as manager started to feel too much like work rather than a daily dose of excitement, anticipation, and participation. I also began feeling some uncertainty about the impact on Kristy and Jeff as they worked through their education and socialization adventure at Holden. Everything was positive for the family, but the uncertainties in terms of the Holden impact on the children and their future began to add to what was really an unjustified anxiety and uncertainty on my part. I know now that the problem was within me and my weariness, not the children. However, as a parent, I had only one opportunity to provide the best learning and living conditions for Kristy and Jeff. Some amount of anxiety was justified.

John and Mary Schramm had publically announced their intention of leaving as Holden directors at the end of the summer of 1984. I would again be faced with resigning my position as manager. If I had a desire to remain I would need to apply for the position with the new director. I had had the privilege of working with directors Carroll Hinderlie, Ron Vignec, Fritz Norstad, and John and Mary Schramm over my twenty years as manager. Perhaps the need to reapply for the manager's position with the next new director was the excuse I needed to finalize my decision. I decided to retire as of September 1983. This would give John and Mary and the board time to select a new manager so Holden wouldn't experience a new director and a new manager during the same year.

Our family moved to our home in Leavenworth in September, 1983 after twenty years living at Holden Village. The Holden board was very generous, extending my employment by one year by adding the one year of consultation. Officially my retirement from Holden was September 1984. This was great for our family. It's true that I possessed a lot of information that had never been documented, but I also understood that the board appreciated my twenty years of service. I shared a lot of ups and downs over those years, working with the board as we dealt with financial challenges and operational challenges, and perhaps the most challenging was dealing with the change in directors.

As manager, I wouldn't normally have had much contact with the board, but Holden was different. During the years Carroll was director, the board at times needed a management contact other than him. It was great to be involved with Holden that final year, to assist the new manager, and to continue working with the forest service and other government agencies on projects that had been underway for several years.

Life for me didn't end when I retired from my employment with Holden Village, but it definitely changed. Although I knew a few people in Leavenworth, it was a very few. I noticed that I could walk through downtown Leavenworth, and no one knew me. No one engaged me in conversation or asked me questions or sought advice about an operational problem. I went from a being person who knew the location of all valves and switches to a person with little purpose in terms of community. For the twenty years working as manager of Holden Village, I had an intense feeling of value. That is a gift. When I retired from Holden, I discovered that I would need to discover daily a sense of value, or at least until I found a work involvement somewhat comparable to Holden.

It was my impression that our daughter Kristy, then thirteen, made a relatively smooth transition. She had played on the girls' basketball team at Holden and played several games against the Leavenworth girls, so she already knew some of them when we moved. New friends introduced Kristy to other girls her age. Stan Winter, a counselor in the Cascade School District, had been on the volunteer staff at Holden Village during our final summer. He provided an excellent contact for Kristy as she entered a new school system. And Kristy had had a brief experience in the Cascade District School when we were on sabbatical from November 1976 until February 1977. This experience had some challenges for her, especially riding the bus in a new living situation with people she didn't know.

Jeff also had some good contacts in Leavenworth, helping his transition at age ten. Jeff and Kevin Rieke were already friends before we moved, and the Riekes knew everyone in and around Leavenworth. When Jeff started school in the fall of 1983, the regular grade school was being remodeled, and all of the students were temporarily being bused to the old school in Dryden. This meant that all the students were in for a new experience, not just Jeff. One of the challenges for Jeff was his desire to join his new friends in Little League. We hadn't played baseball at Holden, and without TV, Jeff had never seen a baseball game. He lacked the normal familiarization with the game that was available to other youth. I don't recall that he and I ever did the normal father-son activity of playing catch while at Holden. Baseball didn't turn out to be his sport.

Jeff did get introduced to golf in the seventh grade, and he seemed to have a natural ability for the sport. I contacted one of the old-time golf pros at the Leavenworth golf club to help Jeff develop his skills. In high school he was on the golf team and competed in the state tournament all four years. He developed close friends with several people working at the golf course. He had a summer job cleaning golf carts, which also meant driving and parking them. The job gave him the opportunity to play the course at no cost.

I appreciated being able to work as a consultant to Holden Village for a year after retiring at manager. I think it was helpful to the village operation but it was also great for me as I made this transition after twenty years of a rather intense involvement with the Holden operation. Prior to retiring I was working on projects that involved several government agencies and it is always difficult for a new person to step in to this kind of work without an opportunity to get personally and professionally acquainted with agencies such as the US Forest Service or the Chelan County Health Department.

Fields Point Landing was one of projects with which I assisted during my consultation year. Discussions involving the forest service and national park service had been in process for several years. Holden was a major player because of the numbers of people who required parking, some of it long-term. There was also the need for a safe and reliable boarding area for uplake travel. Holden Village owned a small house above the Twenty-Five Mile Creek dock. The Holden property had a parking area with solar facilities that is now the Holden Village Bed and Breakfast. It was through these discussions that the concept of Holden operating Fields Point Landing emerged. Fields Point Landing was a joint development by the US Forest Service and the National Park Service to provide an adequate parking area and dock facility to board the commercial boat service. I think Fields Point Landing was one of the first projects in which the US Forest Service and the National Park Service worked together for any development or project. The cooperation between the two agencies was mandated by congress to get the appropriations needed for the development. Since Holden had staff at Twenty-Five Mile Creek assisting with communications in and out of the village, it would be ideal if those people could be part of a contract to operate the new facilities at Fields Point Landing.

I think Holden has operated Fields Point Landing for all but one or two years of its existence. In one of the first years, the forest service and the park service felt the need to open the operational contract to bid so it didn't appear as if anyone was favoring Holden. The people who had the operational contract for a brief time couldn't make it work financially. Since that time it's my understanding that Holden has operated Field Point Landing.

The year I retired, Holden was also in the process of applying for a permit for the new hydro plant on Railroad Creek. I had been involved with the proposed hydro project from its inception, and I continued to have some involvement, especially with government contacts. The forest service was adjusting the forestlands designated as wilderness areas, and I expressed concern that, depending on the new wilderness boundaries, the proposed hydro project would be eliminated. At our request, the Wenatchee National Forest assisted in having the proposed wilderness boundaries adjusted to allow the Holden hydro project to remain alive. This project was eventually dropped, but the concept, the location of the proposed dam, and the adjustment of the wilderness boundaries may now allow the remediation efforts to proceed with their need for additional electrical power for water purification.

During my year as consultant, I responded to many letters from Holden with questions on various items relating to the operation. I also returned to Holden several times for on-the-ground consultation. Over the years I have continued to receive letters or phone calls and now some e-mails. Even during the summer of 2012, when returning for the fiftieth anniversary, I spent an hour or two with operational personnel discussing issues and filling in the blanks concerning some operational and historic questions. My involvement since 1984 partially resulted from my lack of record keeping for many of the projects and operations.

When I arrived at Holden as manager, there were no manuals outlining the locations of valves and switches. Over the years we gradually found everything that was needed for day-to-day operations, but we seldom recorded what we found. We tried to document many of the changes and alterations, but obviously not everything was documented, which left a lot of questions as others took over operational responsibilities.

My excuse was that as business or general manager, for many years I was the only paid employee involved with year-round facility and staffing operation. At the present time, there are multiple paid positions covering essentially what I covered as an individual, including business manager, operations manager, public works manager, facilities manager, volunteer staff coordinator, and utilities assistant. There might be other positions that fit this category. Many of these positions have assistants or administrative assistants. Any organization, even a church related organization, has a tendency to expand operationally as maturity occurs.

I confess that accurate filing and record keeping weren't high on my priority list, but I think I had a reasonable excuse of covering a lot of responsibilities without even a full-time secretary or a part-time assistant. Neither Carroll nor I had assistants. During those years our shared secretary was often seasonal and, depending on the circumstances, was a volunteer or on a stipend-pay basis. During my years at Holden, our challenge was to make it to the next week and especially to the end of the summer program. We weren't thinking about producing an accurate flow chart outlining the operation over the twenty years.

After moving to Leavenworth, I realized that Holden Village could potentially open opportunities for much of my future employment. During the year of consulting, the family financial pressure was decreased, but I also realized that I needed a new job. I had always been intrigued with real estate sales, especially with the option of potentially unlimited income, and began studying to get my associate license. I was added to the staff at Johnson Real Estate. I discovered that sales weren't my forte and realized in less than a year that real estate wasn't my future. I did, however, get acquainted with some great people.

I worked with Cheri Farivar, Mae Hamilton, and for a brief time, Keith Goehner. Cherie is, at this writing, mayor of Leavenworth, Mae is one of the most successful real estate brokers in the area, and Keith is a Chelan County commissioner.

About the time I retired from a rather short stint with real estate, the first Holden-associated job opportunity materialized. The Grunewald Guild needed a manager to work with Rich and Liz Caemmerer. Rich and Liz had been an important part of the Holden Village faculty and community over the years. To a great extent because of their Holden experience, they decided to leave their work at Valparaiso University and begin a community of artists someplace in North Central Washington.

They purchased an abandoned Grange Hall building and acreage in Plain, a short distance north of Leavenworth, and initiated the Grunewald Guild. The guild has been in operation for over twenty-five years and has continuously expanded its program and facilities. It was great to work with Rich and Liz. I felt that I made some minor contributions because of my Holden experience and my contacts in the area.

Faith Lutheran Church has been an interesting ministry with definite Holden connections. I shared part of its story in Chapter 9. Shortly after we moved to Leavenworth, Carl Florea arrived as the pastor of Faith Lutheran. Carl became a close friend and helped me survive my transition away from Holden Village and a divorce after twenty years of marriage. Carl and I spent many hours together, sharing and encouraging one another. He was one of the best preachers of the gospel I have encountered. I hope that Carl can preach or at least share some thoughts at my memorial service. I'm sure his effectiveness was enhanced because he truly believed and really attempted to live what he was preaching. He struggled within his personal life as a result of his struggling with the gospel. Carl was interested in preaching and teaching. He shared with me that he was going to resign from Faith Lutheran after a few years as pastor because, even though the congregation was small, the administrative part of the work discouraged him. I refused to have him deny us his proclamation, and I offered to enter into a shared ministry with him. I would do all of the administrative work, and he could concentrate on the teaching and preaching. The congregation agreed to this arrangement.

During this partnership Carl had a traumatic experience that involved the start of the first Iraq war, Desert Storm. This really impacted Carl. He elected to protest through civil disobedience and ended up in the Chelan County Law and Justice Center, basically the jail. He began a hunger strike, which lasted almost thirty days. Some members of Faith Lutheran supported Carl; others didn't understand his actions and were upset that he would take this approach, which impacted the congregation and called into question our government's actions. There were candlelight vigils outside the jail, and there were prayer meetings for him.

I learned from Carl that living one's faith and acting on one's convictions is a personal matter. It doesn't always match the desires of family, friends, or even job. The media got involved, and a news service working with National Public Radio came to the church one evening to record comments and conversation of various members. Since I was unofficially Carl's spiritual contact, I visited him in jail almost daily. I didn't even need to adhere to the jail's regular visiting hours since I was his pastor.

After less than a year of our job-sharing arrangement, Carl decided that he needed to leave parish ministry, at least for the immediate future. He had been working with Meet Every Need with Dignity (MEND), which was ready to move beyond a part-time volunteer organization and hire a director. He became director and through his insight into community needs put together a great organization that included the Community Cupboard, affordable housing, and initial work on a home for mentally and physically challenged adults.

At this point, Faith Lutheran was without a pastor, although we had two or three retired pastors within the membership. Fritz Norstad suggested it was time for the congregation to have a nonprofessional or lay pastor, at least for an interim. I think Fritz was honest in his determination. On the other hand, he may have been concerned that he would be called on to preach too frequently during the period of selecting a new pastor. Fritz was always thinking out of the box. He convinced the congregation that I be given the opportunity to be lay pastor. The majority of the congregation was open to this option, and Fritz was instrumental in helping convince some who were concerned about the arrangement to give it a try.

I moved from administrative assistant to lay pastor. This was definitely a result of my involvement with Holden Village. Bishop Keller approved this arrangement and officially authorized me to administer communion. I served as lay pastor while the congregation went through the process of choosing a new pastor, which turned out to take more than a year. It was a great experience and perhaps helped to fulfill my mother's prayers. I really enjoyed the opportunity to serve in this way.

During this period I decided to run for a position on the school board. Our two children were still in school, and I had a sincere interest in providing the best education possible within the Cascade School District. The decision to take a chance on running for the school board was, to a great extent, a product of going through a divorce. For me the divorce was what I considered my first major failure. Since I had now experienced this failure, I felt that if I ran for the school board and lost the election, it wouldn't match the failure of a divorce. I was willing to give it a try.

As it turned out, I served on the school board for eight years. During this time I discovered my thoughts and convictions were at times out of the mainstream and weren't always what was being publically expressed by others. I received encouragement from many people who shared similar thoughts but were afraid to express them. This was exciting for me, and the experience encouraged me to express my thoughts more freely. After my first two years on the school board, Carl ran for an open seat, and we found ourselves again working together. He and I most often thought alike and had very similar concerns.

The superintendent at the time criticized Carl and me since we weren't willing to always vote with the other school board members. The superintendent informed us that he expected a five-to-nothing vote so the people in the district felt that the schools had total support of the board. Carl and I informed the superintendent that we would always vote our conscience and convictions and had no intention of being part of a predetermined five-to-zero board. As I recall, that particular superintendent only lasted one more year.

I was always trying to think of new educational opportunities. This wasn't necessarily the responsibility of a board member. I wrote a draft for an alternative education program that would be located at the Leavenworth National Fish Hatchery. This program would involve students working at the hatchery and learning biology, mathematics, social science, and even business as they interacted with the operation of the hatchery. I wrote into the outline the possibility of the students operating a small aquaculture business, which would provide actual business experience. I unofficially presented this proposal to Greg Pratschner, manager of the Leavenworth National Fish Hatchery and also a community friend. He was excited about the possibility, submitted the proposal to his regional office, and was encouraged to proceed with the concept. The problem was I had never discussed the proposal with Marilyn Baker, Cascade school superintendent, so she was a bit surprised that the proposal was encouraged by the US Fish and Wildlife Service before she even knew about it.

I was given the opportunity to chaperone two Cascade High School students, Audra Ellington and Lance Schott, to New York City to participate in the United Nations Youth Environmental Conference, where they made a presentation on the work they were doing at the hatchery. As part of this trip, we also had the opportunity to visit Washington, DC, and meet Washington State Senator Slade Gordon and John Turner, director of the US Fish and Wildlife Service.

I took a copy of my proposal for the alternative school and gave it to Mr. Turner when we were leaving his office. He read it some days later, and within a few weeks he sent a $10,000 check from the National office of the Fish and Wildlife Service to the Leavenworth hatchery to help finance the program. They didn't implement all of my ideas, but the program was initiated. The alternative school is called the Discovery Program and is still in operation. Part of my interest and ideas for this program came from the experience of starting the aquaculture program while at Holden Village and seeing the interest and the educational opportunities allowing youth to work with functioning projects.

In 1993 I was presented a new and exciting opportunity that would provide employment and an exciting challenge for the next ten years of my life. Harriet Bullitt had purchased some property that had originally been a CCC camp and then for many years operated as a Catholic Youth Camp called Camp Field. It was a thirty-plus-acre parcel of land along

Icicle Creek, several miles outside of Leavenworth. The CYO (Catholic Youth Organization) camp had sixteen buildings, only one building recently constructed. The chapel was the newest of all of the buildings and was beautifully built with native stone. It served Camp Field as a worship space but was also used by the camp and others in the community for concerts.

Harriet and her sister inherited the KING Broadcasting Company, started by their mother Dorothy. KING Broadcasting had extensive radio and TV stations that covered the West Coast from the Canadian boarder to San Francisco. Their holdings also include KING-FM, which was the premier classical music radio station in the Seattle area. When they sold KING Broadcasting, Harriet decided to devote the rest of her life working for local environmental causes. It was just at this time that the Catholic Church decided to sell Camp Field. The Bullitt family owned considerable acreage along Icicle Creek, with the western portion of their property located directly across the river from Camp Field.

Representatives from the Catholic Church contacted Harriet to see if she was interested in purchasing the Camp Field property. She was interested in the property to prevent it from ever being considered for construction of condominiums along Icicle Creek. She purchased the property and decided to develop the property into an environmentally sensitive retreat and conference center.

There was a three-story log cabin on the Bullitt property that Bill and Peg Stark were using for some of the activities associated with an organization they had started called The Extended Family. They provided encouragement for local people interested in the arts, music, drama, and dancing. Reed Carlson, former volunteer staff member at Holden Village now living in Leavenworth, was an active participant of The Extended Family and did some repair work for Harriet on the log cabin as well as other projects for her in Seattle. Historically, this log house had served as a brothel with a still to produce liquor in the basement. Harriet's mother had been concerned with the impact this questionable activity might have on Harriet and her sister when they were young and impressionable, and she purchased the log house in order to eliminate the brothel and still.

When Harriet purchased the Camp Field property, she was given the name of a property manager and also a development firm that could be used in developing the property. She fired the initial project managers when she discovered they assumed her involvement would be paying the bills but not being involved in the planning or construction process. I learned quickly that Harriet was a hands-on type of person and wanted to be part of the team of project management and basically involved on a day-to-day basis.

Harriet hired Reed to be part of the new construction management team, and he suggested that she might also consider inviting me to be a part of this team. In the fall of 1993, Reed contacted me and indicated I might be receiving a call form Harriet. She called me and invited me to Copper Notch for a visit. I had never met Harriet but knew of her background from others in the community. My conversation with her went well, and before the end of November, I was officially working as a member of the Sleeping Lady Mountain Retreat project management team. Following the initial construction, Harriet invited me to remain with the project as general manager and project manager for the continuing development and construction projects. Over many previous years, Harriet had had confrontations with developers in terms of environmental insensitivities. Now she found herself a developer, and she was determined to take a different approach.

Harriet wanted to work with an architect who displayed sensitivity for the environment and had a positive track record on environmental projects. She contracted with Jones and Jones Architects from Seattle. Jones and Jones had a strong reputation in environmental projects and had a world reputation specifically in designing natural environments for large zoo projects. John Paul Jones was assigned as the principal architect to work with Harriet. He was Native American and immediately understood Harriet's sensitivity to the natural. It turned out that during the years we worked with John Paul, he was also selected as one of the lead architects on the Native American Museum in Washington, DC. I had the privilege of working with him for ten years, and it was an honor to be able to call him an associate and a friend.

When Reed and I met with Harriet, she outlined the basic rules that we were to follow:

1. All of the original buildings on the site would be saved and moved to new locations when necessary. No original building would be destroyed.
2. No trees would be cut to accommodate this project. The architects surveyed each tree, even measuring their girth. The buildings would be located to save every tree.
3. We wouldn't haul anything to the landfill, and all materials not used would be recycled.
4. All contractors would participate in the recycling program. All contractors would agree to be sensitive to all of the natural growth on the site and agree to eliminate any pollution possibilities from leaking oil or fluids from their equipment.
5. All materials used in remodeling or new construction would come from recycled material if possible.

Prior to the beginning of construction, we conducted a Native American ceremony to acknowledge that we would be impacting and changing aspects of Mother Earth. About twenty people, including John Paul Jones, gathered for the ceremony, which included smoking a peace pipe and burying sacred items. The explanation was that the power of these sacred items would permeate the ground in the surrounding area. I was very moved by the spirituality of the ceremony and immediately spoke with John Paul, suggesting we build some type of monument on the spot where the sacred items were buried. He very kindly explained to me that the burial point should never be identified in the future. The act of burying the sacred items was meant as recognition of the sacredness of the earth, asking forgiveness and understanding for our making changes to the natural. The ceremony was helpful in understanding our efforts to preserve the natural to the greatest extent possible. The peace pipe never remained lit, but it was passed around the circle.

We finally agreed as a project management team that it would be impossible to eliminate some items being hauled to the landfill. We purchased an eight-foot tub grinder so all of the scrap wood and plaster board could be chipped and pulverized and used in the landscape on the site. Bates House moving was hired to move eleven of the existing sixteen buildings to fit the new building locations. Harriet requested that we use local labor, and we accomplished this to the greatest extent possible. One of the larger projects involved contracting with a construction company that used union labor. Before they were hired, we agreed that both nonunion and union labor would be simultaneously working on the site. We obtained agreements ahead of time that no tensions or disputes would be tolerated.

I recall that at one point we had the choice between burning a pile of wood that couldn't go through the tub grinder or hauling it to the landfill. We consulted Harriet. The decision was that, from an environmental point of view, there was less carbon added to the atmosphere through burning than with multiple trips by diesel dump trucks to haul the material to the landfill. Harriet received criticism for this decision, but it was clear that she was convinced what was best and followed through on her convictions. Harriet had strong environmental convictions, but she was also a very practical person.

We were the first ones in the Northwest to use TREX decking for any large project. TREX is made from recycled plastic sacks and hardwood chips. None of the suppliers had the amount of TREX needed. For our project, TREX was shipped in two railcars from the East Coast.

Recycled cellulose, blown-in insulation, was used in all of the buildings. Two large pine trees had to be removed, but a portable saw mill was brought in to convert the logs to dimension lumber used for interior finishing. We used ground-source heat pumps for 60 percent of the housing units. Coils were buried five feet deep in the meadow and the closed-loop system used the fifty-degree temperature of the earth at that depth to maximize the efficiency of the heat pumps for both cooling and heating. Preheating of domestic water was a side benefit.

Landscaping was used to help cool buildings in the summer. We devised a system of using the cold water running in a regional irrigation ditch to cool several of the small buildings. It also provided a cool-water loop for a heat pump system for air conditioning Canyon Wren, the hundred-seat capacity concert hall. No irrigation water was consumed but only used to cool the water pumped through a continuous loop system.

Through our efforts involving environmental sensitivities, Sleeping Lady Mountain Retreat was recognized by numerous organizations with awards. The American Hotel and Lodging Association presented us with the top national award. I traveled back to Washington, DC, and received the award from Senator Bob Dole at the association's annual meeting. Harriet and I also traveled to Olympia, Washington to receive recognition from Governor Gary Locke and the State of Washington for designing an environmentally sensitive commercial project. We also received a national award from the American Institute of Architects (AIA) for the best environmental design and construction in the western United States. The project was also recognized as the first major project to involve construction recycling in the Northwest.

Harriet valued art in nature, and many of her commissioned art pieces were outdoors. She was convinced that art and nature were important partners, and art needed to be enjoyed surrounded by the natural beauty of nature. Some of her commissioned items included work by Richard Beyer, Gretchen Daiber, Thomas Jay, David Barker, Tony Angell, and Dale Chihuly. It was a unique opportunity to work with these outstanding artists, but there is no doubt that Dale Chihuly was the most unique and interesting.

Harriett commissioned Chihuly to do an original glass sculpture at Sleeping Lady Mountain Retreat, but they hadn't discussed a specific location or design. The day after Thanksgiving, 1996, Chihuly called Harriet and said he was on his way over to talk about an idea. When he arrived, Harriet and I sat in Kingfisher dining room with him while he scribbled his idea on a napkin for a permanently mounted outdoor glass sculpture. He had been inspired by the icicles that form during the winter on the mountain rocks.

The sculpture would be a series of hand-blown glass icicles mounted on an armature with special lighting for night illumination. Harriet had a favorite boulder just to the west of Kingfisher. It was decided the sculpture would be mounted on that boulder. It would be the first permanently mounted outdoor glass sculpture Chihuly ever installed. The sculpture involved 1,040 hand-blown glass icicles mounted on a stainless steel armature. Chihuly intended to have the armature heated when it snowed, so water would drip down the glass icicles, forming natural icicles on the glass icicles. That idea didn't materialize. Since Harriet had already announced the date of the unveiling, the pressure was on Chihuly to produce. He had his crew working 24-7 for three weeks to complete the sculpture. Harriet appeared to know how to deal with temperamental artists. It was a thrill to work with her and Chihuly on this project. We made several trips to the Chihuly studio on Lake Union to observe the creative process in the hot shop.

At Holden we began inviting musicians to provide concerts for the community. We were limited to musicians who were willing to exchange a concert for a couple of days' enjoyment of the village and the mountains. Holden had no money but did provide a unique mountain experience. Ironically, one of the musicians who came to Holden was Lisa Bergman, who years later I would meet again when she became involved with the Icicle Creek Music Center. In fact, she directed the organization for several years.

I mentioned to Harriet the delight I had had sitting around the fireplace in Koinonia at Holden Village listening to teachers share information and stimulate discussions. Harriet asked me to establish a similar idea at Sleeping Lady. We called it the Grotto Club and initially met in the Grotto Bar on the Sleeping Lady site. I was in charge of selecting the speakers and maintaining a list of locals who would be invited to participate. Our first speaker was Harriet's brother, Stimson. His presentation was titled "Reflections on the Shape of Things to Come." The Grotto Club met for four or five years at various locations, including most recently in the living room at Copper Notch lodge.

I was always gratified that Harriet included me as one of her many friends, and I think she enjoyed the opportunity to work together. It was obvious that some of the people who were in contact with Harriet had ulterior motives and would make requests for financial help for personal projects. I made no such requests and refused to act as a go-between for other people wanting access to Harriet. She and I spent many hours in informal conversations, and I was amazed at the breadth of her knowledge in so many fields. I didn't know her religious background, but it didn't appear to me that organized religious affiliation was high on her list of activities. However, she was very spiritual, and God and the Bible came up frequently in our conversations. I was amazed at the depth of her biblical knowledge. She told me that she had taken several classes in biblical studies in college, and she obviously retained what she studied.

One day, more or less out of the blue, Harriet asked me if I wanted to go to Sweden. I, of course, answered in the affirmative. She had read about a conference center in northern Sweden that was owned by the City of Stockholm and used for employee retreats. It was located in Husa, a small community that developed through mining, but its current activity was encouraging tourists. The area had a small ski lift, horseback riding, a great bakery, and wonderful walking trails.

Before I knew it, the person in the Stockholm city government who was in charge of the retreat center was contacting me. He would be meeting me at the airport. I would stay at his home for a few days while getting acquainted with Stockholm, then accompany him for several nights at the conference center. While visiting in Husa, I was able to enjoy a short trip around the area via Icelandic horses, had an interview with the local press resulting in an article in the weekly paper, and spoke to a group that was like a chamber of commerce. It was a memorable and enjoyable trip. I don't know if the experience helped provide any ideas for our own project with the Sleeping Lady Mountain Retreat.

The construction work on the Sleeping Lady Conference Retreat facility as originally planned was more or less completed in the summer of 1995, and the grand opening occurred in July. The first groups were registered for August. Before the construction was complete, Harriet asked me if I would switch over from project management to general operational manager, setting up staffing and the overall operation. I was thrilled and appreciative to continue working with her. Many times, my Holden experience came up in discussions, and the Holden experience definitely gave me a background to help establish the Sleeping Lady operation. I noticed that Harriet hadn't planned for a retail operation, and I urged her to consider a gift shop and bookstore as a service to the guests as well as a source of revenue. She did, and it has since been greatly expanded.

Some of the ideas we discussed never materialized. As the entrance to Sleeping Lady was being developed, we initially added a small deli called O'Grady's Pantry. We also had an exercise room, and then the radio station was added. We investigated adding a microbrewery but didn't pursue it.

It was an enjoyable challenge working with the architects and coordinating decisions with Harriet. Both Reed and I had experience with the snow loads at Holden and the inconveniences of snow sliding off roofs. We fortunately were able to have the architects change some of the roof designs to address this potential problem. During the course of the project, Harriet requested many changes to the original plans as new ideas arose. These changes were always accommodated but significantly increased construction costs.

Holden Village and Sleeping Lady Mountain Retreat had many similarities in terms of environmental sensitivities, the importance of art and music, and the importance of a great staff and serving people. Harriet was definitely sensitive in terms of the construction costs, but her desire to implement her ideas and maintain the environmental integrity always had the priority. Her accountant was always perplexed that the construction costs exceeded the estimates. When one makes frequent changes and pay the extra architectural costs and then at times remove what had been initiated to incorporate a new idea, there's no way to stay within the original estimates.

Reusing old buildings that needed to be moved and then basically rebuilt, with the inefficiencies of accommodating the original structure, made it impossible to accurately estimate costs. It was Harriet's project. Her ideas and requests took priority, although they also added considerable costs.

Before initial construction was complete, the request for remodeling and improving what had just been built began. Harriet decided that architectural planning would begin on what was being called the Icicle Creek Music Center. The music center was established to accommodate a resident string quartet and provide instructional opportunities and even practice facilities for young musicians. By the time the work was completed with the mountain retreat and music center, more than sixty buildings were on the site. From the perimeter road they were hardly visible as a result of landscaping and careful placement in and among the trees.

Originally, the mountain retreat, the Icicle Creek Music Center, and the KOHO radio station were all a part of the Sleeping Lady Mountain Retreat. Eventually the music center and KOHO Radio were separated into their own organizations and operation.

My life was greatly enriched working with Harriet and the Sleeping Lady Mountain Retreat project. However, life was still lacking a full meaning for me even though my employment was exciting. After going through a divorce in 1987, I really wanted to find a partner to enhance my life and especially a person who would enjoy gardening and the mountains. I first noticed the ads for the Matchmaker in the Market in the Mountaineers' newsletter when I arrived in Seattle in 1961. I contacted the Matchmaker for the first time in 1997 and as a result met Claudia Johnson in 1998. It was almost love at first phone call. One of our first official dates was my inviting Claudia to join me in attending a fundraiser at Sleeping Lady for the Icicle Creek Music Center. I had helped put together a raffle for the fundraiser. Dale Chihuly had donated one of his glass art creations in the Seaform collection. The Chihuly listed value was $9,000. The tickets were $125 each, and I thought I'd impress Claudia by inviting her for this social event. She ended up winning the raffle, and I think I proposed to her within forty-eight hours.

Harriet graciously offered the Sleeping Lady chapel for our wedding. Since it was the second marriage for the two of us, we decided to have it basically in the form of a concert. The Icicle Creek Music Center String Quartet—including Scott Hosfeld, Marcia Kaufman, Carrie Rehkoph, and John Michel—offered to play for one part of the concert and two friends of Claudia's, Nadine Sander and Stan Halle, concluded the concert. Stan had an original piano composition, titled "Awakened," that he played on the Steinway.

Carl Florea conducted the marriage ceremony. Claudia is about five inches taller than I am. When I was given permission to kiss the bride, I went to the back of the altar and got a five-inch stool to stand on for the kiss. Who would want to kiss a groom that is five inches shorter? The 150 people in the chapel enjoyed a good laugh, which was a great way to begin a marriage.

Those in attendance at the wedding, besides family, were many of Claudia's friends from the Seattle Mountaineers and from Chehalis, Washington; some of our mutual friends from Sleeping Lady and Leavenworth and also friends from Holden Village. Life is good with a great companion and wonderful friends.

It is always interesting how contacts that develop over years of employment can at times provide new opportunities for others. One of the Holden Village contacts came into play while I was manager of Sleeping Lady Mountain Retreat and resulted in Harriet getting back in the business of commercial radio. Jerry Isenhart had purchased KOZI Radio in Chelan in the mid 1960s. Holden Village rented space in the KOZI studio for a downlake office. I became well acquainted with Jerry, and he frequently was involved in some of our discussions concerning communication challenges at Holden Village.

As former co-owner of KING Broadcasting, Harriet always loved the business of radio communication. It was my impression that she also had a desire to add a more progressive/liberal radio station that would cover North Central Washington. I don't recall what occurred first, but in conversation with Harriet she mentioned an interest in starting a radio station on the grounds of Sleeping Lady. Harriet discovered that Jerry owned the frequency for a radio station in Leavenworth. The Leavenworth station had never been developed, but the license was active. She knew that it was much easier to purchase an existing license than going through the time and expense applying to the FCC for a new license.

I mentioned to Harriet that Jerry was a friend of mine, and I agreed to set up a meeting. Harriet, Jerry, and I met in the Kingfisher dining hall one afternoon to have a get-acquainted conversation. Jerry indicated initially that he wasn't interested in selling the Leavenworth frequency individually but might consider selling KOZI, his station in Chelan, along with his frequency in Leavenworth. The discussions continued over the next few months. At one point Harriet became frustrated with Jerry, and they were about ready to cease further negotiations.

Harriet and Jerry had come to an impasse. I suggested we have one last conversation. I sat with Jerry on the patio outside of Kingfisher dinning hall at Sleeping Lady, looking across at Harriet's Chalet on the other side of the river, and we had an exchange of information on the phone with Harriet, who was in the Chalet. We made sufficient progress that the eventual ownership of KOZI and the Leavenworth station was transferred to Harriet. Jerry operated his broadcasting company in a rather interesting way. Not all of his operation was in the manner that Harriet was accustomed to, and it created some delay in the final sale/purchase. The new station was eventually located on the grounds of Sleeping Lady Mountain Retreat with the call letters KOHO.

Harriet had learned from her mother, who started KING Broadcasting, that the station name was very important. Harriet wanted KOHO and discovered that the name was licensed to a station in Hawaii but wasn't being used as an active station. Harriet arranged to purchase the name, and KOHO- FM Leavenworth was born. As you see, Holden Village even had a connection to the initiation of Icicle Broadcasting, Inc., and KOHO 101.1 FM.

By 2003 the construction of Sleeping Lady Mountain Retreat and the Icicle Creek Music Center was complete. Establishing the operation of the retreat center was well under way. There was still some uncertainty whether the operation could financially survive with its primary mission being conferences. It became evident that increasing the emphasis on individual registrations as well as special functions such as the lucrative wedding business might be necessary.

Since my contributions in my areas of experience were complete, I retired at the end of 2003. Twenty years at Holden Village and ten years at Sleeping Lady Mountain Retreat provided thirty years of exciting work. I'm forever grateful to Holden Village and Harriet Bullitt for the opportunities offered to me. It was a gift to be involved in the design and development of these two unique and meaningful projects.

Upon my retirement, Harriet suggested I consider doing a commentary on KOHO each week. She discovered I had an opinion covering many subjects, and she also appreciated that I didn't hold back from being controversial. When I first began, I asked Harriet if she wanted to read and approve my commentaries. Her comment was, "I don't want to read them prior to broadcast. Be as controversial as you like."

This would be a volunteer effort on my part, but I very much looked forward to this opportunity. My commentaries were called *Consider This*. I continued offering a weekly commentary on KOHO-FM 101.1 for seven years. The only period of time I didn't offer commentaries was during the two periods I was a candidate for Chelan County Public Utility District commissioner and wasn't allowed to broadcast. I ended up with over 250 commentaries.

In 2002, I had met Chris Erickson and Larry Long in the Sleeping Lady Pantry. Chris was retired from the telecommunication industry and had an extensive background with finances, especially as it related to communications. Larry had retired from the Chelan County Public Utility District after twenty-five-plus years. I began joining some of their coffee-and-discussion times, and we discovered a mutual interest and concern over some of the issues and activities related to the Chelan County PUD. For some reason I really got involved in some of the issues. In January 2004 I announced a meeting for concerned citizens at the Riverside Center in Cashmere. Jerry Copp, retired Chelan County PUD general manager, offered to fly back form Green Valley, Arizona, to address the meeting. We also involved Robert Parlette, Wenatchee attorney and friend, and several others as speakers. More than four hundred people turned out, and some couldn't get in the door that evening. The emotions were high over concerns with the Chelan County PUD, especially the way Charlie Hoskins, Chelan County PUD manager was providing leadership in the organization. The consensus of the evening was that Charlie needed to leave.

Following the meeting I was convinced that the PUD board of commissioners had failed to do its job, and I initiated a recall effort against Bob Boyd, one of the commissioners. Jim Lynch, a progressive-minded attorney and former mayor of Wenatchee, shared my convictions and offered to be the pro bono legal counsel for the recall process. The judge ruled against the recall, but many people became more aware of some of the problems within the PUD management structure.

Somehow I hit a nerve with the public. Several months later I submitted my name as a candidate for Chelan County PUD commissioner. I ended up serving with Bob Boyd, the commissioner I tried to recall. Initially our relationship was a bit tense, but we ended up agreeing on a several ideas and at least I think we became cautious friends. I served one four-year term but wasn't reelected to a second term. I think I won the first election because the majority of the voters agreed that something needed to change at the Chelan County PUD, and they were less concerned with my liberal views. I lost the second election because we had accomplished the change in management, and my liberal views were more of a detriment.

Chelan County is conservative, and the religious right has a powerful voting bloc. Since I had worked with Harriet Bullitt, I was labeled a "tree hugger." I was proud to be a tree hugger. I tried my best to encourage residential solar electric application, which was difficult to accomplish for a utility with two major hydroelectric dams on the Columbia River and the second lowest electrical rates in the nation. Even in 2004 it seemed apparent that residential solar was about to make a breakthrough, and I tried to make the point that the more residential solar the Chelan County PUD promoted, the more revenue they could derive from selling hydroelectric generated electricity on the open market at higher prices. I was disappointed to discover that some prominent people within the Chelan County PUD didn't believe climate change was a potential problem and certainly didn't believe human activity was a contributing factor. My cartoon drawing friend, Dan McConnell enjoyed drawing a series of cartoons to illustrate some of the humor involved with my efforts with the Chelan Public Utility District. These were featured in the *Wenatchee World*, our local newspaper.

WERNER VS. GOLIATH

By Dan McConnell, Cashmere

I'm glad I had the experience of being a Chelan County PUD commissioner, but I ended up being one liberal in a conservative stronghold. I enjoyed the opportunity to question policies, especially the major problem of financial arrangements with the fiber optic program. Generally if there was a vote dealing with reviewing the financial aspects of the fiber optic program or supporting the option for residential solar energy, the vote was four to one. There was no way that I could do any more than express my opinion, which I did frequently. Generally, it wasn't a popular opinion, but being an elected commissioner, my opinions often reached the *Wenatchee World* newspaper and allowed the pubic to join the conversation.

My final official association with Harriet Bullitt involved serving as one of five members of the Sleeping Lady Foundation. Harriet established this foundation to bring quality programs to Sleeping Lady and to the valley. The population in the valley is too small to support top speakers or concerts through gate receipts. The Sleeping Lady Foundation covered the cost of the events and then partnered with a local nonprofit, which received the revenue from any ticket sales. Among people who came to Sleeping Lady through foundation support were Temple Grandin, doctor of animal science and autistic activist; Morris Dees, philanthropist and cofounder of the Southern Poverty Law Center; Cesar Millan, self-taught dog trainer known as the Dog Whisperer; Maya Lin, designer and artist perhaps best known for her design of the Vietnam Veterans Memorial; and Luis Urrea, Mexican-American poet and author.

The Sleeping Lady Foundation has brought great speakers and musical events to the Leavenworth Valley. Normally the quality of these events is only possible in large metropolitan areas such as Seattle. Bringing this quality of speakers to a small venue is only possible because of the generosity of Harriet Bullitt.

Claudia and I are enjoying our retirement in Tucson, Arizona. The experience at Holden Village and Sleeping Lady Mountain Retreat definitely influenced my life in many ways. We have solar energy panels on our home and drive a plug-in hybrid car. We continue to use vermicomposting to recycle of our organic waste. We have recently added an eight hundred gallon rain water barrel to utilize the monsoon rains to water our citrus trees. Our small garden supplies some of our salad items. Unfortunately, we have been unsuccessful in growing Jerusalem Artichokes in the desert. However, Life is very good.

I'm truly thankful for the opportunities that I have had and the wonderful people who have been so kind to me. My mother is no longer living, so I will need to handle retirement on my own without her prayers. I'm glad I went to Purdue University and became an aeronautical engineer. Life channels us in many and varied directions and definitely provides unanticipated opportunities. I give thanks that I had the courage to accept the offer to manage Holden Village which shaped my life for the next fifty years. As stated in the

Anglican prayer we also title the Holden prayer, *O God, you have called your servants to ventures of which we cannot see the ending, by paths as yet untrodden, through perils unknown. Give us faith to go out with good courage, not knowing where we go, but only that your hand is leading us and your love supporting us…..*

Peace and Joy

About the Author

FORMALLY EDUCATED AS AN AERONAUTICAL engineer at Purdue University, Werner Janssen decided to follow a completely different career path at the age of twenty-four when he accepted the position of business manager of Holden Village, a unique, isolated, developing retreat center located in the North Cascade mountains of Washington State. After managing and developing the operation from 1963 to 1983, he went on to serve as a school board member for eight years in the Cascade School District and as Chelan Public Utility District Commissioner for four years. In 1993 Janssen joined the project management team developing the Sleeping Lady Mountain Retreat in Leavenworth, Washington, eventually serving as its general manager and becoming a member of the Sleeping Lady Foundation. For seven years he presented the weekly, at times, controversial social commentary *Consider This* on the local radio station KOHO 101.1 FM.

CPSIA information can be obtained
at www.ICGtesting.com
Printed in the USA
BVHW032201091222
653911BV00024B/430